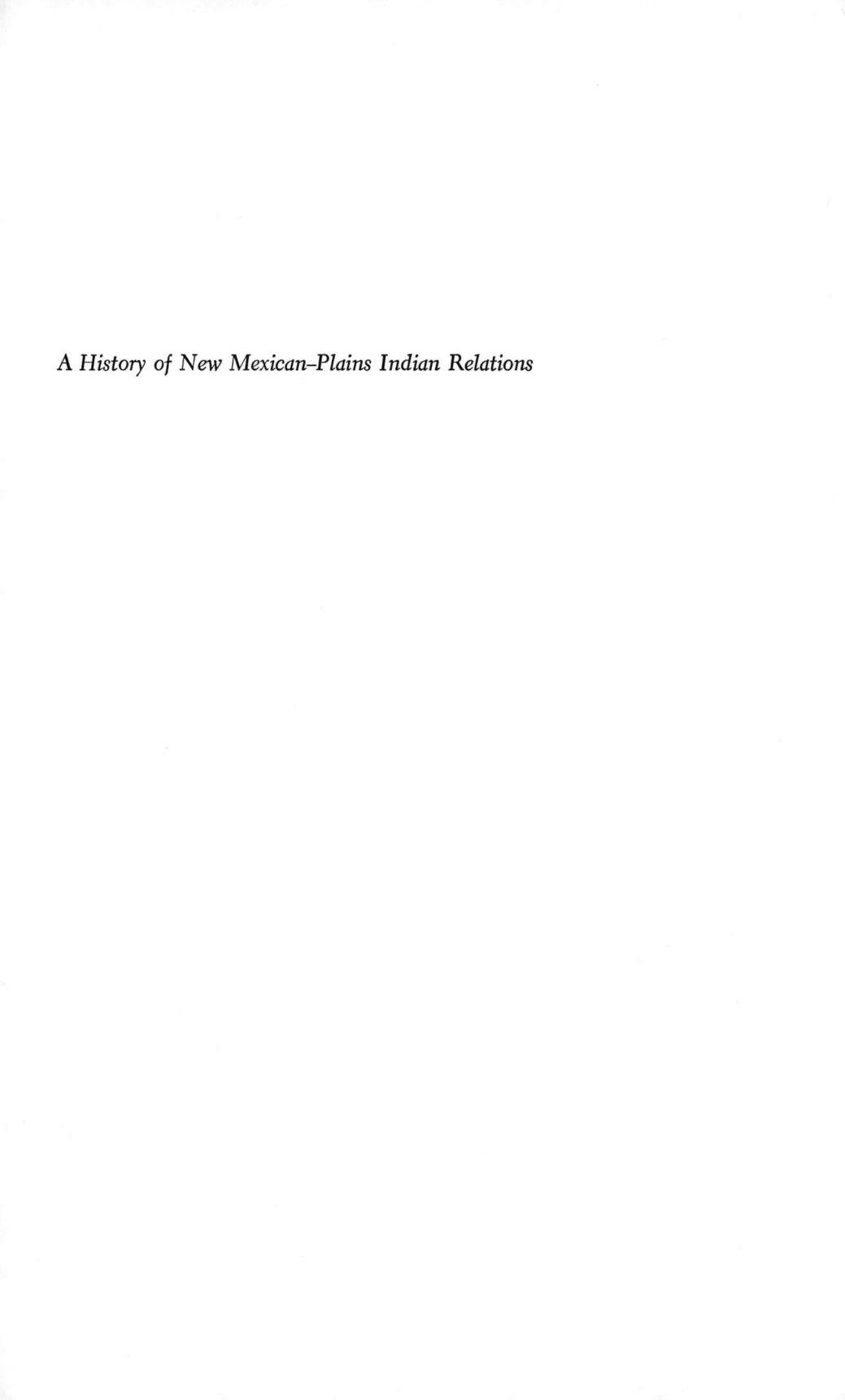

A History of New Mexican–Plains Indian Relations

University of Oklahoma Press : Norman

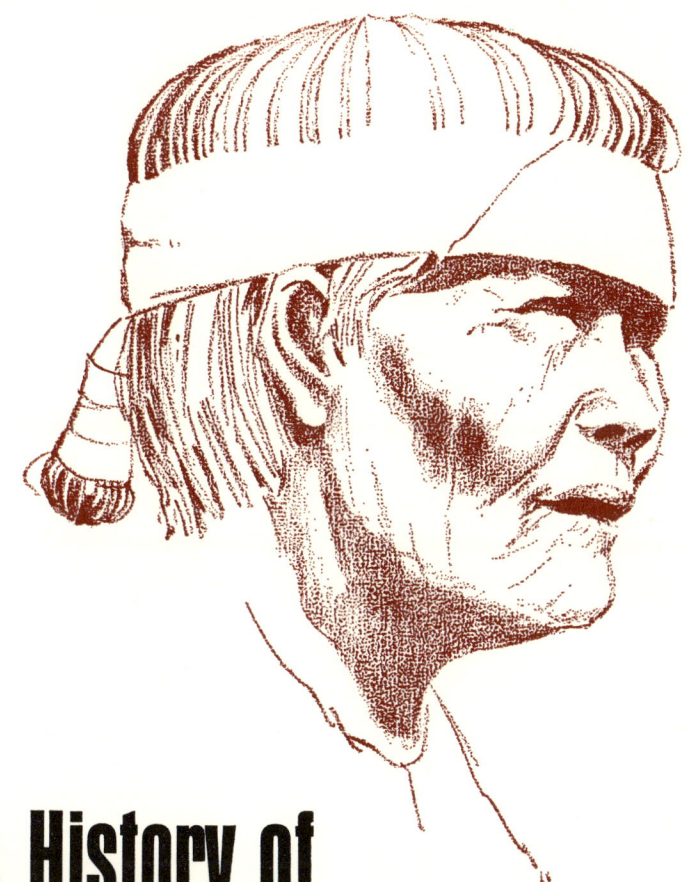

A History of
New Mexican-Plains Indian Relations

by Charles L. Kenner

Library of Congress Catalog Card Number: 68-31375
Copyright 1969 by the University of Oklahoma Press, Publishing Division of the University. Composed and printed at Norman, Oklahoma, U.S.A., by the University of Oklahoma Press. First edition.

Preface

MOST REGIONS OF THE UNITED STATES have undergone the ordeal of being the frontier, the point of conflict between civilization and the wilderness. The impact of the frontier experience, however, was usually ameliorated by the brevity of the episode. Within a decade, or a few score years at the most, law replaced brute force and order, chaos. In sharp contrast, New Mexico was exposed to the rigors of frontier existence for nearly three hundred years. From the time of its founding in 1598 by Juan de Oñate until the Red River War of 1874, the inhabitants were in almost constant contact with unconquered Indians of the plains. This is a study of the profound economic, social, and cultural effects which this long period of interchange produced upon both the New Mexicans and the Indians.

Many historians of the Southwest have sought to find the proper term to apply to the Latin population of New Mexico. "Spanish-Americans," certainly the best term to use for the modern-day Latins, is not to be found in nineteenth-century documents and writings and therefore seems somewhat stilted for a historical work. The terms *Hispanos* and *Nuevo Mexicanos*, although used in recent works, also seem somewhat artificial. For the sake of simplicity, I have chosen to employ the terms "New Mexicans" and "Mexicans." I am quite aware that Anglo-Americans in the territory were also New Mexicans and that after 1848 the native settlers were no longer "Mexicans" from a national standpoint. They had, however, been reared under Mexican rule, had been subjugated unwillingly by foreigners, undoubtedly still thought of themselves as Mexicans, and were so considered by

v

their conquerors. In just as arbitrary fashion, the terms "Anglos" and "Americans" are employed to describe Anglo-Americans.

In the preparation of this study, I have benefited from the labors of many people. Professor Ernest Wallace of Texas Technological College has given so generously of his time and talents that he is due much of the credit for any merit this work possesses. A host of others have also rendered valuable assistance. Professors L. L. Baisdell, J. William Davis, Lawrence L. Graves, and David M. Vigness of Texas Tech have made thoughtful and helpful readings and criticisms. The staffs of the Southwest Collection and the library at Texas Technological College and the Angelo State College Library, San Angelo, Texas, have been very cooperative in obtaining research materials. Cordial aid has also been received from the staffs of the Western History Collection of the Denver Public Library; the Special Collections Division of the University of New Mexico Library; the New Mexico Historical Museum Library, Santa Fe; the Eugene Barker History Center at the University of Texas; the Panhandle-Plains Historical Museum Library, Canyon, Texas; the Library of Congress; and the National Archives. Robert Feynn of the Angelo State College Foreign Language Department lent his considerable talents for the translation of many documents from the Spanish Archives of New Mexico. To all of these and many others go my heartfelt thanks.

CHARLES LEROY KENNER

State University, Arkansas
September, 1968

Contents

		page v
	Preface	
1	The Valley and the Plains	3
2	War, Trade, and Diplomacy, 1700–1786	23
3	The Comanche Peace, 1786–1846	53
4	The *Comanchero* Trade, 1786–1860	78
5	The *Ciboleros*	98
6	The Ascendancy of the Anglos, 1848–1861	115
7	The Civil War and the Adobe Walls Campaign	138
8	The Great *Comanchero* Cattle Trade	155
9	The Suppression of the *Comanchero* Cattle Trade, 1867–1872	176
10	The End of a Long Road	201
	Bibliography	218
	Index	235

Illustrations

Waku Tota, of Pecos Pueblo   *following page* 154
Pueblo of Picuris
Two Men of the Tewa Tribe with a *Carreta*
Vincente Jiron, Chief of Isleta Pueblo
Juan Jesus Leo, Governor of Taos
A Typical *Carreta*
Old Navaho Warrior
A Taos Man
Kit Carson, *circa* 1849   *facing page* 118
Colonel John Irwin Gregg   119
Colonel Ranald Slidell MacKenzie   119
Fort Sumner, New Mexico   134
Fort Union, New Mexico   135
Mow-way's Village   *following page* 198
Mow-way, Kwahadi Chief
Chewing Elk, Comanche Chief
Big Bow, Kiowa Tribe
Kiowa Hunting Camp
Three Former Governors of Taos
Three Taos Men on Horseback
Men from Pueblo of Santa Clara
Two Cheyenne Girls, 1876

Maps

New Mexico, 1600–1700   *page* 13
The Eastern New Mexican Frontier, 1850–1865   125
The Southwestern Frontier, 1865–1875   181

ix

A History of New Mexican–Plains Indian Relations

1
The Valley and the Plains

THERE HAVE BEEN FEW EXAMPLES in American history of neighboring peoples who differed so completely as the Pueblo Indians of the upper Río Grande Valley and the nomadic tribesmen of the South Plains. Originally the natives of both regions had been simple hunters and gatherers, but about a thousand years before Christ, Indians of the Southwest learned to grow corn. Released by this revolutionary step from the constant struggle against imminent starvation, they used their newly acquired leisure to master the arts of building pueblos and making pottery and to develop the other accouterments of a maturing civilization. The Plains Indians, on the other hand, remained so restricted by the never ending search for food that they were never able to make the breakthrough to a richer and more complex culture.

Contrary to what might be expected, the impact that the two peoples had on each other steadily increased as the gulf between their respective ways of life widened. Since each produced desirable goods which the other lacked, some type of intercourse between them became inevitable. To obtain the coveted agricultural products of the Pueblos, the have-nots from the plains at first resorted to raids, but when they saw that these were both costly and uncertain, they gradually turned to peaceful trade to meet their needs. During the long period of commercial contacts thus initiated, both the Plains Indians and the Pueblos acquired cultural traits which significantly affected their entire history.

For the period before 1700, the limited information to be found in the reports of early Spanish explorers and modern archaeologists makes it possible to sketch only an outline of Plains-Pueblo relations. Long before the Pueblos developed their distinctive way of life, the so-called Folsom men—a primitive but brave race who hunted the prehistoric bison of northeastern New Mexico—apparently traded with the Indians of the plains. Among the arrowheads they left intertwined in the skeletons of their kills were many made of a uniquely banded flint found only in outcroppings near the Canadian River in the Texas Panhandle.[1] To get this Alibates flint, the Folsom hunters either made the long, arduous trip deep into the plains to quarry their own or, more likely, bartered for it with the natives who lived there.

The intriguing mystery of the Folsom men notwithstanding, the true Pueblos of New Mexico are not known to have been in touch with plains inhabitants until after 1000 A.D. About that time, the comparatively backward inhabitants of the Río Grande were greatly augmented in population and culture by a mass migration of more advanced peoples from the Mesa Verde region to the northwest. Invigorated by this infusion of fresh blood and ideas, the Pueblo world underwent a rapid expansion that did not spend itself until its outer limits had been pushed beyond the southern fringes of the Sangre de Cristos into the Canadian and Pecos valleys. There, at the edge of the plains, Pueblos built the same style of multiroom adobe- and stone-walled dwellings and manufactured the same types of pottery and culinary ware as their kinsmen in the Río Grande Valley.[2]

About the same time, 1200 A.D., a plains people who settled in the shadows of the Raton Mountains fell under the influence of Taos, the northernmost of the Río Grande pueblos, and acquired from it the knowledge of farming, pueblo building, and pottery making.[3] These otherwise unidentified people, whose incipient culture was soon destroyed by fresh invaders from the plains, would be unworthy of mention except that they were the first of many groups of Plains Indians who succumbed to the attractions and comforts of a sedentary way of life.

[1] James B. Shaeffer, "The Alibates Flint Quarry, Texas," *American Antiquity*, XXIV (October, 1958), 189.
[2] Fred Wendorf, "The Archaeology of Northeastern New Mexico," *El Palacio*, LXVII (April, 1960), 59.
[3] *Ibid.*, 60.

The Valley and the Plains

After 1300, the Pueblos who had moved into the Pecos and Canadian valleys abandoned their homes and retreated up the Pecos River as far as the Pecos pueblo, which would stand as the eastern bastion of Río Grande culture for five hundred years. Although their withdrawal may have been due to a drought, more likely they were forced back by eastern intruders, who soon afterward launched a vigorous assault against the Río Grande pueblos.[4] At first hard pressed, the Río Grandeans eventually weathered the onslaught by abandoning their smaller villages and concentrating in the larger and more defensible communities.

No longer able to steal corn and other coveted foodstuffs easily, the plains invaders, evidently having learned the techniques of crop cultivation during their extensive forays, retired to the comparatively well-watered Canadian Valley and took up agriculture for themselves. They not only succeeded as primitive farmers, but also adopted the Pueblos' style of architecture. Starting with single-room dwellings, they were soon building structures of up to three hundred chambers along various Canadian tributaries in the Texas Panhandle.[5]

Despite the cultural debt that the Antelope Creek people (as archaeologists have designated the Canadian farmers) owed to the Pueblos, commerce between the two groups was insignificant. Of almost five thousand potsherds found in the Saddle-Back excavation in present Oldham County, for example, less than two dozen were of Pueblo origin; and only a few artifacts made of the Alibates flint quarried by the Canadian River residents have been found at Pecos in time levels corresponding to the Antelope Creek focus.[6]

The lack of trade was undoubtedly due to the similarity of the two peoples' ways of life. The Canadian River dwellers produced enough corn to supplement their basic diet of buffalo meat and manufactured their own pottery, crude but serviceable. No longer

---

[4] William C. Holden, "Excavation of Saddle-Back Ruin," *Texas Archaeological and Paleontological Society Bulletin*, V (1933), 50.
[5] *Ibid.*, 51.
[6] *Ibid.*, 49; Dolores Gunnerson, "The Southern Athabascans: Their Arrival in the Southwest," *El Palacio*, LXIII (November, 1956), 350.

nomads, they probably had very little surplus buffalo meat or hides to trade to their western neighbors. The Pueblos, on the other hand, took advantage of the temporary absence of hostile nomads on the plains to roam them freely. Incredible as it seems, so many of their potsherds and artifacts have been found in the sandy region near present Muleshoe, Texas, that archaeologists suspect they even farmed the thin soil there.[7] Pueblos this familiar with the plains undoubtedly hunted their own buffalo and had little need to trade for venison.

Around 1450, the Antelope Creek people vanished without a trace, victims of either war or drought. Although tree-ring studies indicating a severe drought in western Nebraska during the mid-fifteenth century do not necessarily denote similar conditions for the Texas Panhandle, the drought supposition is furthered by the discovery that many of the Canadian ruins filled with wind-blown sand before their walls crumbled away.[8] Quite likely, however, the drought only weakened the ability of the Antelope Creek inhabitants to resist the new wave of nomads who, it is known, moved into the area about the time the pueblo builders vanished.

After obliterating the Antelope Creek culture, this latest group of Plains Indians moved against the Pueblos of the Río Grande. Once again, however, the Pueblos successfully resisted the attacks by erecting larger and more heavily fortified communities. In causing such an unprecedented growth of large towns, the nomads served as the unwitting catalysts for a sudden flowering of Pueblo culture that has caused the entire era to be described as the "Golden Age of the Río Grande."[9]

Of all the pueblos, Pecos, lying squarely athwart the easiest invasion route to the Río Grande Basin, was hardest hit by the nomadic intruders. To survive, its people built houses that towered four stories above the ground and merged them so that sentinels could traverse the rooftops of all without descending. At the second-story level, eaves formed a balcony-like lane that en-

---
[7] Alex D. Krieger, "The Eastward Extension of Puebloan Datings Towards the Cultures of the Mississippi Valley," *American Antiquity*, XII (January, 1947), 143.
[8] Waldo R. Wedel, *Prehistoric Man on the Great Plains*, 145.
[9] Alfred V. Kidder, *The Pottery of Pecos*, I, 154.

circled the entire pueblo. Below the eaves, no opening pierced the adobe walls, for all entrances and exits were made by means of portable ladders. Surrounding the settlement was a low stone wall that secured a large courtyard and a spring that provided the town with an emergency water supply.[10] These protective measures were evidently quite effective because there is no archaeological evidence that Pecos was ever taken by enemies. In addition, the Spanish chronicler, Pedro Castañeda, observed upon arriving there with Coronado in 1541 that "the people of this town pride themselves because no one has been able to subjugate them."[11]

According to Castañeda and Coronado, the Indians who caused the Pueblos to strengthen their defenses had made an amazing adaptation to the plains environment. They ate the buffalo's flesh raw, drank its blood, and used its skin to make their clothes and their conical tents. Upon making a kill, they "cut open the belly of the cow . . . squeeze out the chewed grass and drink the juice . . . saying that it contains the sustenance of the stomach."[12] After satiating their hunger, they deftly skinned the buffalo with their flint tools, sliced its meat into thin strips, dried it in the sun, and then pounded it into a powder that would keep indefinitely. Apparently little handicapped by their horseless state, they went "about like nomads with their tents [loaded on] . . . packs of dogs harnessed with little pads, pack-saddles, and girths." Their hardy way of life agreed well with them: Castañeda thought they were better proportioned, greater warriors, and "more feared" than the Pueblos, and Coronado unequivocally stated that they had "the best physique of any natives of the Indies."[13]

The identity of the nomads is still questionable. Coronado encountered two groups—he called them Querechos and Teyas—who, although hostile toward each other, displayed virtually identical characteristics. While most authorities believe that the Querechos, who dwelt closer to Pecos, were Plains Apaches,

---

[10] "Castañeda's History of the Expedition," in George P. Hammond and Agapito Rey (transs. and eds.), *Narratives of the Coronado Expedition, 1540–1542*, 257.
[11] *Ibid.*; Alfred V. Kidder, *The Artifacts of Pecos*, 3.
[12] "Castañeda's History," *loc. cit.*, 262.
[13] *Ibid.*; "Letter of Coronado to the King, October 20, 1541," *ibid.*, 186.

A History of New Mexican–Plains Indian Relations

opinions vary widely on the Teyas. George P. Hammond stated that they must have been the same as the Tejas of later times;[14] Herbert E. Bolton conjectured that they were "members of the groups" later known as Jumanos;[15] and Jack D. Forbes in a recent study concluded that they were only another branch of the Apaches, perhaps the Lipans.[16] For the purposes of this study, both groups will be referred to as Apaches.

The occupation of the plains by the Apaches forced the Pueblos to discontinue their hunting excursions. With the Pueblos now lacking in meat and hides and the Apaches in corn, there developed a trade that was already well established when the Coronado expedition arrived. According to the Spaniards, the nomads, unable to cope with the scarcity of game and frequency of blizzards during the winter, packed their belongings and trekked to the pueblos, where they found "shelter under the eaves, as the inhabitants do not let them inside."[17] There, under the ever alert guard of the Pueblos, who kept "watch at night with bugles and calls, as in the fortresses of Spain," they passed the winter trading the cattle and deerskins "that they do not need, and the meat dried in the sun" for maize and blankets.[18]

Although the Teyas and Querechos were usually on friendly terms with the people of the towns, occasional hostilities broke out in which the strong walls of the pueblos were not always invulnerable. Hernando de Alvarado, Coronado's chief assistant, found in the province of Tiguex seven other pueblos, "uninhabited and in ruins," which he learned had been destroyed by the "Indians who daub their eyes [Teyas]."[19] Castañeda observed several destroyed pueblos near Pecos and was informed that the Teyas had come out of the north some sixteen years earlier and after an unsuccessful siege of Pecos had destroyed them. Then, before

---

[14] *Ibid.*, 239, n. 2.
[15] Herbert E. Bolton, *Coronado on the Turquoise Trail*, 260.
[16] Jack D. Forbes, *Apache, Navaho, and Spaniard*, 15.
[17] "Castañeda's History," *loc. cit.*, 258.
[18] "Relación del Suceso," *ibid.*, 293.
[19] "Discovery of Tiguex by Alvarado and Padilla," *ibid.*, 183.

The Valley and the Plains

leaving, they had made "friends with all."[20] Such was the completely unpredictable state of Pueblo-Plains Indian relations.

A plausible explanation for the alternating periods of peace and war has been advanced by archaeologist J. Charles Kelley. Kelley conjectures that peace prevailed as long as rainfall was adequate for the farmers to produce an abundance of corn, beans, and squash and for the hunters to obtain plenty of buffalo robes and dried meat. During the periodic droughts, however, the Pueblos produced no surplus corn, and game on the plains became so scarce that the hunters faced starvation. Driven by hunger, the Plains Indians finally raided the pueblos for their seed corn. A few smaller towns might succumb, but the larger ones survived. When the drought ended and corn and game were again plentiful, peaceful trade relations were resumed in a surprisingly short time.[21]

Challenged constantly by the Plains Indians, the Pecos natives responded by reaching heights of military efficiency unparalleled among the Pueblos. Enabled to "dominate the [other] pueblos they wish,"[22] they used their power to become the chief center for the western diffusion of trade goods from the buffalo country. So widely did their traders range that Coronado met some as far west as Zuñi and exchanged glassware and beads for their "dressed skins, shields, and headpieces."[23] The predominant position of Pecos in the plains trade is evidenced further by the abundance in its ruins of plains artifacts, which are rare or absent from sites farther west, "even in the nearby Galisteo Basin."[24]

---

[20] "Castañeda's History," *loc. cit.*, 257-58. Dolores Gunnerson has sought to use this sudden attack on Pecos by the Teyas as evidence to indicate the first arrival of the Apaches in the Southwest. Her reasoning is interesting and worthy of close study, but she does not explain how the close relations existing between the Pueblos and Apaches could have developed within a space of sixteen years. Gunnerson, "The Southern Athabascans," *loc. cit.*, 346-65.

[21] J. Charles Kelley, "Factors Involved in the Abandonment of Certain Peripheral Southwestern Settlements," *American Anthropologist*, N.S., LIV (July, 1952), 384-85.

[22] "Castañeda's History," *loc. cit.*, 257. This indication of occasional interpueblo warfare was also noticed by Suceso, one of Castañeda's comrades, who stated that one of the reasons the pueblos were so compactly built "is due in part . . . to the wars they wage against each other." "Relación del Suceso," *ibid.*, 294.

[23] "Castañeda's History," *ibid.*, 217.

[24] Alfred V. Kidder, *Pecos, New Mexico: Archaeological Notes*, 313.

A History of New Mexican–Plains Indian Relations

It was almost forty years after the Coronado expedition before Spaniards again set foot in New Mexico. During the interim, trade between the Pueblos and Plains Indians seems to have increased. Alfred V. Kidder, after spending years excavating the ruins of Pecos, concluded that the Plains influence shown by eastern specimens "began to be exercised about 1550" and became increasingly stronger during the next hundred years. The greater number of snub-nosed scrapers and two-edged knives made of Alibates flint indicated to Kidder "an intensification of contacts" with the tribes to the east.[25]

In 1581, Fray Agustín Rodríguez and Francisco Sánchez Chamuscado, setting out from the Spanish settlements at the head of the Río Conchos, reopened Spanish contact with the upper Río Grande. Bearing permission from the viceroy to "preach the gospel" in a land to the north where they hoped to obtain "very fruitful results,"[26] they thoroughly explored the Pueblo country. While visiting among the Tompiro pueblos near the salines east of the Manzano Mountains, they were amazed to find their hosts bartering corn and blankets to visiting "people of the buffalo" for deerskins, buffalo hides, and meat.[27] Although long years of intimate contacts had enabled each group to understand the language of the other, the Tompiros were afraid to visit the plains. When the Spaniards asked to be taken to the camps of the wild Indians, the Pueblos refused, warning them that the "Indians who followed the buffalo" were very brave people who used many arrows and that they would kill any trespassers on their domain.[28] In their missionary zeal, Fray Rodríguez and his fellow priests remained behind when Chamuscado returned to Mexico.

The failure of Rodríguez to return enabled a fortune hunter named Antonio de Espejo to obtain permission to lead a rescue expedition to the upper Río Grande. Although he learned early

---

[25] Kidder, *Artifacts*, 43–44.
[26] "Declaration of Pedro de Bustamante, 1582," in Herbert E. Bolton (trans. and ed.), *Spanish Exploration in the Southwest, 1542–1706*, 142.
[27] George P. Hammond and Agapito Rey (transs. and eds.), *The Gallegos Relation of the Rodríguez Expedition to New Mexico*, 267.
[28] Ibid., 267–68.

that the priests had been put to death by the Pueblos, Espejo roamed far and wide across New Mexico, checking on its reputed riches. Concerning relations between the Plains Indians and the Pueblos, Espejo mentioned that the inhabitants of Cochití had many fine buffalo skins which they traded to him for "sleighbells and small iron articles."[29] Since Cochití lay west of the Río Grande, its surplus of robes seems to indicate that the Pueblo trade in these items was very extensive.

Don Juan de Oñate, who in 1598 made the first permanent settlement in New Mexico, found the trade in buffalo robes quite brisk. In September, his nephew and second-in-command, Vicente de Zaldívar, while exploring the region near the Canadian River, met several Indian "herdsmen" returning from Picurís and Taos, "populous pueblos of this New Mexico, where they sell meat, hides, tallow, suet, and salt in exchange for cotton blankets, pottery, maize, and some small green stones which they use."[30] According to another of Oñate's captains, Juan de Ortega, the Vaqueros (as the Spaniards now styled the Plains Apaches) brought meat, fat, hides, and tallow loaded on dogs "a little larger than water-dogs" and set up camp "300 or 400 paces" from Pecos where they traded for maize and blankets. Ortega personally observed the arrival of a party of some four hundred of these plains traders.[31] Oñate, greatly impressed by the trade, noted that most of the Pueblos dressed in buffalo skins, "of which there is a great abundance," and that "this land is plentiful in the meat of the buffalo."[32] Even the Zuñis and Hopis of the western deserts had plenty of buffalo hides for winter wear.[33]

Vicente de Zaldívar later reported that the Vaqueros and the Pueblos formerly had been enemies who killed "each other daily,"

[29] George P. Hammond and Agapito Rey (transs. and eds.), *Expedition into New Mexico made by Antonio de Espejo, 1582–1583*, 112.
[30] "Account of the Discovery of the Buffalo, 1599," in Bolton, *Spanish Exploration*, 226.
[31] "Testimony of Juan de Ortega, July 31, 1601," Mexico, Vol. 26, *Archivo General de las Indias* (cited hereafter as AGI), quoted in Forbes, *op. cit.*, 99.
[32] Oñate to the Viceroy, March 2, 1599, in George P. Hammond and Agapito Rey (transs. and eds.), *Don Juan de Oñate, Colonizer of New Mexico, 1595–1628*, I, 483.
[33] "Diary of Fray Francisco de Escobar," *ibid.*, II, 1014.

but claimed that "by good treatment and many presents" he had persuaded the Apaches to "remain at peace" and trade with his charges.[34] Although Zaldívar seemed to think he had initiated the trade between the two peoples, his statement merely confirms that the long-time commerce between the Pueblos and Vaqueros was still occasionally interrupted by hostilities.

The Spaniards soon jeopardized the intertribal trade by impoverishing the Pueblos, to whom they left, according to a Franciscan friar, "nothing in their houses, no wheat, nothing to eat, nothing that is alive."[35] Thousands of natives, the Franciscans charged, were dying of starvation, and others were staying alive only by eating tree branches or dirt and ashes mixed with a little corn.[36] If these charges were true—or partially so—the Pueblos obviously were left with little to exchange with the Vaqueros.

Two of the pueblos, Ácoma in the west and Jumanas in the southeast, sought to shake off the Spanish tyranny, but Oñate crushed their rebellions with barbarous cruelty. Despite their inability to match strength with the Spaniards, however, other pueblos from time to time plotted to free themselves. In 1609, Picurís, Taos, and Pecos formed an alliance with the Apaches and Vaqueros and threatened to exterminate any Indians who allowed themselves to be converted. Convinced that the Spaniards were "scoundrels" concerned only with their own interests, they sought to persuade the more complacent pueblos that "no benefit" could be gained by co-operation with them.[37] Since all three pueblos in the alliance were located on the eastern fringes of New Mexico and had had long and intimate trade relations with the Vaqueros, it seems likely that the latter were encouraging them to oppose the Spaniards. How long the league lasted or how effective it was is unknown, but there is no evidence of actual hostilities between it and the Spaniards.

[34] "Zaldívar Inquiry, 1602," *ibid.*, 828.
[35] "Declaration of Fray Francisco de San Miguel, September 7, 1601," Mexico, Vol. 26, AGI, quoted in Forbes, *op. cit.*, 97.
[36] *Ibid.*, 97–98.
[37] "Memorial of Fray Francisco de Velasco," in Hammond and Rey, *Don Juan de Oñate*, II, 1024.

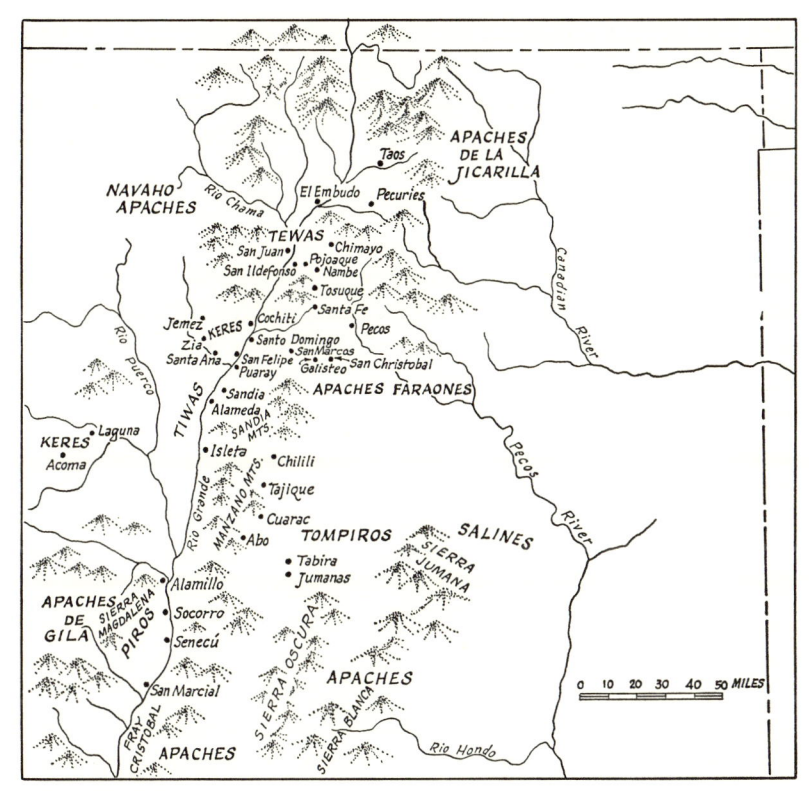

New Mexico, 1600–1700, based on a map from *Apache, Navaho, and Spaniard*, by Jack S. Forlies.

A History of New Mexican–Plains Indian Relations

In the 1620's according to Fray Alonso de Benavides, leader of the Franciscans in New Mexico, the Vaqueros were killing large numbers of buffalo by hiding near water holes and shooting them "as they come by." Then they skillfully dressed the hides, some with the hair on for use as beds and cloaks, and others without, for tents and "other things they are accustomed to use." With their surplus robes packed on the backs of dogs "harnessed in their little pack saddles," entire Vaquero villages—men, women, and children—regularly trekked to New Mexico. In return for cotton fabric and "other things they need," they exchanged robes in such quantities that they provided the dress "commonly worn by both [Pueblo] Indians and Spaniards."[38]

Although Pecos remained the most important trading point for the Vaqueros, the Tompiro towns east of the Manzano Mountains developed such a lively commerce with the Jumano Indians of southwestern Texas that the southernmost settlement became known as Jumanas, "because this nation often comes here to trade and barter."[39] During one of their many trading visits to Jumanas, some of the Plains Indians were quite intrigued by the glittering Catholic medals and crosses. The Spaniards were so encouraged by this incipient expression of interest in Christianity that two friars braved the journey of more than one hundred leagues to the Jumano villages near present San Angelo. Unfortunately, they found the natives more interested in hunting buffalo and fighting Apaches than in learning the catechism.

The Vaquero Apaches also showed curiosity about the new religion of their Pueblo friends, but were speedily rebuffed by the ill-advised actions of the Spaniards. In 1628, according to Father Benavides, a group pilgrimaging toward Santa Fe to view a statue of the Virgin was attacked by Governor Philip de Ossorio "to obtain slaves" to sell in New Spain.[40] To this treachery the Vaqueros retaliated with only a brief flurry of raids; and then they made peace in order to resume trade. Despite the seeming insig-

[38] Peter P. Forrestal, C.S.C. (trans. and ed.), *Benavides' Memorial of 1630*, 54.
[39] Frederick W. Hodge, George P. Hammond, and Agapito Rey (transs. and eds.), *Fray Alonso de Benavides' Revised Memorial of 1634*, 66–67.
[40] Forrestal, *op. cit.*, 55–56.

nificance of this episode, it introduced the most destructive obstacle to good relations between the valley farmers and the plains hunters: the slave raid.

Under Luis de Rosas, who became governor of New Mexico in 1637, the taking of Indian slaves increased greatly. Insatiable in his thirst for money, Rosas sought to monopolize the Indian trade at Pecos and then sent slave raiders deep into the plains, where they killed "a great number of the friendly Apaches" and captured others to sell in Nueva Vizcaya. The Pecos natives protested his barbarity with a "great demonstration" because, they said, the captured Apaches had been living among them and "with them they had their commerce," by which means they clothed themselves and paid their tributes.[41]

Some of the inhabitants of Taos became disheartened at Rosas' misrule in 1639 and fled to the plains, where they took refuge with a friendly group of Apaches living near the present Colorado and Kansas border. In their new homeland they built a pueblo, subsequently known to the Spaniards as El Cuartelejo, and planted crops; but about 1642, Juan de Archuleta, Rosas' assistant, took twenty soldiers to their haven and recaptured most of them.[42] In the early 1660's, another New Mexican governor, Don Diego de Peñalosa, ferreted out the rest of the Taos refugees, who, he reported, were living "as heathens" among the people of El Cuartelejo on the "frontier of Quivira."[43] Although Peñalosa methodically "laid waste" to El Cuartelejo, he could not blot out the fact that the Pueblos and Plains Indians had been living side by side in peace.

Other Pueblo-Apache intrigues called for more drastic resistance to the Spaniards than mere flight. In 1650, the "sorcerers and chief men" of the Pueblos plotted to deliver the "droves" of

[41] "Testimony of Francisco de Salazar, July 5, 1641," Patronato, Vol. 244, AGI, quoted in Forbes, op. cit., 132.

[42] Silvestre de Escalante to Juan Agustín de Morfi, April 2, 1778, in Ralph E. Twitchell, The Spanish Archives of New Mexico, II, 279–80; Forbes, op. cit., 137; Charles W. Hackett (trans. and ed.), Historical Documents Relating to New Mexico, Nueva Vizcaya and Approaches Thereto, to 1773, III, 263–64.

[43] "Trial of Diego de Peñalosa, 1665," in Hackett, Historical Documents, III, 263–64.

mares and horses belonging to the Spaniards to the Apaches, who would then join in an attack "in all districts" on the night of Holy Thursday. Unfortunately for them, their scheme was uncovered when a Pueblo party was detected in the act of driving some mares to the Apaches. Terrified by the narrowness of their escape, the Spaniards ruthlessly arrested "most" of the Pueblo leaders, of whom they hanged nine and sold many others into slavery.[44] Spanish brutality, however, failed to stifle the spirit of revolt. A San Felipe Pueblo declared in 1681 that his people had been planning to rebel ever since the 1650 uprising.[45]

Even in the midst of the intrigues, Pueblo-Plains trade was little interrupted. Fray Agustín Vetancourt, writing some forty years later, stated that more than five hundred Apaches were coming annually to Pecos with their "laden dog trains" to trade for corn, "vari-colored stones," and tobacco.[46] In a similar vein, Fray Alonso de Posada, who was in charge of the Pecos mission in the 1650's, recalled that the Apaches were bringing robes and "captive Indians from Quivira" to trade for horses, the earliest record of the Spaniards' bartering horses to the Plains Indians.[47] Quite significantly, Posada added that the Plains Apaches had always taken particular care to maintain peace with the Spaniards in order to preserve an outlet for their dressed skins and hides. Unfortunately, the Spanish governors failed to perceive this advantage and to give the trade proper encouragement.

A basic change in the trade with the Plains Indians was gradually developing in that an increasing amount was taking place in the Indian camps. Although the origins of this practice cannot be documented, a Spanish captain testified in 1663 that several years earlier he had gone among the "heathen Indians to trade,

[44] "Declaration of Diego López Sambrano, December 22, 1681," in Charles W. Hackett (trans. and ed.), *Revolt of the Pueblo Indians of New Mexico and Otermín's Attempted Reconquest, 1680–1682*, II, 299.
[45] "Declaration of Pedro Naranjo, December 19, 1681," *ibid.*, 247.
[46] Charles W. Hackett (trans. and ed.), *Pichardo's Treatise on the Limits of Louisiana and Texas*, II, 373.
[47] S. Lyman Tyler and H. Daniel Taylor (transs.), "The Report of Fray Alonso de Posada in Relation to Quivira and Teguayo," *New Mexico Historical Review*, XXXIII (October, 1958), 301–303.

The Valley and the Plains

as it was customary for the Spaniards to go as an escort for Christian Indians when the latter go to trade."[48] In 1659, Governor Bernardo López de Mendizábal, who controlled a large portion of the trade at the time, sent Captain Diego Romero among the Plains Indians to barter for buffalo and antelope skins. Upon arriving at the Apache camp, Romero announced that his father "when he came to that land had left a son" and that he desired to do the same.[49] The Apaches, apparently flattered by his request, promptly obliged. After erecting a new tent and furnishing it with a bed of antelope robes, they held a "wedding dance" and brought him a young maiden. The following morning they put a feather in Romero's hair, proclaimed him their "captain," and gave him two bundles of skins and the tent. Thus the Spanish trader, like his later French and Anglo-American counterparts, made use of a temporary marriage alliance to facilitate trade with the Indians.

Trade on the plains was given a tremendous boost in 1664 when Governor Peñalosa decreed that wild Indians, no matter how peaceful, could not come to the pueblos.[50] Although he claimed that his purpose was to keep the Apaches from spying on the strength of the province, it is more likely that he wished to gain a larger share of the trade for himself by eliminating competition from the Pueblos. Whatever his motive, the ban weakened the most important device for maintaining peaceful relations between New Mexico and the Plains Indians.

The growing importance of the trade in Indian slaves also menaced the stability of the frontier. Spanish traders, tempted by the growing demand for laborers in the mines of Nueva Vizcaya and for household servants and sheepherders in New Mexico, bought scores of captives from the Apaches, who obtained them by raiding the Caddoan villages to their east. Although entire villages were decimated, not enough Caddoans were taken to supply the demand. Consequently, the New Mexicans, taking advantage

---

[48] "Hearing for Nicolás de Aguilar, May 8, 1663," in Hackett, *Historical Documents*, III, 140.
[49] "Letter of Fray García de San Francisco, October 13, 1667," *ibid.*, 156.
[50] "Order of Diego de Peñalosa, January, 1664," in Twitchell, *op. cit.*, II, 2.

of a long-standing law that permitted unconverted Indians who made unprovoked attacks on Spaniards to be enslaved, also began capturing the Plains Apaches. As the price of good young Indians rose to as much as forty pesos each in Santa Fe, the slavers used every opportunity to capture Indians, even taking some who were trading peacefully at the pueblos.[51] In 1661, Governor Mendizábal, the most notorious of the slavers, sent an expedition of more than eight hundred Pueblo Indians and Spaniards to capture slaves for the camps and mines of El Parral.[52] Since this occurred during the middle of the harvest season, his greed not only jeopardized the chances for peace, but also deprived his people of badly needed crops.

The Tompiro Pueblos on the southeastern border of New Mexico paid the greatest price because of the avaricious policies of the Spaniards. They had long carried on a lively but dangerous trade with the *Siete Rios* Apaches of the near-by Sierra Blanca Mountains, who, hard put to obtain plenty of buffalo robes and meat to trade, were constantly tempted to steal from their neighbors' fields. Nevertheless, the Tompiros generally maintained until the late 1660's a tenuous peace with the Apaches. Unfortunately, a drought—the Southwest's most persistent opponent of tranquility—which seared southeastern New Mexico from 1666 to 1671 reduced both the Pueblos and Apaches to the verge of starvation. In a series of savage attacks, the Apaches ran off the Tompiros' livestock and forced them to abandon their parched fields to huddle helplessly inside walled pueblos which promised little safety. When Spanish retaliatory campaigns failed to check the Apache attacks, the Pueblos lost hope. Reduced to mere shadows of their former prosperous selves, they gradually drifted away during the 1670's, leaving only emptiness and solitude behind.[53] Their tragic fate was a grim reminder to the other Pueblos of the precariousness of their own position.

[51] France V. Scholes, "Troublous Times in New Mexico, 1659-1670," *New Mexico Historical Review*, XII (July, 1937), 396-97.
[52] "Declaration of Captain Andrés Hurtado, September, 1661," in Hackett, *Historical Documents*, III, 186-87.
[53] Escalante to Morfi, April 2, 1778, in Twitchell, *op. cit.*, II, 269.

The Valley and the Plains

The long-smoldering discontent of the Pueblos flamed up in 1680 in a carefully planned rebellion that quickly drove the Spaniards from the province. It is quite likely that the Apaches *del Acho*, who lived on the eastern edge of the Sangre de Cristos, helped to plan the revolt, since they joined the northern Pueblos in annihilating the Spaniards at Taos and Picurís.[54] Other Apaches participated in the successful siege of Santa Fe. Before allowing Governor Antonio de Otermín to withdraw from Santa Fe, the rebels demanded that he surrender all of his Apache captives, "inasmuch as some Apaches who were among them were asking for them."[55]

Late in 1681, Otermín led an expedition back into New Mexico, expecting to find, according to one of his aides, that "the greater part of the kingdom" had been destroyed and that the Pueblos still alive would submit "most humbly" because of Apache oppression.[56] Since he recalled that in earlier years the Plains Indians, upon entering a pueblo to trade, had maltreated the townsmen "and often their wives and daughters as well," he expected the Pueblos to greet him as a deliverer. Instead, he was shocked to find that the Apaches had neither destroyed a pueblo nor "even damaged one seriously"[57] and that the Pueblos were still determined to resist him. Unprepared to cope with their opposition, he again withdrew to El Paso. He had failed to realize that once the Spaniards were gone, the Pueblos and Plains Apaches would renew their trade alliance.

The near-anarchy that prevailed in New Mexico until Diego de Vargas reconquered the territory in 1693 did not mar the close relations between the eastern towns and the Plains Indians. Pecos became practically a second home for the Faraon Apaches (probably the same tribe as the Vaqueros of Oñate and Benavides), and Taos retained the friendship of the Apaches *del Acho*. Although Picurís, the third pueblo fronting directly on the plains,

---

[54] Hackett, *Revolt*, I, xxiv.
[55] "Letter of Antonio de Otermín, September 8, 1680," *ibid.*, 13.
[56] "Opinion of Fray Francisco de Ayeta, December 23, 1681," *ibid.*, II, 307–308.
[57] *Ibid.*, 308.

was hostile toward the other two, it was able to maintain peace and an active trade with their Apache allies.[58]

During the course of his reconquest, Diego de Vargas encountered some Apache support for the Pueblos. His attempt to surprise Pecos in 1692 failed because "several Apache scouts" warned the Pueblos, who fled into the mountains overlooking their town.[59] Although the Pecos natives at first threatened to take refuge at Taos or among the Apaches rather than to surrender, Vargas managed to win their confidence by his kind treatment of some captive stragglers. When he returned the following year to resume his conquest, Pecos was the first pueblo to submit, and thereafter it actively assisted in the capture of the more recalcitrant towns and encouraged the Faraon Apaches to remain friendly. When Luis Tupatú, the influential chief of Picurís, finally appeared before Vargas to proffer friendship, he explained that he had been away trading with the Apaches for deerskins and that his brother and fellow leader Lorenzo had been on a trip to the buffalo plains.[60] The absence of the two prominent leaders during a crisis indicates that Picurís had become quite dependent on the Plains Indian trade.

Although Vargas relentlessly pressed his reconquest to a conclusion during 1694, his marches, skirmishes, and sieges did not stop the trade between the Pueblos and Apaches. In March, for example, the Faraones came to Pecos to barter as usual. Juan de Ye, the Indian governor there, promptly went to Santa Fe, where he obtained permission to trade from Vargas, who also sent some Spanish soldiers to participate. The fair was, no doubt, a great success inasmuch as the Apaches, upon leaving, promised to return at the end of the wet season and the Spaniards lauded them as having "better behavior [and] a greater perseverance of friendship" than the Pueblos.[61]

In May, Juan de Ye returned to Santa Fe with a Faraon chief and eight warriors. The Apaches gave Vargas three intricately

---
[58] Forbes, *op. cit.*, 238.
[59] *Ibid.*, 239.
[60] *Ibid.*, 251.
[61] *Ibid.*, 254.

The Valley and the Plains

decorated buffalo robes and a tipi, and they asked permission to hold a trading fair at Pecos during the *tiempo de elote* ("when the corn begins to ripen").[62] They informed Vargas that it was a fourteen-day trip to their villages on the Canadian—which would place them in the central part of the Texas Panhandle. Upon leaving, they explained that they had "to attend to their fields." This, the first evidence that any of the Plains Apaches had taken up agriculture, demonstrates the significant extent of the Pecos influence upon the Faraones.[63]

When the Apaches again arrived at Pecos in late August, the Pecos chief asked Vargas to allow the barter and urged the Spaniards to attend in order to emphasize their peaceful intentions toward the Apaches. Although he was about to start on a campaign against some rebellious Tewas, Vargas delayed his departure for a week to enable his followers to visit the fair, enjoining them, however, against the use of horses as a "medium of exchange."[64] War could wait; trade was paramount.

By the end of 1694, Vargas seemingly had completed the reconquest of the Río Grande pueblos, but within two years some of the northern towns had again taken up arms against him. This time, as he methodically crushed the insurgents, Vargas meted out punishment with a cruelty rarely matched—even by Spanish governors. Exaggerated accounts of his barbaric retaliations caused the panic-stricken natives of Picurís to seek refuge among the Apaches on the plains. When he arrived at the deserted pueblo at the foot of the Sangre de Cristos on October 22, his Pecos scouts turned up a straggler who revealed that, three days earlier, his fellow townsmen had "headed toward the place where the bulls run."[65] Determined to prevent their escape, Vargas hurriedly followed along a footpath that was "like a canyon in some

---

[62] Jessie Bromilow Bailey, *Diego de Vargas and the Reconquest of New Mexico*, 169; J. Manuel Espinosa, *Crusaders of the Rio Grande*, 204.

[63] The Hurtado expedition of 1715 substantiated the indication here that the Faraones engaged in small-scale agriculture on the Canadian during this period. *Infra.*, p. 27.

[64] Bailey, *op. cit.*, 149–51; Forbes, *op. cit.*, 256.

[65] "Journal of Events in the Second Uprising of the Pueblos in 1696," in Alfred Barnaby Thomas (trans. and ed.), *After Coronado*, 55.

places and wholly mountainous, and filled with stones." Slowed by their families, supplies, and livestock, the fleeing Indians were overtaken just as they reached the plains. Although they scattered like so many frightened quail, the Spaniards rounded up seventy-one before nightfall. More were captured the following day, but they informed Vargas that Don Lorenzo, their governor, had gone with "the rest, following the Apaches who had moved ahead."[66]

An early autumn blizzard forced Vargas to give up the pursuit. After returning to Santa Fe by way of Pecos at the southern flank of the snow-clogged mountains, he apportioned the forlorn captives among his soldiers for use as bondsmen, "because of their desertion of our holy religion and their royal vassalage."[67] Of the eighty-four prisoners, "counting the suckling babes of the women, and the boys and girls of all ages," however, only five were married braves. Once again the Spaniards had asserted their control over the upper Río Grande region; but their mastery was soon to be challenged by the approach of French traders from the east and horse-seeking Comanches from the north.

[66] *Ibid.*, 58.
[67] *Ibid.*, 59.

2
War, Trade, and Diplomacy, 1700-1786

AT THE BEGINNING of the eighteenth century, the New Mexicans had achieved a remarkable stability in their relations with the Plains Indians. By means of a flourishing trade with the Plains Apaches, they were rapidly inducing the latter to adopt Spanish and Pueblo cultural traits. Unfortunately, these tranquil conditions were eventually destroyed by the intruding Comanches, soon to master the southern plains and become the most serious challenge New Mexico faced before the arrival of the Anglo-Americans. Only after long, painful years of turmoil in which the province was driven to the brink of destruction was a *modus vivendi* reached. Eventually, the sporadic trading between the two peoples transformed the Comanches from hostile marauders into friendly barterers willing to keep a peace treaty.

At the time of the Comanches' arrival, the only Plains Indians hostile to New Mexico were the Faraon Apaches, seminomadic raiders who ranged all the way from the central Texas Panhandle to the Sandía Mountains. Always treacherous, this band of Indians intermittently spread death and destruction deep into New Mexico. Even Diego de Vargas, probably the greatest fighter ever to occupy the Palace of the Governors, was unable to master them. After Vargas died suddenly in 1704 while pursuing a Faraon band, matters grew so desperate that the Santa Fe *cabildo* appealed for aid against the "constant murders and thefts."[1] Before year's end, the ferocity of the raids forced the Spaniards temporarily to abandon Galisteo, which left the southern approaches of both Pecos and Santa Fe wide open to the invaders.[2]

[1] Twitchell, *op. cit.*, II, 125.
[2] *Ibid.*

In his brief administration from 1705 to 1707, Governor Francisco Cuervo made an amazing improvement in the Indian situation. With the aid of the Pueblos "most skilled in war," he won a series of "most happy victories" that forced the Faraon Apaches to make peace.[3] Then, to hold their friendship, he distributed to all who came to Santa Fe presents such as "food, bundles of tobacco, ribbons, hats, needles, beads, and many other trifles."[4] The restoration of peace greatly benefited the Pueblos because it allowed them to renew their trade with "the savages."[5]

Cuervo took advantage of the improved conditions in 1706 to dispatch an expedition under his *sargentomayor*, Juan de Ulibarrí, to bring back the Picurís natives who had fled to El Cuartelejo ten years earlier. The fugitives, disappointed at being subjected by the Cuartelejo Apaches to "labor twice as great" as in New Mexico, had several times petitioned Cuervo for soldiers to "restore" them to their old pueblo.[6] When some of the refugees who returned to Picurís at the beginning of 1706 also urged the sending of a rescue mission, Cuervo finally yielded.

With a force of 132 presidials, settlers, and Pueblos, Ulibarrí left Santa Fe on July 13 on an expedition that introduced to recorded history the inhabitants of a vast area northeast of New Mexico. Marching east from Taos over a trail "very broken, mountainous, narrow and full of many precipices" into the Canadian watershed, he found small groups of Apache farmers, whom he presented with "much" tobacco, knives, pinole, corn, biscuits, and "suitable presents."[7] As he moved north toward Raton Pass, he encountered the Jicarilla, *Flechas de Palo*, and Carlana Apaches, who—belying the appellation of "bad thieves" given them by the Indians farther south—were "busy with the sowing

---

[3] "Certification of Captain Rael de Aguilar, January 10, 1706," in Hackett, *Historical Documents*, III, 367.
[4] *Ibid.*
[5] "Mandamiento of the Viceroy Duke of Albuquerque relative to New Mexico, July 30, 1706," in Twitchell, *op. cit.*, II, 139.
[6] Cuervo to His Majesty, October 18, 1706, in Hackett, *Historical Documents*, III, 384.
[7] "Diary made by Ulibarrí of his trip to ransom the Picuríes Indians, 1706," in Thomas, *After Coronado*, 61.

of corn, frijoles, and pumpkins." After giving the Indians some worn-out horses and other "good presents" to ensure their friendship, Ulibarrí continued on his way.[8]

Reaching the Arkansas River on July 30, Ulibarrí turned eastward toward El Cuartelejo, following a trail over savannas so featureless that, according to him, even the Apaches sometimes got lost. Although his Pueblo guides took their "direction from hummocks of grass" placed a short distance apart on the trail by the Apaches, they lost their way three times before stumbling upon the nearest of the Cuartelejo villages. To Ulibarrí's relief, the Cuartelejos received him with "peace and friendship" and then conducted him to their principal town, the storied El Cuartelejo itself. Here he was greeted with cries of joy by the Picurís natives, who came running out of their "huts of little houses." To cap his success, the Apaches readily agreed to surrender the captives.

Ulibarrí soon realized that the Cuartelejos' amiability stemmed from their need for support against the Pawnees, who, armed with French muskets, had been worsting them in their long-standing warfare. Liberally embellishing the facts, his hosts informed Ulibarrí that French soldiers were fighting side by side with the Pawnees, and as proof they produced a rusty gun supposedly taken from a slain Frenchman. In bringing up the specter of a French intrusion, they had accidentally struck upon the one thing most likely to command Spanish attention.

During the few days necessary for all the Picurís to be brought in from the various Apache villages, Ulibarrí was intrigued to see that the majority of the Apaches wore around their necks crosses, medals, and rosaries. Inquiring the reason, he learned that during "many years" of trading with New Mexico the Cuartelejos had come to attribute the Spaniards' valor to their religious symbols. Reasoning therefore that the medals would "help them in their own wars,"[9] the Apaches sallied forth to battle with the images of Spanish saints hanging from their necks. True to their word,

[8] *Ibid.*, 64.
[9] *Ibid.*, 72.

the Apaches delivered to Ulibarrí all the Pueblos except a few absent on a buffalo hunt who, it was promised, would be returned to New Mexico the following year when the Apaches "came in for ransom." Before leaving the Apache camp, however, Ulibarrí gravely performed a time-honored ritual intended to instill in the Indians loyalty for Spain. He selected a "young Indian of fine body and countenance" to serve as chief of all the Cuartelejos and gave him a baton to symbolize his authority.[10]

Ulibarrí's report disclosed that, under New Mexican influence, the Apaches throughout a vast area northeast of the Pueblo settlements had developed a surprising skill in agriculture to supplement their dependence on the buffalo. His observations have been confirmed by archaeological reports that an Indian village excavated in Scott County, Kansas, contained a multiroomed stone structure, irrigation works, and other features "clearly inspired by, if not the actual work of, Pueblo Indians." Waldo R. Wedel, a leading authority on the archaeology of the Great Plains, concluded that if this village was not the Cuartelejo *ranchería* from which Ulibarrí rescued the Picurís refugees, it was a simultaneously occupied community in which Pueblo Indians from the upper Río Grande and Plains Apaches were residing.[11]

The Cuartelejos were only one of several Apache groups influenced by the Spaniards and Pueblos to adopt a semisedentary way of life. Archaeologists have discovered between the eastern slope of the Colorado Rockies and the Nebraska Sandhills many sites similar to El Cuartelejo that were the homes of Plains Apaches. These sites, designated as the Dismal River Complex and dated by means of tree rings or by cross finds of datable southwestern potsherds "at approximately A.D. 1700 plus or minus 25 to 50 years,"[12] were occupied by a hunting people who, like the Cuartelejos, had adopted a rudimentary form of agriculture from the Pueblos. Evidence of Pueblo influence includes their baking

[10] Ibid., 74.
[11] Waldo R. Wedel, *An Introduction to Kansas Archeology*, 468.
[12] Wedel, *Prehistoric Man*, 113.

pits, identical to those found in post-Spanish levels at Pecos, and their pottery, which "strongly resembles the utility pottery made at Taos, Picurís, and other frontier pueblos on the upper Rio Grande."[13] Wedel asserts that the Pueblos must have speeded up, if they did not initiate, the adoption of crop growing among the Plains Apaches hundreds of miles northeast of New Mexico.[14]

Of all the Plains Apaches, only the Faraones resisted the New Mexicans' blandishments. Like their kinsmen, the Faraones traded regularly at Pecos and Taos, but, unlike the others, they took advantage of their visits to "commit thefts of animals."[15] They had become so troublesome by 1715 that Captain Juan Páez Hurtado, a veteran of Vargas' reconquest, was dispatched to punish them. While planning the expedition, Hurtado was warned by the Taos Indians not to let the natives of Pecos know of his plans because they would inform the Faraones. The Taos spokesmen claimed that the Pecos natives and the Faraones were "almost the same" and that the Faraones had even lived at Pecos until Vargas reduced it in 1693. Then they had gone to live on the plains.[16] The best time to attack the Faraones, the Taoseños continued, would be in the middle of August, "when the moon is almost full," because then they would be threshing the grain from their corn. If the expedition did not strike them then, it would be too late, for after the harvest they cached their grain in the ground and followed the buffalo herds until it was time to plant their crops during the following spring.

Hurtado's campaign was a dismal failure. His Pueblo guide fruitlessly sought the Apache camps for eighteen days until Hurtado, deciding the guide did not know where he was "nor where he ought to go," had him lashed for "such negligence."[17] After a group of Taos Indians whom he sent in search of the Faraones

[13] Ibid.
[14] Ibid., 115.
[15] "Diary of the Campaign of Captain Juan Hurtado against the Faraon Apaches, 1715," in Thomas, After Coronado, 80.
[16] Ibid., 81.
[17] Ibid., 94.

returned empty handed, Hurtado, concluding that his quarry probably had been warned of his expedition by the Pecos Indians, reluctantly turned back.[18]

Although the Faraones continued for a time to be a nuisance, the Comanches replaced them as the major menace on the eastern frontier of New Mexico. This tribe, native to the mountainous region far to the north, apparently had learned of the attractive southlands from their Ute kinsmen and allies, who regularly attended the Taos trade fairs. The Comanches made their first recorded visit to Taos in 1705, ostensibly to trade; but the very next year, they were reported by Ulibarrí to be threatening to attack that pueblo.[19] On his campaign through southern Colorado, moreover, Ulibarrí observed the possible commencement of Comanche pressure on the Apaches of the plains when he met some Penxaye Apaches who were hurrying to join "the rest who live along those rivers and streams in order to defend themselves together from the Utes and Comanches."[20]

The Comanches evidently had been impelled to leave their homeland by pressure from northeastern tribes armed with muskets. Once on the move, they were lured toward New Mexico by their desire for Spanish horses and trade goods.[21] In the first agreement they made with New Mexico, about 1709, they asked for and received permission to trade at Taos.[22] Apparently having had little intention of honoring this original treaty, the Comanches, according to a report of Captain Cristóbal de la Serna of the Santa Fe presidio in 1719, took advantage of the "shade and cloak of *peace*" to steal "on whatever occasion that offered itself."[23]

Serna's statement not only indicates the extent of the Comanches' stealing but also casts doubt on the authenticity of an alleged campaign against the Comanches in 1717. As originally

[18] Ibid., 98.
[19] Twitchell, *op. cit.*, II, 301; Thomas, *After Coronado*, 60.
[20] "Diary made by Ulibarri," *loc. cit.*, 65.
[21] Ernest Wallace and E. Adamson Hoebel, *The Comanches*, 10; Rupert N. Richardson, *The Comanche Barrier to South Plains Settlement*, 19.
[22] "Opinion of Xptoval de la Serna, August 19, 1719," in Thomas, *After Coronado*, 105.
[23] Ibid.

described in 1906 by Amado Cháves, an amateur New Mexican historian, the citizens of Santa Fe, incensed by the Comanche raids, selected Don Juan de Padilla, Don Carlos Fernández, and Don Pedro Pino to lead them against the marauding Indians. After a long pursuit, the Spaniards surprised the Comanches in a beautiful valley southeast of present Anton Chico, killing "hundreds" and capturing seven hundred others whom they sent to die in the sugar-cane fields of Cuba. In concluding this narrative, Cháves solemnly stated that the Comanches were so subdued by their defeat "that they never again went on the war path against the Spaniards."[24] Although accepted by many southwestern historians,[25] Cháves' account was only the garbled rendition of the folk traditions of a victory won over the notorious Comanche chief Cuerno Verde in 1774.[26]

By 1719, the mounting Comanche depredations, including a destructive raid on Taos, and their interference with the impor-

---

[24] Amado Cháves, "The Defeat of the Comanches in 1717," *Historical Society of New Mexico Publication No. 8* (1906), 6-10.

[25] See, for example, Warren A. Beck, *New Mexico*, 94; Cleve Hallenbeck, *Land of the Conquistadores*, 207; Alfred B. Thomas, *The Plains Indians and New Mexico, 1751-1778*, 8.

[26] *Infra.*, p. 47. Although Cháves did not document his article, he based it on a folk drama "written in verse by one of the members of the expedition" (Cháves, "Defeat," *loc. cit.*, 10). He possessed one of the few extant copies of this drama and lent it to Aurelio Espinosa, who edited and published it in 1907 ("Los Comanches," *University of New Mexico Bulletin*, Language Series, No. 1 [1907], 18). Like Cháves' article, the folk drama lists Fernández and Pino as being among the New Mexican leaders—but both were residents of the last half of the eighteenth century and could not have led an expedition in 1717. Since Padilla, otherwise little mentioned in New Mexican history, was a direct ancestor of Cháves (Twitchell, *op. cit.*, II, 198-99), the latter may also have relied upon family tradition in writing his account. For an interesting analysis and translation of the folk drama, see Arthur L. Campa, "Los Comanches: a New Mexican Folk Drama," *University of New Mexico Bulletin*, Language Series, No. 7 (1932). Although both Espinosa and Campa have shown the impossibility of the 1717 campaign referred to by Cháves, no notice of their findings has ever been taken by southwestern historians. The victory described in "Los Comanches" most likely was that of Don Carlos Fernández in 1774 over an unnamed chief (quite feasibly Cuerno Verde, since he was the Comanche leader at that time). The possibility that it was Don Juan Bautista de Anza's victory in 1779 over Cuerno Verde (*infra.*, pp. 50-51) is weakened by the fact that Anza is nowhere mentioned in "Los Comanches." In addition, the drama clearly indicates that Cuerno Verde survived the battle, whereas he perished in the 1779 defeat.

tant barter between New Mexico and the Plains Apaches[27] led Governor Antonio de Valverde to take the field against them with more than six hundred men. Although Valverde was unable to locate his elusive enemy, he discovered the gravity of the Comanche onslaught against the Apaches and perceived the serious consequences this could have for New Mexico. East of Taos in the valley of La Jicarilla he found the Jicarilla Apaches living in small villages composed of adobe houses with flat roofs that sometimes bore "a most holy cross"—a pathetic protection against the Comanches. The Jicarillas, like the Pueblos, raised maize on small, fertile fields irrigated by "many ditches and canals;"[28] but, unfortunately, their crops had attracted Comanche raiders. Valverde visited many "depopulated *rancherías*" where only ruins were to be seen. He noted also that the discouraged Apaches abandoned their houses at night and hid in the hills "to insure their lives."[29]

Between the Raton Range and the Arkansas River, Valverde encountered some Carlana Apaches, shattered remnants of a once powerful tribe, in full retreat before the Utes and Comanches.[30] He was heartened, however, to meet near the Arkansas a large Cuartelejo war party that was also in search of the Comanches. Although he hopefully joined the Cuartelejos, Valverde was unable to track down the Comanches, who had vanished, with hardly a trace, into the vast expanses north of the Arkansas River.

During the joint expedition, Valverde learned that the Cuartelejos were under attack from all sides. One band, the Palomas, had recently been driven from the South Platte region by the Utes, and the entire tribe was subject to devastating raids from the east by the Pawnees. Repeating the charges made earlier to Ulibarrí that Frenchmen were fighting side by side with the Pawnees, the Cuartelejos pleaded for aid, but the approach of winter forced Valverde to return to New Mexico.[31]

[27] "Opinion of Captain Miguel de Coca, August 19, 1719," in Thomas, *After Coronado*, 104-105.
[28] "Diary of the Campaign of Governor Antonio de Valverde against the Ute and Comanche Indians, 1719," *ibid.*, 113.
[29] Valverde to Valero, November 30, 1719, *ibid.*, 142.
[30] "Diary of the Campaign of Valverde," *ibid.*, 114.
[31] *Ibid.*, 119.

The following year, Valverde sent his lieutenant governor, Don Pedro de Villasur, to investigate the reports of French encroachments. With forty-two Spanish soldiers and sixty Pueblo auxiliaries, Villasur followed the well-known trail from Taos to the Cuartelejo villages, then marched northeastward to the South Platte River and descended it until he reached a Pawnee camp on August 7. After trying unsuccessfully for three days to learn the location of the elusive Frenchmen, he became alarmed over the growing belligerency of the Pawnees and withdrew some distance to consider his next move. On the following morning, his camp was surprised by the Pawnees, and he and all but thirteen of his men were killed. The survivors, all wounded, fled pell-mell across the plains to El Cuartelejo, where the Apaches received them "with much kindness" and shared with them their "poor provisions."[32] Clinging pathetically to the only possible source of aid, the Cuartelejos begged the Spaniards to "return to these frontiers" and join them in an offensive against the French and Pawnees. It was a forlorn hope.

Thoroughly alarmed by the Villasur massacre, the Spaniards debated possible means of aiding the Apaches and countering the French movements. The viceroy, perhaps too encouraged by reports that the Cuartelejos were trustworthy and ready to accept Christianity, proposed the establishment at El Cuartelejo of a presidio manned with twenty-five soldiers. However, Valverde vigorously objected, arguing that a 25-man garrison was too small, that El Cuartelejo was lacking in wood and other essentials, that the winters were too rigorous, and that the site was surrounded by "a great number of savages."[33] He maintained that the valley of La Jicarilla, which could be more easily reinforced and provisioned, would be a better location. Unfortunately, neither site was occupied, and the Apaches, bereft of Spanish aid, were unable to check the Comanche advance.

Significantly, the Apaches' inability to withstand the Comanche advance was not due to a marked deficiency in either guns or

[32] Valverde to Valero, October 8, 1720, *ibid.*, 142.
[33] "Council of War, Santa Fe, June 2, 1720," *ibid.*, 157.

horses. It is true that the Apaches were denied guns by the Spaniards, but the Comanches likewise were unable to secure firearms from the French until they had defeated the Apaches. Valverde reported in 1719 that a war party of sixty-nine Apaches that joined him had 103 mounts, a respectable number by almost any standard. That same year, Bénard de La Harpe, a French trader blazing a trail through what is now Oklahoma, stated that the main advantage of the Faraon Apaches in war was that "they have good horses, whereas the other nations have very few."[34]

The Apaches were unsuccessful in defending themselves largely because they lived in small, isolated farming communities that were easy to overwhelm by surprise attacks. On the other hand, Apache retaliatory expeditions were usually unsuccessful because the Comanches were difficult to locate and had better organization and discipline. According to Inspector Don Pedro de Rivera, who visited New Mexico in 1726, the Comanches conserved "such solidarity that both on the marches which they continually make . . . as well as in the camps which they establish where they settle, they are formidable in their defense."[35] Two courses of action might have enabled the eastern Apaches to withstand the Comanche onslaught: by abandoning agriculture and reverting to their former status of nomadic bison hunters, they could have met the Comanches on equal terms; or, by concentrating—like the Pueblos, the Pawnees of eastern Nebraska, and the Taovayas on the Red River—into larger, fortified villages, they could have repulsed the attacks.[36] They failed, however, to make either of these adjustments.

Of the Plains Apaches who were driven back on New Mexico, the defeat of the Jicarillas is the best documented. Governor Juan Domingo de Bustamante, who visited their village in 1723, learned that the Comanches had recently killed many young Jica-

---

[34] "Diary of the Campaign of Valverde," *ibid.*, 128; Anna Lewis (trans.), "LeHarpe's First Expedition in Oklahoma," *Chronicles of Oklahoma*, II (December, 1924), 346.
[35] Rivera to Casa Fuerte, September 26, 1726, in Thomas, *After Coronado*, 212.
[36] Frank E. Secoy, "Changing Military Patterns on the Great Plains," *Monographs of the American Ethnological Society*, No. 21 (1953), 32.

rilla men and carried off many of their women and children.[37] Although Bustamante recommended the establishment of a presidio among the Jicarillas and personally selected a logical site for it, he was unable to obtain authorization for the project. Soon afterward, the Jicarillas despaired of aid and abandoned their homes, some going to the Navahos, others to Taos, and a few—strange as it may seem—"to the extensive plains of Los Cibolos."[38] In 1733, a group settled around a mission established for them on the Río Trampas near Taos and gave up hope of reclaiming their old homeland. According to a report of 1748, "the few that remained" were living peacefully near Taos and Pecos.[39] Too late, the Spanish officials realized that in abandoning the Jicarillas, they lost control of "the pass" through which the Comanches had easiest access to the province.[40]

Because the Comanches were basically a mountain people, the Cuartelejo Apaches, located farther out on the plains than the Jicarillas, were able to hold out a while longer. An Apache report in 1727 placed the Comanches in "El Almagre [the Front Range of the Rockies] or a little farther away"—no immediate threat to the Cuartelejos.[41] Indeed, the Cuartelejos apparently entered into a loose alliance with some French traders. In 1726, they sold to the New Mexicans some Comanche captives who claimed that their captors had been accompanied by white men who, "according to their narrative," were French. About a year later, the Cuartelejos were reportedly joined by five Frenchmen in an expedition against the Comanches.[42] The efforts of these few Frenchmen, however, were short lived and unavailing, for the Cuartelejos were forced to abandon their homeland. Unfortunately, there are no extant records pertaining to their defeat. When next officially

---

[37] Bustamante to Casa Fuerte, January 10, 1724, in Thomas, *After Coronado*, 201.
[38] Rivera to Casa Fuerte, September 26, 1726, *ibid.*, 216; Bustamante to Casa Fuerte, August 26, 1727, in Hackett, *Pichardo's Treatise*, III, 246.
[39] Joaquín Codallos y Rabal to the Viceroy, March 4, 1748, in Twitchell, *op. cit.*, I, 20.
[40] *Ibid.*
[41] Bustamante to Casa Fuerte, April 30, 1727, in Thomas, *After Coronado*, 256.
[42] *Ibid.*, 257.

A History of New Mexican–Plains Indian Relations

mentioned, in 1752, they were living near Pecos, allied with the inhabitants there against the Comanches.[43] They did not immediately give up all contact with the plains, however, for a report in 1754 stated that they roamed the country east of Pecos "as far as the boundaries of Texas."[44]

The Faraon Apaches, found along the Canadian in 1715 by a Spanish expedition and mentioned by La Harpe in 1719 as living west of the Taovayas, were soon afterward set upon by the Comanches. Although there are no contemporary accounts of their defeat, Teodoro de Croix stated in 1781 that some time earlier, a portion of the Mescalero Apaches had been forced to flee "from their old pueblos of El Norte,"[45] almost certainly a reference to the Faraones. And three years later, Governor Domingo Cabello of Texas reported that a group of Apaches who lived three hundred leagues northwest "from the province of Texas" had been defeated in a nine-day battle with the Comanches in 1723 and forced to seek safety in flight.[46] Once driven from the plains, the Faraones cut their ties with the area; in the early 1750's, they were living near the Río Grande about midway between El Paso and Albuquerque and were purchasing buffalo meat and robes from the Cuartelejo Apaches rather than doing their own hunting.[47]

Despite the turbulence on the plains, the Spaniards managed to preserve much of their Indian trade. The importance of the barter, as well as the fact that a surprisingly large portion of it was conducted on the plains, is revealed by the records of early French explorers. Claude Du Tisne, a young French adventurer who visited the "Black Pawnees" (Wichitas) along the Arkansas River

---

[43] Vélez to the Count of Revilla Gigedo, September 29, 1752, in Thomas, *Plains Indians*, 124.

[44] "Instruction of Vélez to His Successor, Don Francisco Marín del Valle, August 12, 1754," *ibid.*, 135.

[45] "General Report of 1781 by Teodoro de Croix," in Alfred B. Thomas, *Teodoro de Croix and the Northern Frontier of New Spain, 1776–1783*, 126.

[46] William E. Dunn, "Apache Relations in Texas, 1718–1750," *Texas State Historical Association Quarterly*, XII (January, 1911), 218.

[47] "Instruction of Vélez," *loc. cit.*, 135.

in southern Kansas in 1719, was told that New Mexican traders had formerly reached their villages, but that the Padoucas had recently "barred the road."[48]

With the Padoucas,[49] the masters of the Kansas plains, the Spaniards had a significant commerce. La Harpe observed in 1719 that whoever controlled the trade with them would be the "master of the region."[50] In 1724, the Frenchman Étienne Veniard de Bourgmond, veteran of long years of trading among the Plains Indians, visited the Padoucas in an attempt to open communications with Santa Fe. During his very amiable stay among them, he learned that the Spaniards came to their villages "every spring" with horses, knives, awls, and axes to trade for buffalo robes. "A great number of warriors" who were preparing to go to New Mexico "to buy horses" had gathered a large number of buffalo hides because, they explained, the Spaniards "give us one horse for three hides."[51] Although the Padoucas offered to take Bourgmond to New Mexico, which they said was only twelve marching days away, he declined the offer because of his poor health and the proximity of winter.

The available references at this time indicate that New Mexico conducted a comparatively peaceful trade with all of the Plains Indians. In 1730, Bishop Benito Crespo, reporting on a visit he had made to New Mexico, was quite impressed with the amount

[48] Du Tisne to Bienville, November 22, 1719, in Pierre Margry (ed.), *Découvertes et Establissements des Francais dans l'Ouest et dans le Sud de l'Amerique Septentrionale*, VI, 313, quoted in Henri Folmer, "French Expansion towards New Mexico in the Eighteenth Century" (Unpublished M.A. Thesis, University of Denver, 1939), 71.

[49] There is a considerable amount of controversy concerning the identity of the Padouca Indians. Many historians of the Plains Indians—including Rupert N. Richardson, Ernest Wallace, Alfred B. Thomas, and Henry Folmer—have concluded they were probably the Comanches. Two other scholars, Frank E. Secoy ("The Identity of the 'Paduca': An Ethnohistorical Analysis," *American Anthropologist*, N. S., LIII [January, 1951], 525-47) and George E. Hyde (*Indians of the High Plains*), vigorously contend that they were in reality the Plains Apaches. I am in agreement with the latter two, but it is not essential to this study to attempt to identify them.

[50] Lewis, "LeHarpe's First Expedition," *loc. cit.*, 347.

[51] Folmer, "French Expansion," 184.

of "bartering and trading" being conducted with the "pagans on the borders."[52] Significantly, he made no mention of Indian hostilities. Don Pedro de Rivera, in a report published in 1736, blandly observed that a "barbarous, warlike nation called the Comanches . . . always on the move," appeared annually in New Mexico to barter and then disappeared, not to be seen again until the next trading season.[53] The first Frenchmen to cross the plains to New Mexico, the Mallet brothers in 1739, also reported that the Comanches (Laitanes) were trading peaceably with the Spaniards.[54] The most probable reason for the Comanches' peaceful behavior was that the Spaniards were their only practical source of European goods until the 1740's, when French traders reached the plains in appreciable numbers.

Most of the trade with the Comanches took place in the New Mexican villages because it was more convenient and because Spanish laws forbade traders to visit the villages of the "wild" Indians.[55] Occasionally, foolhardy individuals ignored the ban,[56] but with increasing risk. In 1768, for example, five settlers and a Pueblo who went to a Comanche camp near Taos to gain an advantage over their fellow traders were killed by their hosts.[57] As a consequence of this and similar incidents, traders generally remained within the safety of their villages.

Throughout the century, Taos dominated the Indian trade by means of great summer fairs to which New Mexicans from far and near and of all classes, hues, and reputations flocked. In its dusty plaza a governor often rubbed shoulders with lowly peons,

---

[52] "Bishop Crespo to the Viceroy, September 25, 1730," *New Mexico Historical Review*, XXVIII (July, 1953), 230.

[53] Quoted in Ernest Wallace, "The Habitat and Range of the Kiowa, Comanche and Apache Indians Before 1876," 65.

[54] Folmer, "French Expansion," 236.

[55] One such edict was issued December 12, 1712 (Twitchell, *op. cit.*, II, 169), another on April 3, 1723 (Hubert H. Bancroft, *The History of New Mexico and Arizona*, 239.)

[56] In 1735, Diego de Torres was accused of trading with the Comanches before the time set and as a result had to forfeit the buffalo hides he had purchased. Twitchell, *op. cit.*, II, 205.

[57] Thomas, *Plains Indians*, 160.

all keenly anxious to reap profits from their Indian visitors. The spirit of the fairs was brilliantly but scathingly captured by a reform-minded priest, Fray Serrano:

> When the Indian trading embassy comes to these governors and their alcaldes, here all prudence forsakes them . . . because the fleet is in. The fleet being, in this case, some two hundred, or at the very least, fifty tents of barbarous Indians.[58]

The New Mexican traders were able to offer an increasing list of European goods. In return for their buffalo hides, meat, tallow, and captives, now the Comanches could obtain cornmeal, bread, and other foodstuffs, and also could choose from an array of beads, trinkets, and a wide variety of ironware ranging from knives and axes to bridle bits and cooking utensils.

Horses also changed hands at the fairs, although at times Spanish officials attempted to prevent their sale to the Indians. Governor Tómas Vélez Cachupín once forbade the settlers to take a single horse to the fair for fear that he would be forced to allow the Comanches "to buy mares and studs."[59] Other governors, however, saw nothing wrong with the practice. Fray Serrano stated in 1761 that New Mexican officials, in preparing for the fair, "gather together as many horses as they can," and fifteen years later another priest observed without reproach that his countrymen were trading horses for slaves and "she-mules"[60] (horse trading in a classical sense). As their horses increased in numbers, the Comanches became sellers instead of purchasers. As early as 1760, Bishop Tamaron noted that they brought horses to trade "out of the plunder they obtained elsewhere," and in the 1770's they were reportedly bringing "a thousand or more animals" with them to Taos. On a more modest scale, Governor Juan Bautista

---

[58] "Report of Fray Serrano to the Viceroy, the Marquis of Cruillas, 1761," in Hackett, *Historical Documents*, III, 486.

[59] "Instruction of Vélez," *loc. cit.*, 133. Hereafter Vélez Cachupin will be referred to simply as Vélez.

[60] "Report of Fray Serrano," *loc. cit.*, III, 486; Fray Francisco Atanasio Domínguez, *The Missions of New Mexico*, 1776 (trans. and ed. by Eleanor B. Adams and Fray Angelico Chavez), 251.

de Anza in 1786 purchased fifteen "riding beasts" from the Comanches.[61]

The rigidly enforced Spanish ban on trading guns to the Indians did not entirely eliminate the traffic, for there was no barrier against the Comanches' selling firearms to Spaniards. Mentioned as early as 1760, this peculiar reverse gunflow was still going on in 1776 when Fray Domínguez stated matter-of-factly that the Comanches sold "good guns," pistols, powder, and balls which they obtained from the Jumano Indians. Although the friar implied that the trade in guns was considerable, the only specific numerical reference is Anza's report in 1786 that he had purchased three from the Comanches.[62]

The propriety of ransoming slaves from the Comanches at the fairs created a furious controversy. Most New Mexican governors maintained that the practice was "laudable" because the redeemed captives were educated and "brought into the fold of the church," and because its discontinuance would cause the Comanches to kill their captives.[63] Some clerics defended the trade as a potential means to save souls. For this reason, Father Claramonte "astutely cultivated" a Comanche chieftain with the intent of getting some Apaches "out of captivity."[64]

Other priests argued that the captives were only being delivered from one bondage into another. Their protests ranged from a mild rebuke that the "ransomed Indians were not well treated by their new masters"[65] to a fiery charge that the governors were enriching themselves by the trade in human bodies, or, as Fray Serrano put it, "gorging themselves first with the largest mouthfuls from this table, while the rest eat the crumbs." To

---

[61] Eleanor B. Adams (trans. and ed.), "Bishop Tamaron's Visitation of New Mexico, 1760," *New Mexico Historical Review*, XXVIII (July, 1953), 217; Alfred B. Thomas, *Forgotten Frontiers*, 317.

[62] Adams, "Bishop Tamaron's Visitation," *loc. cit.*, 210; Domínguez, *op. cit.*, 251; Thomas, *Forgotten Frontiers*, 317.

[63] Vélez to the Marquis of Altamira, January 14, 1751, in Hackett, *Pichardo's Treatise*, III, 332.

[64] Domínguez, *op. cit.*, 251.

[65] "Report of Fray Miguel de Menchero, May 10, 1744," in Hackett, *Historical Documents*, III, 487.

Serrano, the trade was brutal, vicious, and degrading, and he denounced it in ringing terms:

> It is the truth that when these barbarians bring a certain number of Indian women to sell, among them many young maidens and girls, before delivering them to the Christians who buy them, if they are ten years old or over, they deflower and corrupt them in the innumerable assemblies of barbarians and Catholics . . . without considering anything but their unbridled lust and brutal shamelessness, and saying to those who buy them, with heathen impudence: "Now you can take her—now she is good."[66]

The outrageous behavior of the Comanches at the fairs was matched by the larcenous conduct of the Spaniards and Pueblos. On several occasions, even the governors were shocked by their excesses. Governor Tómas Vélez complained that the New Mexicans and Pueblos caused trouble by robbing the Comanches of their robes, horses, or "some other priceless possession."[67] Fray Serrano, even more critical, predicted darkly that the traders, "with their wrongs and injustices [which] stir up these barbarous nations," would inevitably bring on a war.[68] Regardless of the risk, however, the New Mexicans could not resist the temptation to defraud their gullible visitors, who, "as soon as they buy anything . . . usually sell exactly what they bought; and usually they keep losing, the occasion when they gain being very rare, because our people ordinarily play infamous tricks on them."[69]

A few governors seriously endeavored to forestall trouble by regulating the trade. Early in the 1750's, Vélez, who always tried to attend the fairs to keep the settlers from doing their visitors "the slightest injury,"[70] issued a "superior decree" listing the prices assigned to the trade effects of both Comanches and Spaniards. Although the decree has long since been lost, a few of its rates were casually mentioned by Fray Domínguez: for a tanned buffalo robe or "white elkskin," a Comanche received a "beldique,

---

[66] "Report of Fray Serrano," *ibid.*, 487.
[67] "Instruction of Vélez," *loc. cit.*, 134.
[68] "Report of Fray Serrano," *loc cit.*, III, 487.
[69] Domínguez, *op. cit.*, 251.
[70] "Instruction of Vélez," *loc. cit.*, 134.

or broad knife made entirely of iron, which they call a trading knife here"; for two robes he obtained "a very poor bridle, but garnished with red rags"; and for a pistol he got a bridle.[71] The decree was still in effect, at least nominally, in 1786 when Governor Anza received permission to modify it because the value of New Mexican goods "had fallen since then and that of hides had increased."[72] The only changes he made, however, were that two beldiques were to be valued as one robe and that one Spanish horse was to equal thirteen buffalo robes. In conducting the fair at Pecos in 1786, Anza set a high standard. He abolished the practice of requiring contributions from the "pagans" as a fee for permission to trade and marked off two lines "so that the contracting parties, placed on the outside of both, could exhibit and deliver to each other in the intermediate space" the goods to be exchanged.[73] By enforcing these regulations, Anza succeeded in having a peaceful and orderly fair.

The fairs were of inestimable importance to the New Mexican economy. Provincial traders took robes and Indian slaves acquired at them directly to the great Chihuahua fairs to exchange for the manufactured items not produced in their agrarian homeland. Indeed, Taos and Pecos were not the only settlements dependent on the trade. The settlers at La Cañada (present Española), a thriving town on the Río Grande about twenty miles north of Santa Fe and the main trade center for the Utes, reportedly "could not provide for themselves" without the Indian trade, "for they have no other commerce than that of these skins."[74] Conditions probably differed little at other frontier villages.

It would have been extraordinary had not peoples as heterogeneous as the New Mexicans and Comanches had occasional misunderstandings and hostilities. Upon leaving the fairs, the Comanches did not always overcome the urge to help themselves to their hosts' livestock. A contemporary priest wryly observed: "The Comanches always carry off all they want, by purchase in

[71] Domínguez, *op. cit.*, 251.
[72] Thomas, *Forgotten Frontiers*, 318.
[73] *Ibid.*
[74] "Instruction of Vélez," *loc. cit.*, 130.

peace and by theft in war."[75] Furthermore, the Comanches' lack of unity led to situations in which one group might be trading peaceably at Taos while another was raiding elsewhere. Upon being upbraided for this apparent perfidy, one friendly Comanche chief replied: "Don't be too trusty. Remember, there are rogues among us, just as there are among you. Hang any of them you catch!"[76] On the other hand, Comanches desiring access to the Taos fairs too often blamed the raids on "certain warlike captains they cannot control."[77]

In combating the Comanches, the New Mexicans, when well led and adequately armed, were more than able to hold their own. Had they been as timid and cowardly as many Anglos have claimed, their province could never have endured two centuries of constant exposure to Indian attacks. According to a veteran Spanish military observer, New Mexican youths grew up "well prepared for war, for they learn to use weapons and ride horses when they are very young." Their weapons, however, were both poor in quality and inadequate in quantity. The Pueblos generally relied upon the bow and arrow, pikes, and lances and, as a crude sort of armor, wore leather jackets.[78] The Spanish settlers, handicapped by a lack of gunpowder for their few firearms, used similar weapons, the most effective being the lance. Not until the late 1770's was the serious shortage of guns partially alleviated.

The Comanches made few raids on the Spaniards and Pueblos until the 1740's. Then they began assailing Pecos and Galisteo with unprecedented fury, killing 150 at Pecos between 1744 and 1749. Soon after Governor Vélez assumed office in 1749, however, he sought to stop these attacks by garrisoning Pecos with thirty presidials, surrounding it and Galisteo with "intrenchments, with towers at the gates," and stationing "spies" on their eastern approaches.[79] These measures notwithstanding, the inhabitants re-

---

[75] Domínguez, *op. cit.*, 112.
[76] Adams, "Bishop Tamaron's Visitation," *loc. cit.*, 216.
[77] Vélez to Don Juan Francisco de Guemes, March 8, 1750, in Hackett, *Pichardo's Treatise*, III, 328.
[78] Lawrence Kinnaird (trans. and ed.), *The Frontiers of New Spain*, 93.
[79] Vélez to Don Juan Francisco de Guemes, March 8, 1750, *loc. cit.*, III, 328.

mained in constant danger. In 1751, for instance, a French trader named Jean Chapius, who had failed to find a single Comanche while crossing the plains, had no sooner reached the environs of Pecos when he discovered a band of them "spying" upon a forlorn party of Pueblo hunters.[80]

The relentless attacks on Pecos and Galisteo were probably in retaliation for the support these two pueblos had given the Plains Apaches. So "neighborly" were they with the Apaches in 1752 that the latter often left their women and children in their care when they went to the plains to hunt buffalo.[81] The Spanish officials, however, failed to associate the Comanche hostility against Pecos with the presence of the Apaches, whom they welcomed enthusiastically. Governor Vélez actually schemed, "with whatever guile" necessary, to keep the Apaches near Pecos to augment its defenses and for use as spies. Apaches would venture as far as one hundred leagues onto the plains, a feat "very rare and risky" for the Pueblos.[82]

The Plains Apaches and the Jicarillas both served the Spaniards faithfully as soldiers and scouts. In 1760, Bishop Tamaron was introduced by the Santo Domingans to the leader of the "peaceful Apache Indians," who was "esteemed in the kingdom" because he loyally warned of the approach of Comanche marauders and was a safe ally in war.[83] As late as 1779, the inhabitants of Taos were notified by Apache "friends" of an imminent Comanche attack and were thus enabled to repulse it with little loss.[84] But for all their loyalty, the Plains Apaches lacked the strength and numbers to be of great assistance against the Comanches.

The New Mexicans did not associate the Comanche raids on Pecos with the presence of the Apaches because they were convinced that the French were the instigators. In 1748, a number

[80] Hackett, *Pichardo's Treatise*, III, 354.
[81] Vélez to the Count of Revilla Gigedo, September 29, 1752, *loc. cit.*, 124.
[82] *Ibid.*
[83] Adams, "Bishop Tamaron's Visitation," *loc. cit.*, 203.
[84] "Governor Anza's Diary of His Campaign Against the Comanches," in Thomas, *Forgotten Frontiers*, 138. These statements do not pertain to the Apaches of southern and western New Mexico, who continued to attack the province, although their main targets were in Chihuahua and Sonora.

War, Trade, and Diplomacy, 1700-1786

of forays occurred soon after rumors reached New Mexico that thirty-three Frenchmen were on the east side of the Sangre de Cristos, not far from Taos, trading the Comanches "plenty of muskets for mules."[85] Governor Vélez was certain, therefore, that the French had alienated the Comanches "from our friendship and trade."[86] Since the factors promoting war were largely counterbalanced by the mutual need for trade, the New Mexican frontier had alternating periods of peace and war throughout the period from 1750 to 1786. Battles, treaties, trade fairs, and raids occurred in perplexing array.

Vélez, on the whole, was the most successful governor before Anza in dealing with the Comanches. Upon taking office in 1751, he used conciliation and diplomacy to stop an Indian war which he had inherited from his predecessor, but when the Comanches raided Galisteo in violation of their pledges, he surprised and annihilated one of their *rancherías* east of Pecos.[87] Winning the respect of the Comanches with his show of strength, he gained their confidence by his lenient treatment of those whom he had captured and held it by his fairness in subsequent trade relations.

Don Francisco Marín del Valle, the successor to Vélez, maintained an uneasy peace with the Comanches from 1754 to 1760. In August, 1760, however, a large force of Comanches swept down into the Taos Valley and attacked a Spanish ranch house in which many settlers had gathered for protection. After a desperate struggle, the Indians broke into the house, killed all the men, and carried off fifty-six women and children.[88] Although Governor Marín, at the head of a punitive expedition, trailed them as far north as the Arkansas River, the raiders escaped unscathed.

Early in 1761, Marín was succeeded by Don Manuel del Portillo, who was infatuated with the idea that the Comanche problem could be solved by a quick, decisive victory. Soon after his arrival, Portillo proclaimed that no Comanches would be allowed

---

[85] Twitchell, *op. cit.*, II, 149.
[86] "Instruction of Vélez," *loc. cit.*, 134.
[87] *Ibid.*, 78. Since the reports of this campaign are very vague and probably exaggerated, it does not seem necessary to describe it in detail.
[88] Adams, "Bishop Tamaron's Visitation," *loc cit.*, 216.

to trade until every Spanish captive had been released. For some inexplicable reason, the Taos alcalde nevertheless admitted a large number of Comanches to a fair upon their promise to ransom seven captives. Learning of this, Portillo rushed to Taos and imprisoned the Comanche chiefs when they refused to comply with his demand that they immediately return all their prisoners. The following day, he coolly ordered the leaderless Comanche braves to hand over their horses and "remain on foot" for the duration of the fair. Angered by such arrogance and bent on avenging the seizure of their chiefs, the Indians charged—straight into a trap. Portillo, shrewdly anticipating their action, shattered their ranks with a salvo from a grapeshot-loaded cannon and a "close volley" of shotguns. The Spaniards, piously "invoking the Queen of Angels and men," were joined in the slaughter of the terrified Comanches by some Utes and Apaches who were present for the fair. After the melee ended, Portillo proudly boasted that more than four hundred Comanches had been killed and about three hundred women, "large and small," had been captured.[89]

Although the elated governor predicted that his "glorious" victory would bring peace to New Mexico because of the fear it had inspired in the "heathen" tribes, he had little time to enjoy the triumph. In February, 1762, he was replaced by former Governor Tómas Vélez, who thought Portillo's attack both unjust and unwise. Vélez promptly reinitiated his old peace policy and claimed that he thereby prevented a general attack by the Comanches. Again he sought to win the good will of the Comanches by releasing some of their prisoners and promising to regulate the Taos fairs. Thus reassured, the Comanches pledged to return their Spanish captives and to restrain their young braves.[90] Although information on the mid-1760's is sparse, the peace, except for a few minor misunderstandings, apparently remained in effect until Don Pedro Fermín de Mendinueta became governor in 1768. Don Nicolás Lafora, who in 1766 inspected the province in company with the Marqués de Rubí, found that New Mexico suffered

[89] *Ibid.*, 220.
[90] Thomas, *Plains Indians*, 155.

"some small annoyances" from the Comanches but that the benefits gained from trade with them were far more impressive.[91]

Soon after Governor Mendinueta arrived in New Mexico, a Comanche chief named Cuerno Verde, the most implacable Indian foe the province ever had, again led his people to war. First noticed by Mendinueta in October, 1768, because he wore "a green horn on his forehead," Cuerno Verde reportedly had the "appearance and accoutrements of a little king" with a bodyguard and pages to attend him while he mounted and dismounted and to hold "a canopy or shade of buffalo skins for him in which he takes his seat."[92] A decade later, Governor Juan Bautista de Anza, who labeled Cuerno Verde "the cruel scourge" of New Mexico, theorized that the chief held an intense hatred for New Mexico because his father had been killed there.[93] In his war against the Spaniards, Cuerno Verde had the support of the Taovayas, enterprising middlemen of the border, who sold him guns obtained from illicit English traders from east of the Mississippi. A Taos Indian who escaped from the Comanches in 1768 reported to the New Mexican officials that "not many months ago the Jumanos [as the New Mexicans called the Taovayas] brought seventeen loads of guns and munitions to the Comanches" and traded them for horses that had doubtlessly been stolen from the Spaniards.[94] The Taovayas were more dangerous than the French traders of earlier years because they purchased captive people as well as horses. In 1778, they held captive ten Spaniards from New Mexico whom they had bought from the Comanches.[95]

The chief target of the Comanches during 1768 was Ojo Caliente, a strategically located settlement on the west side of the Río Grande about forty miles north of Santa Fe. Governor Mendinueta, convinced that "none of the districts of Santa Cruz de la Cañada would be secure" without Ojo Caliente, sent fifty pre-

---

[91] Kinnaird, *op. cit.*, 94.
[92] Thomas, *Plains Indians*, 166.
[93] Thomas, *Forgotten Frontiers*, 135.
[94] Mendinueta to Croix, June 18, 1768, in Thomas, *Plains Indians*, 161–62.
[95] Athanase de Mézières to the Commandant General, April 19, 1778, in Hackett, *Pichardo's Treatise*, II, 247.

sidials to garrison it. Fortunately, they arrived in time to foil an ingenious Comanche plot. The Indians announced that they would arrive at Taos on June 2 to trade and make peace, knowing that the Ojo Calienteans would hasten to attend the proposed fair. Then they dispatched one hundred men to destroy the defenseless town. Only the arrival of Mendinueta's presidials thwarted their scheme.[96]

Nevertheless, the Comanches continued their raids against the frontier village so fiercely that the panic-stricken settlers began abandoning their homes "to live in different places of this kingdom." Mendinueta ordered the refugees to return or suffer a fine of two hundred pesos and the forfeiture of their land. Many refused to obey, and one, Diego Gomes, expressed their despair when he explained that because in "his presence five of his relatives had been killed and he was not able to prevent it, he yields the right to the house and lands which he has at said Ojo Caliente."[97] By the next year, however, the attacks having subsided, the settlers ventured back to their village and Mendinueta suspended his harsh decree. A tragic reminder of the Ojo Calienteans' plight was contained in the Miera map of 1780, which labeled the entire Caliente Valley below their village tersely and simply: "Settlements destroyed by hostile Comanches."[98]

The troubles at Ojo Caliente were repeated many times in other villages. In 1770, the Spanish settlers at Taos were forced to abandon their separate plaza and take refuge in the Taos pueblo "with the consent" of the Indians.[99] Since the Taos natives had always zealously guarded their privacy, the situation was obviously one of grave danger.

In 1771, Mendinueta concluded with the Comanches another of an apparently unending series of peace treaties; yet by the middle of 1772, he complained that five hundred marauders had

---

[96] E. Boyd, "Troubles at Ojo Caliente, a Frontier Post," *El Palacio*, LXIV (November, 1957), 353-56.
[97] *Ibid.*, 356.
[98] A copy of the Miera map is printed in Thomas, *Forgotten Frontiers*, 87.
[99] Domínguez, *op. cit.*, 219.

attacked Pecos, and others had raided Picurís and Galisteo. After noting this, he naïvely reported an incredible sequel to the raids:

> ... the Comanches did not find it inconvenient to present themselves peacefully at Taos to trade their buffalo skins, horses, mules, some guns and captives in exchange for bridles, awls, knives, colored cloth and maize, from which the settlers of the province benefited.[100]

After trading peacefully for more than a year, the Comanches renewed the war in 1774 with a massive and unceasing assault. At first the New Mexicans resisted quite successfully. In August, 1774, nine Santa Clara Pueblos, without suffering the slightest injury, put to flight fifty Comanches.[101] Then, in September, a New Mexican force led by Don Carlos Fernández, a shrewd old Indian fighter, won a decisive victory in which more than four hundred Comanches were killed or captured and about a thousand "beasts of burden" seized.[102]

Mendinueta, who fervently hoped that Fernández' victory would halt the attacks, since the Indians had never before "been given an example of how our arms in attack could succeed in destroying a *ranchería*," was sadly disappointed.[103] The Comanches retaliated with such fury that Viceroy Antonio María de Bucareli wistfully suggested that instead of teaching them a lesson, the punishment may have exasperated them and "thus be the motivating reason for their uniting" to seek vengeance.[104]

Bucareli's harried fears became reality as the Comanches, swarming into the province "by all routes," stamped out effective resistance. Although New Mexico still had an abundance of men "very fit for war," the lack of arms and horses made them almost useless for fighting.[105] To remedy the shortage of guns, the Spanish officials encouraged the presidial soldiers to barter

---

[100] Thomas, *Plains Indians*, 43.
[101] *Ibid.*, 170.
[102] *Ibid.*, 174.
[103] *Ibid.*
[104] *Ibid.*, 177.
[105] "Bonilla's Notes Concerning New Mexico, 1776," in Charles W. Hackett, George P. Hammond, and J. Lloyd Mecham (eds.), *New Spain and the Anglo-American West*, I, 195.

their old firearms to the settlers for foodstuffs. A survey that later showed only 600 guns and 150 pairs of pistols "in all the realm" seemed to satisfy everyone.[106]

The acquisition of sufficient horses was more difficult. Raising a supply was impossible because of the unending Comanche raids. The problem had grown so acute by the summer of 1775 that Mendinueta warned Viceroy Bucareli that if New Mexico did not receive fresh horses, "perhaps to the number of fifteen hundred," it would be desolated.[107] Faced with this danger, the penurious bureaucrats in Mexico City reacted with uncharacteristic haste. A royal council quickly agreed to forward the horses "at the account of the royal treasury."[108] but Bucareli, for reasons unknown, failed to send them. The delay was tragic. On June 23, 1775, a Comanche party ran off most of the stock of the Sandía pueblo. The Sandíans bravely pursued the marauders on foot, but when they became "most worn out," the Comanches turned upon them and killed thirty-three.[109] Nor was this an isolated incident. According to Mendinueta's reports, the ratio of New Mexican losses to those of the Comanches during the summer of 1775 was almost six to one.[110]

Pecos and Galisteo were the hardest hit. Handicapped by a searing drought that left them without sufficient food, their inhabitants were unable to withstand the raids. At Pecos, the irrigated lands could not be farmed because the pueblo was so constantly besieged, and crops planted in the small dry-land fields immediately under the pueblo's walls failed because of the lack of rain. Therefore, in the doleful words of Fray Domínguez, "what few crops there usually are do not last even to the beginning of a new year . . . and hence these wretches are tossed about like a ball in the hands of fortune."[111] The seriousness of the food shortage

[106] Thomas, *Plains Indians*, 184.
[107] Mendinueta to Bucareli, August 19, 1775, *ibid.*, 184.
[108] *Ibid.*, 50.
[109] Mendinueta to Bucareli, August 18, 1775, *ibid.*, 181. The Sandía church records confirm this disaster. See Fray Angelico Chavez, *Archives of the Archdiocese of Santa Fe, 1678–1900*, 234.
[110] Thomas, *Plains Indians*, 181–83.
[111] Domínguez, *op. cit.*, 213.

during the summer of 1776 is poignantly revealed in a priest's terse notation that the parents of a child he had baptized were absent because they were "looking for something to eat."[112]

At Galisteo, smaller and even more demoralized than Pecos, many residents were killed by Comanche raiders and the survivors were so terrorized that they would not venture to the fields. By 1776, the forays and lack of rain had combined to produce a famine so acute, according to a priestly chronicler, that the natives were forced to beg for food elsewhere: "Now the men alone, now the women alone, sometimes the husband in one place, his wife in another, the children in still another, and so it all goes."[113] Those who remained at the pueblo sustained life only by eating "the hides of cows, oxen, horses, etc., in a sort of fried cracklings" or, when these failed, by stripping the "vellum from the saddle trees" or by toasting "old shoes." They longed to abandon the pueblo and divide themselves "as best they might among the pueblos with good supplies," Domínguez reported, "but they have not done so for fear of the government." The populations of the two pueblos declined drastically during the war. Galisteo had scarcely half the people in 1776 that it had boasted in 1760, and at Pecos the population dropped from 446 in 1750 to 269 in 1776.[114]

In 1777, the situation grew worse. The Comanches unleashed a rash of raids that left twenty-three New Mexicans dead at Valencia, eight at Taos, fourteen at Isleta, and many others elsewhere.[115] The following year, Cuerno Verde's raiders, bolder and more ruthless than ever, killed or captured 127 settlers and Pueblos.[116] No letup seemed to be in sight.

At this darkest hour of New Mexico's history, the Spanish officials in faraway Madrid finally became aware that continued procrastination might cause the loss of not only New Mexico but also its neighboring provinces. Accordingly, they placed the entire northern region of New Spain under a new military govern-

[112] Chavez, *op. cit.*, 205. [113] Domínguez, *op cit.*, 219.
[114] *Ibid.*, 213; Kidder, *Pecos, New Mexico*, 327.
[115] Thomas, *Plains Indians*, 51.
[116] "General Report of 1781 by Teodoro de Croix," *loc. cit.*, 111.

ment called the Commandancy-General of the Interior Provinces and appointed Don Teodoro de Croix to head it as commander-general. Because of a lack of funds and jurisdictional differences with Viceroy Bucareli, Croix did not reach the northern frontier until late 1777. At Chihuahua in June, 1778, he formulated plans for the defense of New Mexico, Nueva Vizcaya, and Sonora in a council of war attended by Mendinueta, worn out by eleven years of combating the Comanches in New Mexico, and by Don Juan Bautista de Anza, fresh from the colonization of California and already named to succeed Mendinueta. The provincial governors at the council, bothered by Apache attacks almost as much as by Comanche raids, decided that instead of fighting both tribes simultaneously, they would adopt the Marqués de Rubís proposal of 1768 to seek an alliance with the Comanches against the Apaches. Croix, who had already dispatched the fifteen hundred horses requested by Mendinueta, assured the governors he would do everything possible to back them up.[117]

Arriving in New Mexico in late 1778, Governor Anza immediately turned to the Indian situation. Concluding that a lasting peace could never be gained until the Comanches had learned that nowhere, not even in their southeastern Colorado homeland, would they be safe from Spanish punishment, he mustered a motley force of six hundred soldiers, settlers, and Pueblos in August, 1779, for a surprise attack. Since he realized the impossibility of marching up the eastern side of the Sangre de Cristos undetected by the Comanches, he led his force northward through the Ute-controlled San Luis Valley. En route he augmented his ranks with two hundred Utes and Jicarillas, anxious to settle old scores with the Comanches and familiar with their favorite camping places.

Near present Colorado Springs, Anza crossed to the eastern slopes of the mountains, having reached unobserved the rear of the enemy camps. He marched southward to the vicinity of present Pueblo, where he came abruptly upon Cuerno Verde's village. Since that fiery chief and most of his warriors were absent on a

[117] *Ibid.*, 17-18.

raid against Taos, Anza easily captured the camp, together with about fifty women and children; then he continued down the lee of the Rockies in quest of the returning raiders. At the foot of Greenhorn Mountain, which perpetuates his memory, Cuerno Verde, disheartened by the failure of his raid and by reports of the destruction of his village, stumbled into a trap set by Anza. Finding himself surrounded and outnumbered more than ten to one, he led his warriors in a last defiant assault on the Spaniards. The battle did not end until Cuerno Verde and all of his warriors lay dead.[118]

Anza's successful campaign all but ended the Comanche threat to New Mexico. Seeking easier prey, the Comanches during the following year turned upon Texas with a series of attacks "so horrible and bloody" that Croix feared their continuance would lead to the complete destruction of the province.[119] In New Mexico, on the other hand, Comanche attacks in 1781 were repulsed with such losses that the Indians "swallowed their pride" and solicited peace in the pueblo of Taos. Although Croix was urgently pressing Anza to reach an agreement, the governor concluded that the Comanches had not come in "good faith" and rejected their overture. He informed them that there would be no peace until all the tribe would agree to it. Otherwise, he concluded, "whatever infractions occurred, the subterfuge would remain of attributing them to the opposing party."[120]

The Comanches were strongly divided over the issue of war or peace. A faction led by Chief Toroblanco insisted on resuming war, but another under the leadership of Chief Ecueracapa demanded peace. Toroblanco's inability to win a striking success against the Spaniards seems to have caused many of his supporters to defect to the peace party. Since Anza still insisted on unanimity as a prerequisite for negotiation, the peace faction brutally murdered Toroblanco in 1785 and terrorized his adherents into compliance.[121]

[118] Thomas, *Forgotten Frontiers*, 119-42.
[119] Thomas, *Teodoro de Croix*, 74, 112.
[120] *Ibid.*, 114; Thomas, *Forgotten Frontiers*, 299.
[121] *Ibid.*

News of the change of sentiment was carried to New Mexico by a Taos buffalo hunter who had been captured by "Comanche spies" and later released. Soon afterward, Josef Manuel Roxo (possibly a trader) journeyed to the Comanches on his own initiative and urged them to ask Anza for peace once more.[122] The Indians agreed and chose as their representative Ecueracapa, a remarkable leader later described by Anza in ecstatic terms as "distinguished . . . by his adroitness and intelligence in political matters" and "without equal in military achievements."[123] In a brilliant maneuver, Ecueracapa invited the Pecos natives to visit his camps on the plains and "magnanimously entertained" the many who accepted. At one stroke he won their good will and, of more importance, impressed them with his power and strength. Upon returning home, the Pueblos reported that the Comanches "were so many that they doubted if all the people of this province would equal their number."[124] Obviously, peace would be as advantageous to the New Mexicans as it would to the Comanches.

In a conference held at Pecos on February 28, 1786, Anza and Ecueracapa quickly agreed on a deceptively simple set of peace terms. By the perpetual and unbreakable agreement, the Comanches could move closer to New Mexico—with the governor's approval—in return for a promise to be peaceful toward all Indians friendly to Spain. Ecueracapa asked for and received the "establishment of free trade and fairs" at Pecos and the right to travel through Pecos to Santa Fe at any time to present grievances of his tribe. He agreed also to join the Spaniards in an offensive war against the Apaches.[125] With the presentation of a "token of credential" to Ecueracapa to symbolize his authority over the Comanches, the treaty was concluded. A major landmark in the history of both New Mexico and the Comanches had been reached.

[122] *Ibid.*, 385, n. 109.
[123] *Ibid.*, 295.
[124] *Ibid.*, 313.
[125] *Ibid.*, 313–16.

3
The Comanche Peace, 1786–1846

INDIAN AFFAIRS DURING THE LAST YEARS of the Spanish regime in New Mexico were characterized by a remarkable stability. The New Mexican officials, conducting Indian policy in a realistic and dispassionate manner, maintained with the Comanches an equilibrium that was strikingly similar to the understanding reached with the Plains Apaches a century earlier. Confronted by Plains Indian tribes so powerful that they could have destroyed the province, the Spanish leaders secured the greatest degree of peace and prosperity that New Mexico had ever known. Although the intrusion of Anglo traders eventually upset the delicate balance of New Mexico's Indian relations, matters never degenerated into chaos, as they did in Texas, Chihuahua, and the other North Mexican provinces.

Guidelines for preserving the peace negotiated between Anza and Ecueracapa were lucidly formulated in 1786 by Bernardo de Gálvez, viceroy of New Spain, conqueror of West Florida during the American Revolution, and nephew of the great visitor-general, José de Gálvez. Viceroy Gálvez, stating that the earlier peace treaties had broken down because they contained no "advantages" for the Indians, boldly proposed to prevent hostilities by satisfying the Indians' legitimate grievances. Giving them gifts, he asserted, would cost less than what "is now spent in considerable and useless reinforcements of troops."[1]

To preserve the peace, he emphasized the need for a revised and realistic trade policy that would allow the bartering to Indians of such controversial items as horses, guns, and ammunition.[2]

[1] Bernardo de Gálvez, *Instructions for Governing the Interior Provinces of New Spain, 1786* (trans. and ed. by Donald E. Worcester), 40–43.
[2] *Ibid.*, 46.

He contended vigorously that the trading of horses and other livestock in return for buffalo robes would lessen the Indians' incentive for stealing; that firearms, instead of increasing the Indians' strength, would make them reliant upon the Spaniards for repair and replacement; and that, in time of war, it would be a simple matter to cut off their supply of gunpowder. Further revealing his Machiavellian thinking, Gálvez suggested that the guns traded to the Indians should be extra long so they would be awkward to carry on horseback, resulting in continual damages and need for repairs or replacement. In addition, they should have "superficial adornments which delight the sight of ignorant persons," and barrels, stock, and bolts made of steel without the "best temper" so they would be unreliable.[3]

Although the bloodshed and suffering produced during subsequent decades by the trading of guns to the Indians seem to indicate that Gálvez was wrong, it should be remembered that he envisioned Spaniards trading them under strict supervision in return for buffalo robes and meat. The gun trade brought unrest only after firearms were introduced illicitly by American traders who encouraged the Indians to steal Spanish horses. Until these outsiders intruded, the policies of Gálvez were remarkably successful.

Turning to the specific problem of the Comanches, Gálvez based his recommendations upon a keen appreciation of Indian mentality. In deference to their pride, for example, he ordered the New Mexicans to refrain from punishing Comanche lawbreakers. Instead, they were to let the "tribunal of Ecueracapa or council of captains" judge the offenders. The Comanches would accept chastisement by their own chiefs, Gálvez declared, but they would resent punishment by the Spaniards, "even though it were more moderate and pious."[4]

To help retain the Comanches' friendship, Gálvez instructed the New Mexicans to entertain Indian visitors liberally. He decreed that all Indians who presented themselves in peace should

[3] Ibid., 48–49.
[4] Ibid., 51–52.

*Courtesy of the Smithsonian Office of Anthropology,
Bureau of American Ethnology Collection*

Waku Tota, possibly the last survivor of Pecos Pueblo.
By John K. Hillers, 1880.

*Courtesy of the Smithsonian Office of Anthropology,
Bureau of American Ethnology Collection*

Pueblo of Picuris, a general view from the east.
By A. C. Vroman, New Mexico, 1900.

*Courtesy of the Smithsonian Office of Anthropology,
Bureau of American Ethnology Collection*

Two men of the Tewa tribe with a *carreta*, Pueblo of Tesuque, New Mexico. By John K. Hillers, 1880.

*Courtesy of the Smithsonian Office of Anthropology,
Bureau of American Ethnology Collection*

Vincente Jiron (spelled Garron in the text), chief of Isleta Pueblo. By John K. Hillers, prior to 1886.

*Courtesy of the Smithsonian Office of Anthropology,
Bureau of American Ethnology Collection*

Small Feathers of the Eagle, also known as Juan Jesus Leo, governor of Taos. Photograph made prior to 1877. Note similarity to Plains Indians in appearance.

U. S. Signal Corps Photograph, The National Archives

A typical *carreta*, at Jemez, New Mexico.

*Courtesy of the Smithsonian Office of Anthropology,
Bureau of American Ethnology Collection*

An old Navaho warrior with lance and shield. Photographed by James Mooney near Keams Canyon, Arizona, in 1893.

Courtesy of the Smithsonian Office of Anthropology,
Bureau of American Ethnology Collection

A Taos man wearing Plains-type leggings and blanket, *circa* 1910.

receive presents ranging in value from one or two pesos for a common warrior to fifteen or twenty pesos for a chief.[5] These meager sums, when multiplied by the numerous visits, added up to 5,906 pesos in 1789. Of this total, 4,248 pesos went to the Comanches, 842 to the Navahos, 416 to the Utes, and 320 to the Jicarillas.[6] In 1795, 3,323 pesos were spent on Indian gifts and it was estimated that 3,900 would be needed for the following year.[7]

This generous treatment of Comanche visitors, even though it suggests an element of bribery, apparently led to the development of a warm relationship between the Indians and the New Mexicans. In 1812, Don Pedro Bautista Pino, the only delegate from New Mexico who ever attended the Spanish *cortes*, claimed that the "continued" state of peace and friendship with the Comanches was the result of the presents given them and asserted that the Comanches had originally tried to return gift for gift. When told that this was not necessary, their "esteem" for the Spaniards had "increased mightily."[8]

In conducting relations with the Comanches, New Mexican governors leaned heavily upon specially trained interpreters: two based at Taos and one each at Santa Fe and Pecos. At least one was to be among the Comanches at all times "to give an account of their movements."[9] For eight pesos a month, the interpreters handled a wide range of duties somewhat akin to those of modern diplomatic representatives. They had to be hardy enough to accompany Comanche campaigns against the Apaches and shrewd enough to handle commercial matters. Governor Don Fernando

[5] *Ibid.* For evidence that the New Mexican governors relied upon Gálvez' instructions, see Fernando de la Concha to Pedro de Nava, November 1, 1791, MS, Document 1164, Spanish Archives of New Mexico, Santa Fe. This document, together with other documents from the Santa Fe Archives, was examined in photostatic form in the Coronado Room, University of New Mexico, Albuquerque.

[6] Frank D. Reeve, "Navaho-Spanish Diplomacy, 1770-1790," *New Mexico Historical Review*, XXXV (July, 1960), 233.

[7] Fernando de Chacón to Pedro de Nava, July 8, 1796, MS, Document 1367, Spanish Archives of New Mexico.

[8] H. Bailey Carroll and J. Villasana Haggard (transs. and eds.), *Three New Mexico Chronicles*, 135.

[9] Don Fernando de la Concha, "Advice on Governing New Mexico, 1794" (trans. by Donald E. Worcester), *New Mexico Historical Review*, XXIV (July, 1949), 240.

de la Concha, for example, would never allow New Mexican traders to visit the Comanche camps unless an interpreter was available to "take charge of governing them" while they were among the Indians.[10] Interpreters also accompanied all official and many unofficial expeditions to the plains, particularly the larger buffalo-hunting parties.[11] Their most important task, however, was to serve as an avenue of communication between the Palace of the Governors and the Comanche camps.

The crowning achievement of the New Mexicans in their relations with the Comanches was to persuade them that their chiefs should be "confirmed" by Spanish officials in the name of the king. This practice, a standard Spanish device for influencing friendly Indians, apparently was not extended to the Comanches until 1786 when Anza confirmed Ecueracapa. Thereafter, confirmation became common. In 1797, for example, a band of Comanches came to Pecos upon the death of their chief and requested Governor Chacón to preside over the election of a new leader. After a Kotsoteka warrior named Canagiap was elected "by a plurality of votes," Chacón recognized him in the king's name and gravely invested him with the proper symbols of his authority: a silver-handled baton, a silver medal, and an ornate scarlet cloak.[12] As late as 1818, some Kotsotekas who came to Pecos with news that their chief had recently died were told by Governor Facundo Melgares that after they had decided "in council" on a successor, he would "confirm him accordingly."[13]

[10] Ibid., 246.
[11] Manrique to Salcedo, March 31, 1810, MS, Document 2311, Spanish Archives of New Mexico. This was not the first use of such officials by the Spaniards. In 1778, Athanase de Mézières wrote of the Taovaya Indians that "in each of these villages there resides a Spanish merchant of Natchitoches skilled in the language of the Indians with whom he deals. . . . It is his duty to watch over their conduct, maintain the general union, and report without delay anything of interest to the service of his Majesty and to the peace of his subjects." Herbert E. Bolton, *Athanase de Mézières and the Louisiana-Texas Frontier, 1768–1780*, I, 109.
[12] Chacón to Nava, November 18, 1797, MS, Document 1404, Spanish Archives of New Mexico.
[13] Facundo Melgares to Don Alexo García Conde, October 8, 1818, in Alfred B. Thomas (trans. and ed.), "Documents Bearing Upon the Northern Frontier of New Mexico, 1818–1819," *New Mexico Historical Review*, IV (April, 1929), 156.

The Comanche Peace, 1786-1846

According to Don Pedro Bautista Pino in 1812, confirmation had become so essential to the Comanches that a chief would feel "deeply reproached" if he were denied such recognition.[14]

The silver-handled baton and scarlet cloak issued to Chief Canagiap were not unusual accessories for a Comanche chief. In 1808, Don Francisco Amangual, while en route from San Antonio to Santa Fe, visited a Comanche village in western Texas in which he was greeted by chiefs in "long, red coats, with blue collars and cuffs, white buttons, and yellow imitation gold galloons."[15] One Indian, more outlandish than the rest, sported a short red coat, blue trousers, white stockings, English spurs, and an "ordinarily cornered hat" that clashed violently with his chalk and ocher facial paint. As late as 1822, Thomas James, an observant pioneer in the Santa Fe trade, described Cordero, a famous Comanche chief, as coming to Santa Fe "dressed in his full regimentals."[16] Ludicrous as Comanches in war paint and dress blues might seem, their attire strikingly exemplifies the strength of the Spanish influence on them.

The New Mexicans were also able to influence the Comanches through the education of their children in Santa Fe. Ecueracapa sent his son to Governor Anza in 1786, asking that the boy be instructed in the Spaniards' language and customs as if he were the governor's own child. Anza accepted the boy but cautioned that he might not make such progress as his father desired.[17] In 1812, Pino reported that the son of a chief named Maya had also learned to read at a school in Santa Fe. Eventually succeeding his father as chief, the youth afterward had "held the Spaniards in the highest regard."[18]

As a result of the Comanche peace, Spanish explorers were able to travel the plains freely and safely. When Pedro Vial, most

[14] Carroll and Haggard, *op. cit.*, 136.
[15] Francisco Amangual, "Diary of the Incidents and Operations which took place in the Expedition made from the Province of Texas to the Province of New Mexico [1808]" (typescript translation by J. Villasana Haggard).
[16] Thomas James, *Three Years Among the Indians and Mexicans* (ed. by Milo Milton Quaife), 134.
[17] Thomas, *Forgotten Frontiers*, 314.
[18] Carroll and Haggard, *op. cit.*, 130.

noted of the trail blazers, prepared to leave Santa Fe for St. Louis in 1792, Governor Concha confidently stated that "he will meet no other tribes than those of our allies the Comanches on whose aid and knowledge he can count with all safety."[19] Soon after leaving Pecos, Vial met some Comanches who (exclaiming "it was a long time since they had seen" him) made him return to Pecos and visit with them. "Consequently," he moaned half-seriously, "we lost the march of the day."[20] In 1799, Don José Cortéz reported that travelers were "hospitably entertained, respectfully served, and treated with greatest friendship" by the Comanches. They were escorted courteously from one village to the next and their horses were carefully guarded.[21]

A small minority of Comanches, however, remained hostile toward the Spaniards. In an Indian village in 1787, Vial observed the return of some Comanche youths from an unsuccessful horse-stealing foray into New Mexico. The raiders' elders berated them sharply, however, for attacking "their friends," the Spaniards.[22] While Vial was visiting another Comanche camp, there arrived two Indians who claimed that the Spaniards were conspiring against the Comanches and that Vial "was leading them to New Mexico in order that they all might be killed."[23] Fortunately for Vial, his hosts refused to believe the story.

For a brief time, the Comanches seemed ready to succumb to the comforts of a sedentary life. In July, 1787, a Jupe Comanche chief named Parunarimuco asked Anza to help his people build a pueblo on the Arkansas River in eastern Colorado. Anza immediately dispatched thirty New Mexican workers, and by Septem-

---

[19] "Concha's Instructions to Vial, May 21, 1792," in Archer B. Hulbert (ed.), *Southwest on the Turquoise Trail*, 47.

[20] "Vial's Diary, May 25, 1792," *ibid.*, 49.

[21] "Report of Don José Cortéz, 1799," translated in "Lt. A. W. Whipple's Report upon the Indian Tribes," *Explorations and Surveys for a Railroad Route from the Mississippi River to the Pacific Ocean*, III, 119.

[22] Vial's Diary, November 11, 1787," *Archivo Nacional de la Nación, Historia,* Vol. XLIII, Part 14.

[23] "Vial's Diary, April 7, 1787," quoted in Carlos E. Castañeda, *Our Catholic Heritage in Texas, 1519–1936*, V, 154.

ber, nineteen houses had been completed and occupied.[24] Elated by this development, Don Jacobo Ugarte y Loyola, commander-general of the Interior Provinces, reported to the viceroy that the Comanches were building houses on their own to such an extent that their pueblo would "constitute a considerable settlement." Careful to stress the traditional Spanish concern about the Indians, he piously intoned that "putting the gentiles in pueblos would open the door easily to the preaching of the gospel."[25]

Ugarte's optimism was without foundation. In January, 1788, a full two months before he had written his hopeful letter to the viceroy, the Comanches had abruptly deserted their pueblo because a favorite wife of Chief Parunarimuco had died. In accordance with Comanche custom, the chief abandoned the site of his grief. The Spaniards, chagrined by the collapse of their hopes, concluded that "unless Divine Providence performs a miracle," the Comanches would never "come out of their barbarity."[26]

The Spaniards' disappointment over the failure of the colonization project was undoubtedly tempered by their success in obtaining the aid of the Comanches against the Apaches. To whet the Comanches' natural appetite for fighting, the New Mexicans supplied them with horses, guns, and ammunition; paid salaries to their chiefs;[27] and in 1788 offered them "a horse with bridle and two large knives" for each Apache brought to Santa Fe.[28]

Most of the fighting—if the few extant documents are reliable indicators—was on a relatively small scale. Near Tucumcari Peak in 1787, José Mares, returning from San Antonio to Santa Fe, encountered some Comanches who had recently killed five Apaches and captured thirty.[29] In June, 1792, Ecueracapa, provisioned by the Spaniards and accompanied by a New Mexican

---

[24] Anza to Don Jacobo Ugarte, October 20, 1787, in Alfred B. Thomas (trans. and ed.), "San Carlos on the Arkansas River, 1787," *Colorado Magazine*, VI (May, 1929), 86.
[25] Ugarte to Don Manuel Antonio Florez, March 13, 1788, *ibid.*, 88.
[26] Concha to Ugarte, June 26, 1788, *ibid.*, 90.
[27] Ecueracapa, for example, reportedly received two hundred pesos a year. Bancroft, *op. cit.*, 267, n. 30.
[28] Reeve, "Navaho-Spanish Diplomacy," *loc. cit.*, 232.
[29] "José Mares Diary, 1787," quoted in Castañeda, *op. cit.*, V, 155.

interpreter, led five hundred Comanches against the "Apaches Lipanes, Lipiyanes, y Llaneros." Near the Bosque Redondo, on the Pecos, the Comanche party divided into two groups, with one, led by Ecueracapa, moving toward the Sierra Blanca Mountains and the other, under a chief named Geranucano, going toward the plains. Ecueracapa's force killed five Apache warriors and captured four women and a few horses. Geranucano, after a fourteen-day march to the east, located a considerable Apache camp. Since he failed to surprise it, however, his men killed just six Apache warriors and captured only thirteen women and children.[30]

Indecisive as these campaigns were, they eventually led to a conclusive Comanche victory over the Plains Apaches. About 1790, Don Manuel Merino, secretary to the commander-general of the Interior Provinces, reported that the Llanero Apaches (perhaps the same group as the Cuartelejo Apaches of earlier decades), who occupied "the plains and sandy country" lying between the Pecos and Canadian rivers, fought the Comanches in "frequent skirmishes and actions," especially during "the time of buffalo killing."[31] According to a report by Don José Cortéz at the end of the decade, however, the Llaneros had been driven west of the Pecos.[32] There, the survivors eventually were absorbed by the Mescaleros.

New Mexican forces often fought side by side with the Comanches against the Apaches. In 1797, an expedition of four hundred Comanches, presidials, settlers, and Pueblos campaigned against the Mescaleros in the Sand Hills country of southeastern New Mexico. According to the plan of operations, all booty, such

[30] Concha to the Count of Revilla Gigedo, July 20, 1792, MS, Document 1200, Spanish Archives of New Mexico; Concha to Nava, November 10, 1792, MS, *ibid.* Although the Comanches usually confined their activities to the plains, eight accompanied a New Mexican expedition against the Gila Apaches of Arizona in 1788. Don Fernando de la Concha, "Diary, 1788" (trans. by Adlai Feather), *New Mexico Historical Review*, XXXIV (October, 1959), 289.

[31] Don Manuel Merino, "Report Made to the King Concerning the Lands of the Apache Nation, Its Division, the Sites Which They Occupy, and Their Manner of Waging War and Perpetrating Their Robberies [c. 1790]," in Hackett, *Pichardo's Treatise*, III, 213.

[32] "Report of Don José Cortéz," *loc. cit.*, 119.

as livestock and weapons, was to be divided equally among the allies, but all Apache prisoners were to be taken to Santa Fe. The commander of the New Mexican contingent was advised to be careful not to antagonize the Comanches and to avoid giving them arbitrary orders except during the actual battles.[33]

In 1810, the Kotsoteka chief Cordero traveled to New Mexico to join his kinsmen "and their Spanish allies" against the Apaches.[34] On this campaign the Comanches were told that they could keep all unbranded or unclaimed horses taken from the Apaches, while identifiable animals would be returned to their former owners in New Mexico and Chihuahua.[35]

Joint campaigns took place as late as 1822, when Thomas James encountered a force of fifty Spaniards and three hundred Comanches returning from one.[36] Although it is difficult to appraise the value of the Comanche aid, Don Pedro Pino declared in 1812 that the "Apache, roaming around in every direction, has no other check to his depredations than that of his fear of the brave and honest Comanche."[37]

On at least one occasion, the New Mexicans repaid the Comanches for their assistance by helping them against their own enemies. In 1790, Governor Concha sent a small Spanish force with a Comanche band on an ineffectual expedition against the Pawnees. When the Spanish officials in St. Louis complained that this action complicated their own Indian problems, Pedro de Nava, Concha's superior, reprimanded the Governor and warned him that he might give "distant and little known nations" reasons to attack his province.[38] Concha replied that the Comanches had long presented "themselves to work either alone or united with our people against the Apaches" and thus would have

---

[33] Nava to Real Alencaster, October 19, 1797, MS, Document 1399, Spanish Archives of New Mexico.
[34] Richardson, *op. cit.*, 67.
[35] *Ibid.*
[36] James, *Three Years*, 134.
[37] Carroll and Haggard, *op. cit.*, 135.
[38] Concha to Nava, November 1, 1791, MS, Document 1164, Spanish Archives of New Mexico, translated in A. P. Nasatir (ed.), *Before Lewis and Clark*, I, 147-48.

been deeply offended if he had refused their request for aid. He reassured Nava that as long as the Comanches were friendly, New Mexico had little to fear from any other Plains Indians.[39]

At the same time that they encouraged the Comanches to fight the Apaches, the New Mexicans sought to keep them at peace with their other allied tribes—the Navahos, Utes, and Jicarillas. This policy almost collapsed in late 1792 when the Utes and Navahos, smarting to avenge earlier humiliations, organized a raiding party that surprised a Comanche village while the warriors were absent on a buffalo hunt. The raiders captured a large number of women, children, and horses, but the Comanches soon retaliated by destroying a Ute camp. Although these forays had taken place a "long distance" from New Mexico, the officials were alarmed that the province would be caught in the middle of the budding Indian war and "the peaceful state of affairs now existing" would end. To forestall this, Governor Concha ordered the Navaho chiefs to deliver their prisoners to the Comanche leaders at a council in Santa Fe.[40] His best efforts to foster friendly relations between the two nations, however, resulted only in a temporary truce.

In contrast to this unsatisfactory settlement, the New Mexicans, according to Indian tradition, helped to forge a lasting peace between the Comanches and Kiowas about 1790. Groups from each of these traditionally hostile tribes by chance visited a New Mexican village on the same day. In some undisclosed manner, their worried hosts persuaded them to negotiate. A few days later, the Kiowa leader, accompanied by one or two Mexicans, visited the Comanche camps on the plains, where an alliance, never to be broken, was "patched up."[41]

The colorful Comanche trade fairs which had meant so much to the province underwent a significant change after the advent

[39] *Ibid.*
[40] Concha to Nava, June 12, 1793, *Archivo General de la Nación, Provincias Internas*, Vol. CII, Part 2, pp. 40–43.
[41] James Mooney, "Calendar History of the Kiowa Indians," *Seventeenth Annual Report of the Bureau of American Ethnology*, 163; see also Wilbur S. Nye, *Bad Medicine and Good*, 84–88.

of peace. In 1786, the Comanches announced they were transferring, "if not all, the greater part of their fairs to Pecos,"[42] and there is no further mention of their trading at Taos. The Pecos trade fairs, although gradually overshadowed by the small-scale barter small groups of Comanches and New Mexicans were constantly conducting in each other's villages, continued well into the nineteenth century. Eight Comanches who arrived at the settlement in 1808 announced that their chief was on his way to the annual "ransom" held there.[43] Ten years later, Governor Melgares reported the arrival at Pecos of more than a thousand Indians under Chief Soguara, "to trade in this province, according to custom."[44] There is no indication that fairs were still being held after Mexico achieved its independence.

One of the most significant results of the years of peace with the Comanches was the slow expansion of the New Mexican frontier toward the plains. In 1794, Pecos ceased to be the eastern outpost for the first time in five hundred years when settlers located at San Miguel del Vado farther down the Pecos Valley.[45] Early in the nineteenth century, other villages were founded lower down on the Pecos—San José del Vado, La Cuesta, and (about 1822) Antón Chico, which remained the eastern gateway to the province until the Civil War.

These towns were inhabited largely by *genízaros*—Indians who had been ransomed from the Comanches and other wild tribes as children.[46] The practice of buying children from the Indians had been so prevalent that by 1790 the province contained a large number of *genízaro* Apaches, Comanches, Navahos, Utes, and Kiowas, all lacking land and status because the New Mexicans considered them "children of the enemy" and would not "admit them to their pueblos." According to a Franciscan friar, the *genízaros* were reduced to living without "land, cattle, or

[42] Thomas, *Forgotten Frontiers*, 306.
[43] "Diario de novedades desde 1 de Julio de 1808 hasta 13 de Septiembre," MS, Document 2134, Spanish Archives of New Mexico.
[44] Melgares to Alexo García, November 9, 1818, MS, Document 2771, Spanish Archives of New Mexico.
[45] Twitchell, *op. cit.*, I, 266; Carroll and Haggard, *op. cit.*, 8.
[46] Domínguez, *op. cit.*, 42, n. 42.

other property with which to make a living except their bows and arrows."⁴⁷ Abandoned, they lived "like animals" and were fast becoming a problem. To alleviate their deplorable plight, Governor Chacón began settling them along the Pecos River in the 1790's. Once there, these Comanche and Kiowa neophytes, of whom so little is known, established contact with their old tribes and even induced some of their wild kinsmen to take up residence among them along the Pecos. Fray Angelico Chavez, a modern investigator, has discovered that the baptismal books at the eastern missions indicate that a "large number of Comanches" were baptized at San Juan and "a large number of Plains Indians" at Taos during the last few years of the eighteenth century.⁴⁸ In 1812, José Cristóbal Guerro, a San Miguel *genízaro* of Comanche extraction, claiming to represent 230 families, petitioned the bishop of Durango for a resident priest. His account of the settlement led the bishop to believe that the "Comanches are joining San Miguel and San José and getting baptized, so that these towns are expected to become the most populous in New Mexico."⁴⁹

Two of the Comanche settlers in New Mexico are mentioned in the reports of American travelers. In 1825, Major George C. Sibley, who surveyed and marked the Santa Fe Trail to Taos, engaged an old Comanche Indian named Francisco Largo (who spoke "Spanish very well, but no English") to find a wagon route across the Sangre de Cristos where previously only pack trains had passed. Within four days' time, Francisco had found a wagon route through a pass south of the "usual mule route." Sibley, obviously pleased, noted in his diary that the Indian had discharged his duty faithfully and "very much to my satisfaction, & so I told him."⁵⁰ A few years later, Josiah Gregg encountered another New Mexican Comanche, known simply as "Manuel el Comanche," who had lived a nomadic life on the plains until he visited San Miguel, where he married a Mexican girl and had

---

⁴⁷ Fray Damian Martínez to Fray Juan Agustín de Morfi, 1792, *Archivo General de la Nación, Historia*, Vol. XXV, Folio 138.
⁴⁸ Chavez, *op. cit.*, 232.
⁴⁹ *Ibid.*, 75.
⁵⁰ Kate L. Gregg (ed.), *The Road to Santa Fe*, 107.

resided there for the last ten or twelve years as "a sober, 'civilized' citizen."[51] Manuel achieved considerable reputation as a guide. In 1833, he was hired by Albert Pike, the Arkansas poet-journalist, to guide him across the plains.[52] Seven years later, he led Gregg from Santa Fe to Van Buren, Arkansas, and in 1849 conducted Captain Randolph B. Marcy for six hundred miles over the plains "quite reliably."[53]

The eastward expansion of the New Mexican frontier was not limited to the Pecos Valley. Settlers from Trampas, Embudo, and Picurís took advantage of the Comanche peace to move up the Tres Ritos Canyons to the crest of the Sangre de Cristos and beyond into the untilled valley of the Mora River. By 1818, a sufficient number had silently moved across the mountains to begin petitioning for a church.[54] In contrast to the *genízaros* on the Pecos, the Morans proudly called themselves *todos castellanos* —all Castilians.

There is some dubious evidence that settlement even leapfrogged far into the plains. One Antonio Ortiz received a land grant on the Gallinas River east of present Anton Chico in 1819 and reportedly "occupied it for many years with his cattle, flocks, and herds" until Indians forced him to abandon it.[55] More intriguing is the story of Pablo Montoya, who in 1824 obtained a grant far to the east on the Canadian River near the future site of Fort Bascom. According to the later testimony of one of his friends, Montoya "occupied the place with his stock" about four-

[51] Josiah Gregg, *Commerce of the Prairies* (ed. by Max Moorhead), 316.

[52] Albert Pike, "Narrative of a Journey on the Prairie," *Arkansas Historical Association Publications*, VI (1906), 96-97.

[53] Randolph B. Marcy, *Thirty Years of Army Life on the Border*, 99. Concerning the influx of Comanche blood into eastern New Mexico, John P. Harrington, an early anthropologist who made a detailed study of the Pueblo Indians, stated that the natives of Pecos, many of whom "spoke Comanche as well as their own tongue," contained "much Comanche blood." John P. Harrington, "The Ethnogeography of the Tewa Indians," *Twenty-Ninth Annual Report of the Bureau of American Ethnology*, 478.

[54] Fray Angelico Chavez, "Early Settlements in the Mora Valley," *El Palacio*, LXII (November, 1955), 319.

[55] "Abstract of Title to the Antonio Ortiz Grant Situated in San Miguel County, New Mexico," typescript copy in Coronado Room, University of New Mexico, 12.

teen or fifteen years. After his death, his family abandoned the grant because of Indian hostilities.[56] Unlikely as the story seems, it is barely possible that Montoya, alleged also to have been an Indian trader, maintained a ranch in the very heart of the Comanche country during the 1820's and 1830's.

The New Mexican sheep industry, which had always fluctuated according to the state of Indian affairs, likewise benefited from the peaceful conditions. During the incessant Comanche wars of the 1770's, Governor Mendinueta was compelled to forbid the export of sheep in order to conserve the remnants of the decimated flocks, but after the Comanche peace treaty of 1786, the sheep industry climbed to unprecedented prosperity. By the last decade of Spanish rule, according to Josiah Gregg, 200,000 to 500,000 sheep were being driven to Chihuahua each year.[57] His estimate, seemingly too high, was dwarfed by the claim of J. Francisco Chávez, scion of a great sheep-raising family and New Mexico's territorial delegate to Congress in the early 1870's, that 1,000,000 sheep were driven annually to Mexico during this period.[58] Even if these estimates were somewhat exaggerated, the happy condition of the sheep industry was perhaps the most remarkable attestation to the success of Spanish Indian policy in New Mexico.

The first cracks in the façade of New Mexico's successful Indian policy originated in the acquisition of Louisiana by the United States in 1803. This act initiated a keen rivalry for the loyalty of the Plains Indians as both the Spaniards and the Americans recognized the strategic importance of the Plains tribes to the control of the expanses between Louisiana and New Mexico. In 1805, James Wilkinson, the schemer who commanded the American forces in Louisiana, stated that the Comanches "have it in their power to facilitate or impede our march into New

[56] Deposition of Rafael Romero, "Private Land Claims in New Mexico," 36 Cong., 2 Sess., *House Exec. Doc. No. 28*, 24–26.

[57] Gregg, *Commerce*, 134.

[58] Statement of J. Francisco Chávez, "The Pastoral Lands of America," 43 Cong., 2 Sess., *House Exec. Doc. No. 13*, 309.

Mexico should ever such movement become necessary."[59] When Zebulon M. Pike left on his fateful expedition up the Arkansas River the following year, Wilkinson instructed him to attempt to win the friendship of the Comanches.[60] However, Pike was unable to carry out the order because the Pawnees, his intended intermediaries, were at war with the Comanches.

In response to the American challenge, the New Mexicans stepped up their own activities among the Plains Indians. Confident of Comanche loyalty, they concentrated on extending their influence to the Pawnees. Spurred on by rumors about the impending Pike expedition, Lieutenant Facundo Melgares, after marching from Chihuahua with one hundred regular troops and recruiting five hundred settlers in New Mexico, moved eastward in August, 1806, with the most imposing force to penetrate the plains since Anza's march against Cuerno Verde in 1779. After following the Canadian River deep into what is now Oklahoma, he turned north to the Arkansas, where he met the Pawnees one month before Pike. In a solemn conference with the tribe, he stressed the power of Spain, liberally distributed flags, medals, and other gifts, and then left,[61] having (in the words of some American traders) "influenced the Indians much" in New Mexico's favor.[62]

In order to exploit the groundwork laid by Melgares, the New Mexican officials appointed two veteran French traders, Jean Chavet and Pedro Vial, to serve as interpreters for the eastern Indians. Although very little is known of their work, it was quite likely that Governor Meriwether Lewis of Louisiana alluded to them in 1808 when he nervously reported that the Osages, Kansas, and Pawnees were assembled at "the Great Saline" in northern Oklahoma "to hold a council with the Spaniards and as it is un-

[59] Wilkinson to Henry Dearborn, July 27, 1805, in Clarence E. Carter (ed.), *The Territory of Louisiana-Missouri, 1803–1806*, 169.
[60] W. Eugene Hollon, *The Lost Pathfinder*, 101.
[61] Elliott Coues (ed.), *The Expeditions of Zebulon Montgomery Pike*, II, 413–15.
[62] William Clark to Henry Dearborn, June 1, 1807, in Clarence E. Carter (ed.), *The Territory of Louisiana-Missouri, 1806–1814*, 127.

derstood by the invitation of the latter."[63] Lewis feared that the results of the conference would not "be favorable to the quiet of our frontier." It was also probably Chavet and Vial who in 1808 persuaded the Pawnees to make peace with "part" of the Comanches.[64]

Nevertheless, New Mexican influence over the Pawnees soon waned, perhaps because Spain, then occupied by Napoleon's troops, was unable to support Indian affairs on its distant frontiers. In 1811, Major John Sibley, an American Indian agent, visited the Pawnees to ascertain whether they had dissolved their former allegiance to the Spanish authorities. Although they had a letter from the governor of New Mexico as well as Spanish medals and flags, the Pawnees informed Sibley that New Mexican agents no longer came to their camps and that they seldom went to Santa Fe because of the distance.[65]

New Mexico's influence over the eastern Plains Indians remained weak after the close of the Napoleonic Wars because of the serious shortage of Indian trade goods. In 1818, Governor Melgares complained that a visit to Santa Fe by some Comanches had left him with too few "Indian presents" to satisfy any other visitors.[66] That same year, an astute foreigner observed that the New Mexicans had neither the trade goods nor the market to meet the needs of the Plains Indians, who, consequently, were doing "everything possible" to attract American traders. He also warned that the Indians might turn against the Spaniards.[67] The prediction was somewhat belated, for the Anglo influence had already led to a renewal of Comanche raids against Texas and Chihuahua.

Counteracting the efforts of the Americans called for all the diplomatic skills that the New Mexicans could muster. In 1816,

[63] Meriwether Lewis to Henry Dearborn, July 1, 1808, *ibid.*, 199.
[64] "Diario de novedades desde 1 Julio de 1808 hasta 13 de Septiembre," MS, Document 2134, Spanish Archives of New Mexico.
[65] "Extracts from the Diary of Major Sibley," *Chronicles of Oklahoma*, V (June, 1927), 205.
[66] Melgares to Conde, October 8, 1818, in Thomas, "Documents," *loc. cit.*, 136.
[67] Alfred B. Thomas (trans. and ed.), "Anonymous Description of New Mexico, 1818," *Southwestern Historical Quarterly*, XXXIII (July, 1929), 58.

Juan Lucero, the most experienced of the New Mexican interpreters, visited the Comanche camps in an effort to bolster the waning friendship. Lucero warned the Comanches that the American gifts were only intended to entice them into stealing from the Spaniards and that the Americans would eventually seek to take their lands. He suggested that any who doubted this should go to the United States, where they could see that the Americans had wiped out the other Indian tribes, "as they will do to the Comanches."[68]

It was only natural that the eastern Comanches would break away from New Mexico's influence much earlier than their western kinsmen. By 1819, the "Cumanches Orientales" were raiding so openly in Chihuahua and Durango that Governor Melgares of New Mexico was ordered to send an expedition of 255 men down the Pecos in an effort to intercept them on their return. Significantly, his instructions emphasized that he was not to attack the "Cumanches Occidentales," who lived peacefully near the borders of New Mexico, but rather to call their principal chief to Santa Fe, assure him of the Spaniards' good will, and warn him not to go close to the "territories in which the campaign will be, lest our troops attack him by mistake."[69]

Although the eastern tribes were steadily falling out of the Spanish orbit, New Mexican agents, to the consternation of American officials, made sporadic efforts to regain their allegiance. In March of 1819, the Indian agent at Fort Smith became highly alarmed over the intrusion of "Spaniards from Santa Fe" into the lower Canadian Valley, although he did not know whether they were an official expedition or only a large trading party.[70] A month later, Agent John Fowler in southeastern Oklahoma complained that the New Mexicans had given the head chief of the Caddos "new presents" and "old advice," which had encouraged him to

[68] Bonavia to Allande, August 13, 1816, MS, Document 2672, Spanish Archives of New Mexico.
[69] Conde to Melgares, May 11, 1819, MS, Document 2819, Spanish Archives of New Mexico.
[70] William Bradford to John C. Calhoun, March 28, 1819, in Clarence E. Carter, (ed.), *The Arkansas Territory*, 59.

be very insolent and "full of threats."[71] However, it is difficult to see how either of these affairs could have posed a challenge to the Americans for control over the eastern Indians.

The New Mexicans continued to wield a very strong influence over the western Comanches until the end of the Spanish regime, as is vividly illustrated by the harrowing experience of American trader Thomas James. While en route to New Mexico in early 1822, James and his companions were seized by a band of Comanches, who decided to kill them the following day. Before the execution could be carried out, six Spaniards rode madly into the camp, crying, "Save them! Save them!" When the leader of the party, who had ridden twenty miles to rescue the Americans, demanded to know why the Comanches desired to kill the Anglos, he was told that the Spanish governor at Santa Fe had commanded them not to allow any Americans to pass. The New Mexican then explained that Mexico had become independent and that the New Mexicans now considered themselves to be "brothers to the Americans."[72] James, so intensely anti-Mexican that he had no sooner related this miraculous rescue than he stated that the Comanches "entertained a strong aversion and dislike" for the New Mexicans,[73] would hardly have made up this striking testimonial to the close co-operation between the New Mexican officials and the Comanches.

Under the administration of Mexico, Indian relations in New Mexico steadily deteriorated. The rapid turnover of officials (there were no less than ten different governors during the first twelve years of Mexican rule) made it impossible to maintain any continuity in policy. The inexperienced officials, moreover, were handicapped by inadequate financial resources. The meager appropriations for Indian affairs, which in 1826 totaled only 698 pesos, were made less adequate by the high price of Indian goods—46½ *varas* (one *vara* equals 33 inches) of a heavy blue cloth valued by the Indians for cloaks and decorative purposes, for

---

[71] John Fowler to John Jamison, April 16, 1819, *ibid.*, 70.
[72] James, *Three Years*, 134.
[73] *Ibid.*, 151.

example, cost 310 pesos.[74] Thus far fewer gifts were available than previously.

As the influence of the New Mexicans waned, the western Comanches in 1825 began to raid in Chihuahua. Upon hearing this, the New Mexican officials dispatched interpreter Manuel Mestes to reprimand them. Although they readily admitted to Mestes that they had participated in the raids, the Comanches blamed the Kiowas for instigating them. To show their good will, they warned Mestes that the Kiowas were talking of an attack upon New Mexico itself and pledged assistance if this occurred.[75] Since the raid did not develop, their aid was not required.

For the balance of the decade, the New Mexicans strove in vain to stop the western Comanches from raiding Chihuahua and Durango. At a council held on the Gallinas River in 1828, Kotsoteka Chiefs Cordero and Paranquita glibly promised, in return for presents, to keep peace with Chihuahua.[76] The following year, Don Juan José Arrocha, the military commander in New Mexico, with a force of 125 men, conferred with Comanche Chief Parvaquivista at the Bosque Redondo on the Pecos River below present Fort Sumner. After the father chaplain of the expedition had celebrated Mass in the midst of the Comanches to impress upon them the solemnity of the occasion, Arrocha began the conference by protesting the damages the Indians had inflicted on Chihuahua. He "energetically" told them to restrain their young braves and chided them for breaking their previous pledges of peace. Parvaquivista and his lieutenants, intent on obtaining the gifts brought by the New Mexicans, promised anew to raid no more. The following morning, Arrocha, having put the agreement into writing, solemnly sealed and delivered a copy of the treaty to the Comanche chief as a token to remind him of

[74] "Cuenta de la fonda de Aliados a los Capitanes Comanches, Cordero, Isaconoso, Estrellas, y los Gandulos que los acompañan," August 19, 1826, MS, Document 1826/720, Mexican Archives of New Mexico.
[75] Severino Martínez to Bartolome Baca, June 14, 1825, translated in Twitchell, *op. cit.*, I, 347.
[76] Don Juan José Arrocha to Don José Antonio Chávez, August 31, 1828, MS, Document 1828/943, Mexican Archives of New Mexico.

his pledge.[77] The Spaniard then returned home; Parvaquivista and his warriors avidly began to lay their plans for their autumnal excursions to the rich southlands.

There is no record of further negotiations with the Comanches. The New Mexicans may have realized the futility of such efforts, or the chaotic condition of national affairs may have prevented any co-ordination of Indian policy. When it finally became a matter of every province for itself, New Mexico managed to maintain peace with the Comanches; Chihuahua and Durango did not.

Despite the general tranquillity with the Comanches, New Mexicans endured a few minor depredations. In 1827, for example, the alcalde at Taos sent frantic word to Santa Fe that a party of Comanches, in whom he recognized "much malice," had killed twenty cows near the pueblo.[78] Before troops who were ordered to the settlement could arrive, however, the Comanches had vanished without further misconduct.

The only report of a major Comanche raid in New Mexico was made by James Ohio Pattie, trapper and inventive fabricator of tall tales. Shortly after Pattie and his fellow Mountain Men arrived in Santa Fe in 1826, the Comanches reportedly captured several women and children, including the governor's daughter. The New Mexicans cowered helplessly as the savages raced away with their victims, but Pattie and his comrades pursued the Comanches, rescued the captives, and returned the governor's daughter to a grateful father.[79] Had not Pattie's editor and rewrite man, a veteran Cincinnati newspaperman named Timothy Flint, published five years earlier a novel containing an almost identical adventure,[80] this episode, uncharacteristic as it is, might merit some credence.

---

[77] Arrocha, Diary of Expedition Led to Bosque Redondo to Negotiate with the Comanches, July 19 to August 31, 1829, MS, Document 1829/460, Mexican Archives of New Mexico.

[78] Manuel Martínez to Manuel Armijo, September 22, 1827, MS, Document 1827/1145, Mexican Archives of New Mexico.

[79] James Ohio Pattie, *The Personal Narrative of James O. Pattie of Kentucky*, 78–81.

[80] Flint's novel, *Francis Berniam*, had opened with the American hero, "fine looking and dignified," at Santa Fe in the act of rescuing from a Comanche band

The Comanche Peace, 1786-1846

Other American visitors to New Mexico not only did not report any Comanche raids, but commented on the peacefulness of the Comanches. Jacob Fowler, a semi-illiterate but shrewd Mountain Man, noted in 1821 that the Comanches were "at Peace with new maxeco and the Spanish in Habetance there,"[81] and Josiah Gregg, a frequent and observant visitor to both Santa Fe and Chihuahua during the 1830's, reported that the Comanches "cultivated peace" with the New Mexicans, although they were continually at war with Chihuahua and Durango.[82]

Precisely why the Comanches remained friendly with New Mexico while they were hostile toward the other North Mexican provinces is difficult to determine. New Mexican diplomacy, astute though it may have been, could hardly have been the only reason. Josiah Gregg, the only contemporary writer to speculate on the matter, conjectured that it was because the poverty of New Mexico offered few temptations to raid and because the Comanches desired to retain some friendly point with which to keep an "amicable intercourse and traffic."[83] Since New Mexico had been even poorer during the period of the Comanche onslaughts, Gregg's first deduction obviously was wrong; but his belief that trade was the key to the Comanche peace unquestionably was correct. In addition, the bonds that had developed between the New Mexicans and Comanches were far warmer and deeper than Gregg realized.

Native New Mexicans explained the Comanches' friendliness in a more romantic way. According to tradition, the Comanches remained tranquil because of a great victory the New Mexicans had once won. The date, the locale, and even the name of their

---

a Mexican governor's daughter, "a damsel of exquisite beauty" whom he later married. (Lennie Merle Walker, "Picturesque New Mexico Revealed in Novel as Early as 1826," *New Mexico Historical Review*, XIII [October, 1938], 326). It would seem, therefore, that Flint, who admitted in the foreword to Pattie's *Narrative* that he had contributed an "occasional interposition of a topographical illustration," was overly modest about his role in the writing of the book. Pattie, *op. cit.*, 25; John Ervin Kirkpatrick, *Timothy Flint*, 189.

[81] Elliott Coues (ed.), *The Journal of Jacob Fowler*, 56.
[82] Gregg, *Commerce*, 437.
[83] Ibid.

commander had been forgotten, but not the victory's magnitude and importance. Father Antonio José Martínez, the famed curate of Taos immortalized in Willa Cather's *Death Comes for the Archbishop*, stated in 1865 that the Comanches "in olden times" had always been at war but that after they "met with a severe disaster" in which a great many of their warriors were killed, "they abandoned the idea of fighting against New Mexico" and were "always faithful in keeping peace with us."[84]

Captain George H. Pettis, who learned of the great victory as an officer in New Mexico in the 1860's, reported that some eighty years earlier, the New Mexicans had found the Comanches in "full force at 'Rabbit Ear Creek,'" and after a two days' fight they 'cleaned them out, cleaner than a shot gun,' killing several thousand of them." The Comanches had never "forgotten the lesson."[85]

Amado Cháves' version of the legend, already described,[86] asserted that the battle had ended the Comanche wars for all time: "Whenever the young bucks wanted to start a war against the Spaniards the gray haired old men would take them to las 'Orejas del Conejo' ... and show to them the pile of bones and skulls [of their ancestors] ... and that would cool their desire to fight."[87]

A new foe, called simply the "Nations of the North,"[88] replaced the Comanches as New Mexico's chief menace from the plains during the 1820's. Although the specific tribes were not named in the records, the new enemies quite likely were the Cheyennes

---

[84] Statement of Antonio José Martínez, July 26, 1865, in "Condition of the Indian Tribes," 39 Cong., 2 Sess., *Senate Report No. 156*, 488.

[85] George H. Pettis to the editor, March 7, 1870, *Daily New Mexican* (Santa Fe), March 24, 1870.

[86] *Supra.*, p. 29 n.

[87] Cháves, "Defeat," *loc. cit.*, 9.

[88] The New Mexicans' use of this term is not to be confused with its use in Texas in the eighteenth century to refer to the tribes living along the Red River. One of the first references to these Indians in the New Mexico archives was in 1801 when the Comanches reported that they had been surprised and attacked by the *Naciones del Norte* on the Arkansas River. "Extracto de las Novedades occuridas en la Prov. del Nuevo Mexico desde 20 de Noviembre de 1801 hasta 31 de Mayo de 1802," MS, Document 1594, Spanish Archives of New Mexico.

and Arapahos, newcomers to the southern plains. Their depredations were usually limited to small-scale raids on the livestock of northeastern New Mexico and posed no serious threat, except at the ancient pueblo of Pecos, which had become too depopulated to defend itself. On June 17, 1828, fifty militiamen had to be sent to drive the "Barbarians of the North" away from it.[89] It was these new raiders, apparently, who forced the survivors at Pecos to join their kinsmen at Jémez, bringing to a dismal end the history of the proudest pueblo in all New Mexico.

The depredations by the Nations of the North led indirectly to the founding of Las Vegas. The petitioners for the Las Vegas grant claimed that the settlement would close to the northern tribes the "entrance" to the Pecos River villages. If this were done, they stated, the people of San Miguel and its environs would have no one to fear but the Comanches, who were "supposed to be peaceful."[90] Thus they could recoup their depleted fortunes. The Las Vegas grant was issued and a settlement was established there in 1835, but even so, the nuisance raids did not cease until after the Civil War.

The troubles with the northern Indians were made worse by the increasingly inept conduct of Indian affairs by the venal politicians who governed New Mexico during the 1830's and early 1840's. Manuel Armijo, the notoriously corrupt governor who later abandoned Santa Fe to the Americans, allowed an unnecessary war to break out with the Arapahos. In 1840, the Utes sold some captive Arapaho slaves to the New Mexicans. The Arapaho chiefs appealed to Armijo through Charles Bent, the trusted co-owner of Bent's Fort on the Arkansas River, for the release of their fellow tribesmen, offering to pay one horse for each captive.[91] When Armijo ignored the request, Bent warned him that both

---

[89] Juan Esteban Pino to Juan José Arrocha, June 17, 1828, MS, Document 1828/624, Mexican Archives of New Mexico.

[90] José Miguel Sánchez to the Ayuntamiento of Santa Fe, February 8, 1832, MS, Document 1831/1123, Mexican Archives of New Mexico.

[91] Charles Bent to Manuel Alvárez, January 30, 1841, MS, Benjamin Read Collection, Santa Fe (microfilm copy in the Special Collections Division, University of New Mexico).

the Arapahos and the Cheyennes—"the most formidable warriors of the North"—would go to war unless the Indians were freed. Armijo's contemptuous dismissal of this notice brought tragedy. On April 30, 1841, Bent wrote Manuel Alvárez, his friend and the American consul in Santa Fe, that a party of Arapahos had come to Bent's Fort with "8 Spanish scalps" and ten horses that they had taken "somewhere east" of the Sangre de Cristos.[92] Unfortunately, there is no further information on the Arapaho War because Bent soon afterward went to St. Louis on a business trip. Although the outbreak apparently was not serious—Bent reported in 1846 that the Cheyennes and Arapahos had "for many years been on friendly terms with the New Mexicans"[93]—the incident reflects the sad state to which New Mexican diplomacy had sunk.

Relations with the Apaches also worsened during the last turbulent years of Mexican rule. Like the northern tribes, however, the Apaches mounted comparatively few large-scale attacks; Gregg stated that in all his travels in New Mexico, he had heard of only one serious incursion by them—near Socorro in the early 1830's.[94] On the other hand, the Apaches insolently stole thousands of sheep. According to Gregg, they boasted that they could have destroyed every sheep in the country, "but . . . they prefer leaving a few behind for breeding purposes, in order that their Mexican shepherds may raise them new supplies."[95]

Although most of New Mexico's Indian neighbors became warlike during the last hectic years of Mexican rule, the Comanches remained peaceful. When asked to inform the Commissioner of Indian Affairs on conditions in New Mexico after the American occupation, Charles Bent indicated that relations had changed little with the Comanches since the 1820's. They had "been at peace for many years with the New Mexicans," although they had

---

[92] Bent to Alvárez, April 30, 1841, *ibid.*
[93] Charles Bent to Medill, November 10, 1846, in Annie Heloise Abel (ed.), *The Official Correspondence of James S. Calhoun While Indian Agent at Santa Fe and Superintendent of Indian Affairs in New Mexico*, 7.
[94] Gregg, *Commerce*, 322.
[95] *Ibid.*, 135.

The Comanche Peace, 1786-1846

carried on an "incessant and destructive" war with Chihuahua, Durango, and Coahuila.[96] In view of the destruction wrought on the more densely populated and inaccessible interior provinces, it might be but little exaggeration to conclude that had there been no Comanche peace in New Mexico, there might have been no New Mexico.

[96] Bent to Medill, November 10, 1846, in Abel, *op. cit.*, 7.

4
The Comanchero Trade, 1786-1860

AMONG THE MOST STRIKING and picturesque of the New Mexicans were the daring individuals who traveled to the plains to trade with the Comanches. The *Comancheros*,[1] as they came to be known, consisted mainly of two groups: the "indigent and rude classes of the frontier villages"[2] and the Pueblo Indians, avid traders from time immemorial. The reputation of the *Comancheros* is quite paradoxical. At first considered harmless rovers of the plains, later they were regarded as notorious villains; yet during the interval, they changed very little. They were the victims of a rapidly changing society in which they, like their red-skinned customers, became a dangerous anachronism that had to be eliminated by the new masters of the plains.

The era of the *Comancheros* opened with the peace treaty negotiated between Anza and Ecueracapa in 1786. Although traders had visited the Indian country previously, the number had been severely limited by official restrictions and by the danger from hostile Indians. After the peace treaty, however, numerous frontiersmen asked permission to trade in the Comanche country, and Governor Fernando de la Concha, Anza's successor, acceded to their requests in order to acquire "knowledge of the waterholes and lands" of the Comanches in the event of a renewal of hostilities.[3]

[1] The term *Comanchero*, unknown in Spanish documents, made its first appearance in print in Josiah Gregg's *Commerce of the Prairies* in 1843. It seems likely, therefore, that Gregg either coined the term or at least popularized it. Most army officers who served in the Southwest during the 1840's and 1850's read Gregg's book to obtain information on the area; hence, when they encountered New Mexican traders on the plains, they promptly labeled them *Comancheros*.
[2] Gregg, *Commerce*, 257.
[3] Concha, "Advice on Governing," *loc. cit.*, 246.

The Comanchero Trade, 1786-1860

The opening of the plains to the traders was not an unqualified success. The *Comancheros*, oblivious to the possible consequences, purchased horses avidly from the Plains Indians in order to resell them in their war-torn homeland. But since this practice encouraged the Indians to steal from one another and therefore threatened the uneasy peace among New Mexico's Indian allies, Concha forbade trading on the plains except when it was specifically requested by the Comanches.[4] It seems likely that this policy continued for the remainder of the century, for goods acquired on an unauthorized trade visit in 1796 were confiscated.[5]

Government hostility toward the *Comancheros* ended abruptly in 1810 after a small party of armed Americans was captured east of Pecos. Governor Joseph Manrique immediately presumed that they were hirelings of Joseph Bonaparte, usurper of the Spanish throne, who was rumored to be planning an invasion of New Mexico from bases in American territory. Critically short of trained troops, Manrique began to grant "continual licenses to the settlers" to trade with the Plains Indians, hoping thus to detect the approach of hostile forces. The attack never materialized, but Manrique's plan apparently brought about a dramatic increase in the trade. On July 20, 1810, he reported that a party of fifty men had just left to visit the Kiowas, another was on its way to the Utes, and a third had just returned from trading with the Comanches.[6]

After the Mexican revolution of 1821, the policy toward the *Comancheros* fluctuated erratically. In 1827 a trader was arrested for going to the Indian country without permission;[7] the following year, the military commander at Santa Fe informed the alcalde at San Miguel del Vado that he desired to send an emissary with the next party of *Comancheros* in order "to treat with the Comanches on important affairs to the national service;"[8] but in

[4] *Ibid.*, 247.
[5] Twitchell, *op. cit.*, II, 277.
[6] Joseph Manrique to Namesio Salcedo, July 20, 1810, MS, Document 2342, Spanish Archives of New Mexico.
[7] Mariano Martín to Don Antonio Narbora, February 26, 1827, MS, Document 1827/224, Mexican Archives of New Mexico.
[8] Jefe Político to Estevan Baca, May 21, 1828, MS, Document 1828/495, *ibid.*

1831, the same San Miguel alcalde was ordered to refrain from licensing settlers to trade with the Comanches because such expeditions were "detrimental to order."[9]

Nevertheless, the trade flourished. Stephen Long, an American officer who explored the Southwest in 1820, reported that a well-beaten trail containing more than twenty parallel bridle paths followed the Canadian River eastward from New Mexico toward the plains.[10] Long also noticed along the river some sandstone cliffs inscribed with figures of men and horses, which he interpreted as recording meetings of the Indians and the Spaniards "for the purpose of trade, when the horses were either given as presents or bartered for other articles." Although he did not meet any *Comancheros*, Long did encounter a group of Kiowa-Apaches on its way to meet some Spanish traders on the upper Canadian.[11]

By the 1840's the *Comanchero* traffic had broadened the pack trails observed by Long into full-fledged cart roads. Lieutenant J. W. Abert, who in 1845 led an official exploration down the Canadian, stated that the trail had "the appearance" of a wagon road.[12] Four years later, Captain Randolph B. Marcy, after guiding a group of Forty-niners from Van Buren, Arkansas, to Santa Fe, described the *Comanchero* trail as "the old Mexican cart-road."[13] A gold seeker with Marcy's caravan was more explicit. Along the upper Canadian, he wrote, "you find large, broad wagon trails made by the *Ciboleros*, or buffalo hunters, and the Comanche traders, which lead you to the settlements."[14]

The first American officials arriving in New Mexico after the

---

[9] Jefe Político to Comandante Principal, September 23, 1831, MS, Document 1831/695, *ibid.*

[10] Edwin James, *James' Account of S. H. Long's Expedition, 1819–1820* (Vols. XIV–XVII of Reuben G. Thwaites [ed.], *Early Western Travels, 1784–1846*), XVI, 87, 95. Another early *Comanchero* trail extended from the Bosque Redondo on the Pecos eastward to *Cañon del Rescate* near present Lubbock, Texas. Pike, "Narrative," *loc. cit.*, 100–101.

[11] James, *Long's Expedition*, XVI, 105.

[12] Lt. J. J. Abert, "Report on the Upper Arkansas and the Country of the Comanche Indians," 29 Cong., 1 Sess., *Sen. Exec. Doc. No. 438*, 49.

[13] Capt. R. B. Marcy, "Report," 31 Cong., 1 Sess., *House Exec. Doc. No. 45*, 42.

[14] Ralph P. Bieber (ed.), *Southern Trails to California in 1849*, 307.

conquest found the *Comanchero* trade in a flourishing condition. Upon assuming his duties as superintendent of Indian affairs in 1849, James S. Calhoun reported with astonishment that the Pueblos and Mexicans had a "constant habit of trading with the Comanches." Although he thought the trade "ought to be gently and quietly stopped," he allowed it to continue under an improvised set of regulations. To Pueblos (for whom he was more responsible) who asked permission to trade, he gave "a simple permit, without charging a fee of any amount." Mexican traders, on the other hand, were required to produce testimonials of good character, to post a bond of up to five thousand dollars, to pledge not to trade in munitions of war, and to state the specific tribes with which they wished to deal. They were also charged a fee of ten dollars for a license.[15]

Calhoun had hoped that the licensing requirements would restrict the trade, but this was not the case. When one trader received a license, he discovered, a dozen or more would "club together" and trade on it. Thus, although he issued only three licenses to Mexicans during his first year in office, "the number of traders going to the plains was never greater."[16] There is some indication, however, that Calhoun's licensing procedures had some effect on the traffic. Two men whom he sent to ransom a captive from the Mescalero Apaches reported upon their return that the Indians had a "large number of captives, horses, and mules which they had not found a market for, as traders did not come to see them as formerly."[17]

Many of the requests for trade licenses were recorded at the Indian agency in Santa Fe by John Greiner and John Ward, secretaries to Calhoun and his successor, William Carr Lane. An analysis of the journal entries from April 1, 1852, to January 1, 1853 (when the records are most complete), reveals that sixteen trading parties were licensed—twelve Pueblo and four Mexican.[18] More significant, perhaps, were the five requests which were

[15] Calhoun to Orlando Brown, January 25, 1850, in Abel, *op. cit.*, 105-106.
[16] *Ibid.* [17] Calhoun to Brown, March 15, 1850, *ibid.*, 161.
[18] Annie Heloise Abel (ed.), "The Journal of John Greiner," *Old Santa Fe,*

denied: one to a Pueblo because he refused to accept responsibility for some Mexicans whom he wished to take with him, two to Mexicans who lacked the necessary documents, one to a Mexican because the agent "didn't like his appearance," and one without a recorded reason.[19] The licensed expeditions, however, were probably only a minority of those that actually went to the plains. Many Mexican traders could not hope to fulfill the requirements for a permit and thus were forced to trade illicitly. Moreover, only the Pueblos who lived near Santa Fe bothered to obtain licenses. Such inveterate traders as the natives of Taos, Picurís, and Isleta went directly to the plains without asking leave of anyone.

The entries of Greiner and Ward also indicate that August and September were the chief trading months. More than half of the recorded requests for trade permits in 1852 were made between August 11 and September 8. This data is substantiated by the report of Lieutenant A. W. Whipple, who traveled the Canadian route to New Mexico in September, 1853. While crossing the Panhandle, he met five Mexicans on September 8, six or eight Pueblos from Santo Domingo on the twelfth, "traders in search of Comanches" on the fifteenth, a party of fifteen on the eighteenth, and twenty-two persons on the twenty-second. In addition, he reported there were "other parties in the vicinity." Whipple concluded in amazement that he had "no previous idea of the extent of this Indian trade, or of the impunity with which defenseless traders could mingle with the savage and treacherous tribes on their own soil."[20]

As they made their way across the plains, the *Comancheros* often presented a bedraggled sight to the few Americans whom they encountered. In 1845, Lieutenant Abert met a "poor and shabby" group of traders dressed in "conical-crowned sombreros,

---

III (July, 1913), 189–242; *idem*, "Indian Affairs in New Mexico Under the Administration of William Carr Lane; From the Journal of John Ward," *New Mexico Historical Review*, XVI (April, 1941), 206–32.

[19] *Ibid.*

[20] "Lt. A. W. Whipple's Report upon a Route near the Thirty-Fifth Parallel," *Explorations and Surveys for a Railroad Route*, III, 31–39.

jackets with the stripes running transversely; large bag breeches extending to the knee; long stockings and moccasins." Abert was considerably more charitable, however, than Captain Lemuel Ford of the First Dragoons, who, upon meeting *Comancheros* in eastern Colorado, confided to his diary that "these Spaniards are the meanest looking race of People I ever saw, don't appear more civilized than our Indians generally. Dirty filthy looking creatures."[21]

Even veteran Anglo traders were sometimes taken aback at the alien appearance and habits of the *Comancheros*. Jacob Fowler, upon encountering a party of sixty at a Comanche camp in southeastern Colorado, immediately judged them to have "far less sence" (like many early travelers, his spelling did not match his perception) than the Comanches. He also claimed that the Comanches issued orders to the New Mexicans "much as we command our negroes." To gratify Fowler's whim, the Comanches bade the Mexicans to pray so that he could "see their fashion." The traders obligingly "went through the Catholic prayers, and afterwards prayed fervently" for the American. During the course of the prayers, Fowler gaped when he saw the leader of the *Comancheros* casually catch "a louse and eat it." When the actual trading began the next day, Fowler again professed to be shocked to see that the Mexicans, "were painted like the Indians,"[22] but it is difficult to believe that any occurrence—unless it were observing traders who "prayed fervently"—would have shocked an experienced American plainsman.

Strangely enough, the early travelers on the plains seldom mentioned Pueblo traders. Lieutenant Abert saw some whose "jet black hair was tied up in stumpy queues with some light-colored ribbon," and Lieutenant A. W. Whipple, leader of one of the Pacific railway surveys in the 1850's, recorded that he met a group from Santo Domingo who were wrapped in blankets and had headbands around their hair.[23]

[21] Abert, "Report on the Upper Arkansas," *loc. cit.*, 53; Nollie Mumey (ed.), *March of the First Dragoons to the Rocky Mountains in 1835*, 72.
[22] Coues, *Journal of Jacob Fowler*, 72–73.
[23] Lt. J. W. Abert, "Report of Lt. J. W. Abert of His Examination of New

A History of New Mexican–Plains Indian Relations

Unkempt and tattered though they might be, the *Comancheros* had an abundance of trade goods eagerly coveted by the Plains Indians: bread, flour, and corn meal. These products became such an integral part of the commerce that they were inseparably linked with it. Long afterward, some Pueblos who were questioned about the barter recalled:

> When the men were going to the plains to trade with the Comanches, the women used to grind whole loads of meal for them to carry. Several women would grind together at night; they ground the corn successively on three or four metates ranging from rough to smooth. On the first they broke up the corn, and reduced it to fine flour on the fourth, toasting it after each grinding. Meanwhile, the men sang the grinding song, or beat a drum, and the women kept time to the music with slow, regular strokes.[24]

The New Mexicans carefully baked the trade bread in their rounded ovens until it was dark, dry, crisp, and almost imperishable. They knew that the Indians regarded it as a great delicacy and would pay as much as a good pony for a "sack" of the hard but nutritious loaves.[25] Years later, the Cheyennes, cooped up on a reservation, wistfully recalled that the traders had brought them "foods" that were very good.[26]

Early American observers differed greatly about the quality and taste of the bread. Josiah Gregg stated that the loaves, although "exceedingly hard and insipid while dry," became soft and palatable when soaked in water.[27] Young Lewis Garrard, who had his first taste after he had spent a winter eating the cooking of Mountain Men, ecstatically proclaimed the bread to be "light, porous, and sweet—a perfect luxury with a cup of coffee by a mountain-pine fire."[28] On the other hand, a tenderfoot Forty-niner,

---

Mexico," 30 Cong., 1 Sess., *House Exec. Doc. No. 41*, 446; "Whipple's Report upon a Route," *loc. cit.*, 34.

[24] Wilfred W. Robbins, John P. Harrington, and Barbara Freire-Marreco, "Ethnobotany of the Tewa Indians," Bureau of American Ethnology *Bulletin 55*, 86.

[25] Edgar L. Hewett and Bertha P. Dutton (eds.), *The Pueblo Indian World*, 98.

[26] George B. Grinnell, *The Cheyenne Indians*, I, 124.

[27] Gregg, *Commerce*, 67.

[28] Lewis Garrard, *Wah-To-Yah and the Taos Trail*, 242.

not two weeks out of the East, recoiled in disgust from the "hard, black-looking crackers" that a swarthy *Comanchero* offered to sell him for sixpence each.[29]

In addition to their staple stocks of bread, flour, and corn meal, the traders, according to contemporary accounts, carried to the Indians sugar, "saddlary," dried pumpkins, onions, tobacco, barley meal, and dry goods. Manufactured items, such as hardware or cloth, apparently were rarely traded, perhaps because they were too difficult for the *Comancheros* to procure.

Although commonly regarded as "gun-runners," the *Comancheros* had very few firearms to barter until after the arrival of American merchants in New Mexico. Indeed, the Mexican traders were buying more guns from the Indians than they were selling. In 1848, the Indian agent for the Osages reported that his charges were purchasing "guns, blankets, cloth, powder, lead, etc. of the traders in this nation" and trading them to the Comanches for horses. The Comanches, he asserted, "can sell their guns for thrice their value."[30] This indicates that the Comanches were again selling firearms to the New Mexicans as they had done at the Taos trade fairs during the preceding century. The *Comancheros*, however, did sell weapons to the Plains Indians— lances and tomahawks, "more slender and graceful in design than those supplied by English or American traders." They also brought the Indians "iron or steel arrow spikes ready made," which were rapidly superseding the traditional flint points.[31]

In addition to trade goods, the *Comanchero* visits also provided the Indians with an important social diversion in their bleak lives. A Cheyenne story recorded by George Bird Grinnell poignantly illustrates the keen anticipation with which the Indians looked forward to the arrival of the *Comancheros*:

> ... one night the people heard a loud shout saying, "The Mexicans

[29] Lansing B. Bloom (ed.), "From Lewisburg to California in 1849," *New Mexico Historical Review*, XX (January, 1945), 46.
[30] John M. Richardson to the Commissioner of Indian Affairs, February 25, 1848, quoted in Grant Foreman, *Advancing the Frontier, 1830–1860*, 242.
[31] Mooney, "Calendar History," *loc. cit.*, 141; J. Marvin Hunter, *The Boy Captives*, 159.

have come to trade; they are camped here just outside the circle."
All the women jumped out of bed, got together the things that they
had to trade, and rushed off in the direction of the voice. When
they got outside the circle they could see no camp, and looked
around, not knowing what to do. Then from behind them on the
other side of the camp came the shout, "The Mexicans are camped
here, and they have plenty of things to trade." At once the women,
thinking they had made a mistake, turned about and ran in that
direction; but when they reached the border of the camp on that
side, no Mexicans were to be found. Then the cry sounded from
still another direction, saying: "This is where the Mexicans are;
come this way;" and some of the women started, but presently
someone shouted out, "Oh it must be Little Hawk who is calling
us about from one place to another." It proved to be Little Hawk,
and there were no Mexicans.[32]

In return for their goods, the *Comancheros* received horses,
mules, buffalo robes, and meat. With the exception of the traffic
in horses and mules, their commerce of the early nineteenth century was remarkably similar to the barter carried on between the
Plains Indians and the Pueblos during the time of Coronado: a
simple exchange of the produce of the valley for the game of the
plains.

Although most of the trade goods were carried to the Indian
country on pack animals, a significant amount was taken in ungainly ox carts called *carretas*. In 1845, Lieutenant Abert reported
that the *Comanchero* trail along the Canadian "was strewn" with
the broken axletrees of the Mexican carts. Near the Texas line,
however, the road suddenly changed "from a wagon trail to a
bridle path," which led Abert to conclude that the Mexicans
cached their *carretas* at that point and from there traveled with
pack animals to the Comanche villages. Abert was both amazed
and amused at the construction of an abandoned cart found at
the end of the wagon road:

> Two eccentric wheels, not exactly circular, formed by sawing off
> the ends of large logs, and rimming them with pieces of timber to

[32] Grinnell, *op. cit.*, I, 125. For another graphic account of the traders' impact on the Plains Indians, see Alice Marriott, *The Ten Grandmothers*, 16-26.

increase their diameter . . . They were perforated in the neighborhood of the centre, to receive an axletree of cottonwood. A suitable pole, and a little square box of wicker wood completed the laughable machine.[33]

Abert's amusement over the *carreta* was shared by many of his fellow Americans, who regarded its odd appearance and inefficiency as evidence of the cultural backwardness of the New Mexicans. Josiah Gregg claimed that it required four yoke of oxen "to draw the load of a single pair with an ordinary cart." W. W. H. Davis, a federal judge in New Mexico during the 1850's, detected other faults in the vehicle. "The wheels are never greased," he complained, "and as they are driven along they make an unearthly sound . . . being a respectable tenor for a double-bass horse fiddle."[34]

Despite their archaic equipment, the *Comancheros* ranged over an extensive area. To the east, they wandered as far as the Wichita Mountains (Sierra Jumanos) of Oklahoma;[35] to the southeast, as far as the Davis Mountains, where in 1849 a party charged some footsore emigrants fifty to seventy-five dollars each for horses which, according to the Anglos, had probably cost them no more than six dollars apiece.[36] Other traders were going far to the north by the beginning of the century. In 1811, a brigade of trappers sent out by Manuel Lisa, father of the Missouri fur trade, discovered that "the Spaniards of Mexico were going every year to trade with the Arapahoes" near the South Platte River.[37] As late as 1858, a *Comanchero* party was encountered on the Platte "packing flour" to the Indians.[38] Years later, Lieutenant John Bourke, one of the Southwest's first amateur anthropologists,

---

[33] Abert, "Report on the Upper Arkansas," *loc. cit.*, 53.
[34] Gregg, *Commerce*, 147; W. W. H. Davis, *El Gringo*, 212.
[35] Gregg, *Commerce*, 322.
[36] Mabelle E. Martin (ed.), "From Texas to California in 1849," *Southwestern Historical Quarterly*, XXIX (July, 1925), 47.
[37] Herbert E. Bolton (ed.), "New Light on Manuel Lisa and the Spanish Fur Trade," *Southwestern Historical Quarterly*, XVII (July, 1913), 63.
[38] Anselm H. Barker, *Diary of 1858 from Plattsmouth, Nebraska Territory, to Cherry Creek Diggings, the Present Site of Denver, Colorado* (ed. by Nollie Mumey), 56.

questioned an ancient native of San Juan Pueblo about his youthful travels. Eyes misty with nostalgia, the old Pueblo recalled that in addition to the routine excursions to the Comanches and Kiowas, he had gone far to the north and bartered with the Sioux, Cheyennes, Arapahos, Crows, Utes, and Shoshones.[39]

Naturally the time required for making the trading trips varied greatly. Gregg stated that *Comancheros* usually wandered "around for months,"[40] but the journals kept by Greiner and Ward in the early 1850s show that the traders were often gone only a few weeks. On August 15, 1852, for example, Santo Suazo of Tesuque Pueblo received a license to trade with the Comanches; by September 15, he had returned to Santa Fe to report that the Comanches "are all behaving well . . . and are all moving towards the Arkansas in order to hunt buffalo." Similarly, two Indians from Santa Ana Pueblo who received licenses on June 22 returned on July 30 with a report on "conditions among the Comanches."[41] This brevity was not unusual, for licenses granted by Greiner and Ward were often valid for only two months.

The *Comancheros* learned to move skillfully and at will over the featureless landscapes of the plains. Among the earliest Anglos to witness their extraordinary ability were the ill-fated members of the Texan–Santa Fe Expedition. In August, 1841, after the force had virtually collapsed from exhaustion in the vicinity of Quitaque Creek, a vanguard that included George Wilkins Kendall, the youthful publisher of the *New Orleans Picayune*, moved ahead and luckily encountered a handful of *Comancheros*. The traders pointed out to Kendall and his companions the route to New Mexico and then went back for the main party. Kendall was amazed to learn later that the Mexicans had covered in "less than four days" a distance that had taken his party thirteen days to traverse.[42] Thomas Falconer, a young Englishman with the main group, noted with awe that the Mexicans could bring "us

[39] Lansing Bloom (ed.), "Bourke on the Southwest," *New Mexico Historical Review*, XI, (July, 1936), 267.
[40] Gregg, *Commerce*, 257.
[41] Abel, "Journal of John Greiner," *loc. cit.*, 218–41.
[42] George Wilkins Kendall, *Narrative of the Texan Santa Fe Expedition*, 354.

exactly to the places that they told us about yet they led by no trail nor by any visible marks."[43]

In making their lonely trade visits, the *Comancheros* were in constant danger of being robbed by their savage customers. Gregg once met some traders who were fleeing from the Comanches, who, he stated, often recaptured horses they had sold to the *Comancheros*;[44] in a similar incident, Lieutenant Whipple encountered five traders who sought his protection from some Indians who had robbed them of nearly all their goods.[45] In early 1852, Greiner recorded that a trader visiting his office complained that the Kiowas "had stolen all his animals."[46] The following year, a trader named Matias Baca asked John Ward for a pass to "try and recover some of his animals the Comanches had stolen" during his trip among them.[47] It is significant that each of these incidents involved Mexicans rather than Pueblos, who seem to have had a better rapport with the Plains Indians. These outrages, at least as far as the Comanches were concerned, were more likely the result of personal grudges than of any general feeling of antipathy toward the traders.

Although there is no record of the Comanches' having killed any of the traders, the Kiowas, notorious for their treachery and viciousness, were another matter. In 1858, they callously murdered two *Comancheros* who were en route to a small Comanche village.[48] When Adolph Bandelier, the pioneer anthropologist and historian, spent a few weeks at Santo Domingo in 1880, he learned that the Kiowas had long been a menace to traders. About sixteen or eighteen years earlier they had

> attacked a party of forty from San Juan Pueblo but were repulsed after a fight which lasted from midnight till after 3 P.M. The Pueblos had one man killed and one wounded, and their entire stock was

---

[43] As quoted in H. Bailey Carroll, *The Texan Santa Fe Trail*, 145.
[44] Gregg, *Commerce*, 322.
[45] "Whipple's Report upon a Route," *loc. cit.*, 31.
[46] Abel, "Journal of John Greiner," *loc. cit.*, 199.
[47] Abel, "Indian Affairs in New Mexico," *loc. cit.*, 345.
[48] "Report of Lt. John V. Dubois, February 23, 1858," in *Annual Report of the Secretary of War*, 1858, 258.

run off, so that they had to return on foot. The captain of the Kaihua was killed, and they fled, leaving many dead behind them. The Comanche witnessed the engagement from the neighboring hills, but remained neutral.[49]

The Comanches did not always tolerate Kiowa interference with their traders. Once, according to Bandelier, a Pueblo party on its way to the Comanches was stopped by Kiowas who asked to trade. After the bartering was completed, the Kiowas demanded the return of their goods. This the traders refused to do. Before the Kiowas could attack, however, some Comanches "dashed into the camp," ascertained the cause of the trouble, and "had the Kaihuas whipped out."[50]

The Navahos, who often slipped onto the plains in quest of buffalo or Comanche horses, were almost as serious a menace to the *Comancheros* as were the Kiowas. On August 26, 1860, a party of Pueblos from Isleta set out for the Comanche country. According to the crude vernacular of the *Santa Fe Weekly Gazette*, they were winding their way through the *Cañon del Infierno* (Valley of Hell) in the Manzano Mountains when they suddenly found themselves in a " 'hell of a fix' (to use a common expression) surrounded by Navahoes." In the brisk battle that followed, the Pueblos beat off their attackers at a cost of one Isletan killed, five wounded, and sixteen burros stolen. Two of the Navahos were killed.[51]

In trading with the Cheyennes and Arapahos, the *Comancheros* faced considerable opposition from American traders who resided among these Indians. "Uncle John" Smith, an American squawman who exercised a great deal of influence over the Cheyennes, was one of the most notorious of the Mexicans' tormentors. Smith forced all traders coming to "his Indian village" to pay tribute to

[49] Adolph F. Bandelier, "Journal for 1880," MS, New Mexico Museum Library, Santa Fe, entry for October 21, 1880. Typescript copies of the pertinent entries in the journal were furnished by Dr. Charles Lange and Dr. Carroll L. Riley of Southern Illinois University, who prepared the manuscript for publication.
[50] *Ibid.*
[51] *Santa Fe Weekly Gazette*, September 2, 1860.

him before they were allowed to barter. On one occasion, a party of "strange Mexicans" refused. Smith thereupon incited the Cheyenne braves to dump the goods of the "cowering Mexicans" onto the ground and then to help themselves. Ordered out of the camp, the *Comancheros* left, according to Lewis Garrard, who looked upon Smith almost as a demigod, "crossing themselves and uttering thanks to Heaven for having retained their scalps." This was the last time that New Mexicans refused to bribe Smith. Garrard related that the "poor Greasers" were so intimidated that when on one occasion they encountered Smith all alone, instead of dispatching him on the spot, they promised to give him "every third robe" for his permission to trade.[52]

The New Mexican traders were not always so timid and craven in their encounters with Americans. A disreputable Anglo known simply as "Old Bob" once crept into a *Comanchero* camp and stole two horses, keeping one for himself and trading the other for a rifle and ammunition at Bent's Fort. When he returned to the plains, "intent on renewing his depredations," he unfortunately fell in with the traders from whom he had stolen the horses. They took back the remaining horse and then turned their wrath on "Old Bob." Despite his "prostestations of innocence and stout resistance," they stripped him of his weapons, gave him a severe flogging, and then turned him loose, "destitute of everything except the baseness of his own heart!"[53]

The Americans who established trading posts on the plains during the 1830's and 1840's not only competed with the New Mexicans but also furnished them with an important market for their products. Their forts, which lined the foot of the Rockies from the Arkansas to the North Platte, depended almost exclusively upon caravans from New Mexico for foodstuffs. At Fort Lupton in northern Colorado, Rufus Sage observed a party of

[52] Garrard, *op. cit.*, 116; Henry Inman, *The Old Santa Fe Trail*, 280. It is impossible to tell how much Garrard's anti-Mexican bias, which had been whetted by his witnessing the New Mexican and Pueblo revolt of early 1847, colored this story. John Smith was a powerful figure among the Cheyennes from 1838 to 1868 and often served as an interpreter for them.
[53] LeRoy R. Hafen and Ann W. Hafen (eds.), *Rufus Sage* (Vols. V and VI of *The Far West and Rockies Series*), V, 272.

fifteen Mexicans who had come from Taos to trade flour, corn, bread, beans, onions, dried peppers, and salt for robes, meat, moccasins, ammunition, guns, coffee, tobacco, and "old clothes." But in this commerce, too, the Mexicans were subjected to intimidation. Sage observed "an affray" in which a small party of Americans forced the *Taoseños* to reduce their price on flour from twenty dollars per *fanega* (120 pounds) to five dollars.[54] (The same year, 1843, flour at near-by Fort Laramie reportedly was selling for twenty-five dollars per hundredweight.)[55]

Many New Mexican traders remained at the trading posts to guard horses, care for cattle, and perform other tasks in return for wages that ranged from four to ten dollars a month. Although the real value was somewhat less because they were paid in trade goods valued at exorbitant rates, the wages were much higher than the Mexicans could make in their poverty-stricken homeland. It is not known what kind of workers the New Mexicans were as a whole, but at "St. Vrain's Fort on the South Platte" in 1842, Captain John C. Frémont hired a Mexican to act as his personal servant and described him as "an active, laborious man" who was "of very considerable service."[56]

In the 1830's, some of the New Mexican traders established a settlement of their own, named Fort El Pueblo, on the Arkansas River about five miles above Bent's Fort. According to Thomas Farnham, who passed by it in 1839, the inhabitants lived in one-story adobe houses built around a quadrangle, raised grain and vegetables on irrigated plots near the river, and had a few head of livestock.[57] Later in the same year, Matt Field, an impressionable young poet-journalist, ventured to stay overnight at the post, even though he had "some awkward sensations relative to the

[54] *Ibid.*, 62.
[55] Matt Field, *Prairie and Mountain Sketches* (ed. by Kate L. Gregg and John F. McDermott), 81.
[56] John C. Frémont, *Narrative of the Exploring Expedition to the Rocky Mountains in the Year 1842 and to Oregon and North California in the Years 1843-1844*, 26.
[57] Thomas Farnham, *Travels in the Great Western Prairies, the Anahuac and Rocky Mountains, and in the Oregon Territory* (Vols. XXVIII and XXIX of Reuben G. Thwaites [ed.], *Early Western Travels, 1784-1846*), XXVIII, 174.

black-looking fellows" who lived there. After convincing himself that the residents were "of peaceable character," Field became quite inquisitive and learned that they made their living "entirely by hunting and trading now and then with friendly Indians." Once or twice a year they traveled to Santa Fe to sell skins and to buy necessities. Romanticizing the Mexicans as much as other travelers had deprecated them, Field dubbed their settlement "Milk Fort" because of the number of milk goats kept there. To him the men were as brave and daring as the Comanches, had the "fleetest horses," and were "as expert with the bow as the Indians."[58] Field was that rarity among men who could appreciate and idealize alien cultures.

Other parties of *Comancheros* established tiny settlements on the Arkansas where they eked out a precarious existence under the constant threat of Indian attack. On Christmas Day, 1854, for example, a large war party of Utes and Jicarilla Apaches slipped out of their mountain retreats to strike a settlement at the present site of Pueblo, Colorado. The Indians killed fifteen men, captured a woman and her two children, and ran off two hundred head of stock.[59] Such raids kept all but the most restless and daring out of the region.

One of the most controversial aspects of the *Comanchero* traffic was the ransoming of captives, a practice rooted centuries in the past. Originally, the New Mexicans had purchased only Indian captives—to obtain servants and mine workers—but after the increase of Comanche raids in Chihuahua and Durango in the nineteenth century, they began purchasing Mexican prisoners also. As had been the case with ransomed Indians, a purchased Mexican remained the property of his redeemer until and unless the latter received compensation, either from relatives in Old Mexico or from the American officials. Some traders, it was

---

[58] John E. Sunder (ed.), *Matt Field on the Santa Fe Trail*, 152.
[59] Lt. L. H. Nichols to Col. T. T. Fauntleroy, January 11, 1855, Dept. of N. Mex., Letters Sent, Vol. 9, 265, U.S. Army Commands, Record Group 98, National Archives. Hereafter, the abbreviations LS, LR, RG, and NA will be used for Letters Sent, Letters Received, Record Group, and National Archives, respectively; U.S. Army Commands will be shortened to Army Commands.

charged, profited greatly from buying highborn captives from the Comanches and holding them for an "adequate" reward. A group of traders from Mora returned from the Indian country in March, 1850, with four newly ransomed captives for whom they had paid exorbitant amounts. To free a twelve-year-old boy had cost four knives, one plug of tobacco, two *fanegas* of corn, four blankets, and six yards of red Indian cloth. Another boy of the same age had cost one mare, one rifle, one shirt, one pair of drawers, thirty small packages of powder, some bullets, and one buffalo robe. And a young woman had required two striped blankets, ten yards of blue cotton drilling, ten yards of calico, ten yards of cotton shirting, two handkerchiefs, four plugs of tobacco, one bag of corn, and one knife.[60] Although these prices may have been exaggerated in order to get a larger reward, the items vividly illustrate the fondness of the Comanches for a variety of small goods.[61]

Although Governor Calhoun was horrified to learn that the traders purchased their own "kith and kin," he overcame his disapproval of the trade in captives whenever his own countrymen were involved. In late 1849, some Apaches ambushed a wagon train on the Santa Fe Trail, killing five of the men and fleeing with a Mrs. White and her small daughter. As soon as news of this tragedy reached Santa Fe, Governor Calhoun hastened to a "daring, fearless, and . . . discreet" Mexican trader and offered him a reward of one thousand dollars for ransoming the Whites.[62] Although the trader left on his mission less than an hour after Calhoun talked to him, Mrs. White had already been murdered before he located the Apaches. Efforts to save the daughter were likewise futile.

The New Mexicans, however, did succeed in rescuing an impressive number of prisoners. In 1837, a native of San Miguel bartered Mrs. Sarah Ann Horn from the Comanches for "a horse,

[60] Calhoun to Brown, March 31, 1850, in Abel, *op. cit.*, 183.
[61] Among the travelers who noticed this quirk of the Comanches in regard to trade was W. B. Parker, who wrote: "They . . . prefer a variety rather than a quantity, even though the goods may not be so valuable." W. B. Parker, *Notes Taken During the Expedition Commanded by Capt. R. B. Marcy U.S.A., Through Unexplored Texas in the Summer and Fall of 1854*, 234.
[62] Calhoun to Medill, October 29, 1849, in Abel, *op. cit.*, 65.

four bridles, two looking-glasses, two knives, some tobacco, and some powder and balls." In contrast to the Mexican's generous payment, an Anglo trader to whom the distraught woman had first been offered had been willing to give only "a poor old horse" that looked like an "aged rack of bones." Compared to the American, Mrs. Horn reported, the Spaniards "of whom I was so much afraid were kind ... they brought me enough of food and drink."[63] Other *Comancheros* during 1837 also liberated a Mrs. Harris, who had been captured at the same time as Mrs. Horn.[64]

Few border captives owed more to the New Mexican traders than Mrs. Jane Wilson, a young Texas farm wife whose husband had been killed by Indians in the summer of 1858 while they were en route to California. While Mrs. Wilson was returning to East Texas with a small wagon train, she and her two young brothers-in-law were captured by Comanches. After twenty-five days of brutal maltreatment, she escaped, only to face quick and certain starvation on the barren plains. After being reduced to "a mere skeleton," she met a small party of *Comancheros*, who tended her "in every possible manner," clothed her in men's apparel, and secreted her with some provisions in a hollow tree. Then they went on to the Comanche camp, hoping to ransom her young brothers-in-law. By the time they returned eight days later, unsuccessful in their quest for the boys, Mrs. Wilson was so weak that they had to pack her on an Indian travois. They turned her over to an American family at Fort Union and were rewarded with forty dollars by David Meriwether, the new superintendent of Indian affairs in New Mexico.[65]

Meriwether was satisfied and Judge W. W. H. Davis stated that the conduct of the leader of the *Comancheros* was "such as to entitle him to all praise,"[66] but Colonel Philip St. George Cooke, commander at Fort Union, dourly condemned the traders

[63] Carl C. Rister, *Comanche Bondage*, 168–71.
[64] *Ibid.*, 165.
[65] Meriwether to George W. Manypenny, December 13, 1853, N/306, New Mexico Superintendency, Office of Indian Affairs, LR, RG 75, NA. Hereafter, Office of Indian Affairs will be abbreviated OIA and New Mexico Superintendency to N. Mex. Supt.
[66] Davis, *op. cit.*, 110.

because they did not also "rescue or redeem" the two boys. Cooke expressed a deep suspicion of such "friendly intercourse with these aggressive savages,"[67] but he did not explain what might have been Mrs. Wilson's fate had the *Comancheros* not found her. Meriwether dispatched the *Comancheros* on a mission to rescue the two boys, but the attempt was unnecessary. Both had already been ransomed by other traders of the plains, one by a group of Chickasaws and the other by some Kickapoos. Congress later appropriated one thousand dollars to reward the rescuers of the boys,[68] a generous sum compared to the forty dollars doled out to the *Comancheros* for Mrs. Wilson.

Nelson Lee, another of the survivors of Comanche captivity, also owed his rescue to Mexican traders, who found him in the New Mexican mountains, more dead than alive, and concealed him from the Indians until they could return to the settlements.[69] These are only four of several Americans who owed their survival to the kind and compassionate efforts of a people whom too many of their countrymen considered to be the "weakest . . . most concontemptible servile objects to be seen."[70]

Although most of the early *Comancheros* were of the simple and comparatively harmless type already described, others—backed by wealthy *ricos* and unscrupulous Anglos—introduced guns and whisky to the Indians in exchange for horses and mules stolen in Mexico. In 1831, Josiah Gregg witnessed the departure from Santa Fe of a large trading party "freighted with engines of war and a great quantity of whisky" to be given to the Apaches for "mules and other articles of plunder which they had stolen from the people of the south."[71] Gregg evidently did not classify these nefarious traders as *Comancheros*. In a similar vein, Governor Calhoun complained that sinister groups were trading arms and ammunition to the Indians in such quantities that he believed that five-sixths of the mules in New Mexico had been

[67] Cooke to Meriwether, December 4, 1853, C/117, Dept. of N. Mex., LR, Army Commands, RG 98, NA.
[68] Foreman, *op. cit.*, 283.
[69] Nelson Lee, *Three Years Among the Comanches*, 65.
[70] Garrard, *op. cit.*, 272.
[71] Gregg, *Commerce*, 203.

brought in by them.⁷² George Ruxton, a young Englishman (somewhat prone to exaggerate) who traveled northward through Chihuahua and New Mexico in 1846, even stated that some New Mexicans disguised as Indians accompanied the Apaches on their raids in Mexico. He observed the capture of two such raiders during his visit to Chihuahua.⁷³

Other New Mexicans covertly introduced whisky on a large scale among the Cheyennes and Arapahos. In 1844, Thomas H. Harvey, the superintendent of Indian affairs at St. Louis, charged that New Mexico had become "a new source of supply." The liquor peddlers Harvey castigated were not the rude and simple *Comancheros* encountered by Gregg and Abert, but rather desperate characters, most of whom had deserted from the trading companies and "now form a reckless band of desperadoes," engaged in illicit and destructive trade with the Indians.⁷⁴ Equally active in purveying alcohol to the Plains Indians were Anglo traders from Missouri who used the border tribes, such as the Osages and Kickapoos, as middlemen.

As the years passed, the distinction between the hitherto law-abiding *Comancheros* and the lawless gun and liquor runners steadily grew more tenuous. Almost imperceptibly, the *Comancheros* of the frontier villages exchanged their role as peaceful purveyors of foodstuffs among the Plains Indians for a new one as inciters of tribal resistance to the Anglo intruders. As early as 1857, the Indian agent for the Cheyennes complained bitterly about the immense number of Mexican traders who were roving over the country, ostensibly to trade provisions to the Indians but in reality to "introduce among them their miserable Mexican whiskey, using their influence, which in many instances is great, to keep up the hostile feeling against the whites."⁷⁵ This report was the forerunner of many allegations of evil deeds perpetrated by the *Comancheros* during the post–Civil War period.

⁷² Col. John Munroe to Adj. Gen. R. Jones, June 11, 1850, in Abel, *op. cit.*, 109.
⁷³ LeRoy R. Hafen, *Ruxton of the Rockies*, 161.
⁷⁴ "Report of Thomas H. Harvey, October 8, 1844," in *Annual Report of the Secretary of War*, 1844, 437.
⁷⁵ "Report of R. C. Miller, October 14, 1857," in *Annual Report of the Commissioner of Indian Affairs*, 1857, 436.

5
The Ciboleros

PUSHING BOLDLY ONTO THE PLAINS side by side with the *Comancheros* were the New Mexican buffalo hunters, the *ciboleros*. Indeed, the two groups were closely related, for it was not uncommon for hunters to carry trade goods to the plains, for traders to return with their *carretas* laden with buffalo meat, or for a person to hunt and trade alternately. But the primary object of the *Comanchero* party was to trade; that of the *cibolero*, to hunt.

The *ciboleros*, although relatively unimportant until the nineteenth century, had pursued their vocation sporadically for untold ages. Pre-Spanish hunters had ventured forth whenever their relations with the people of the plains permitted. When the peaceful Antelope Creek people occupied the Canadian Valley during the fourteenth century, for example, the Pueblos had hunted extensively, but with the arrival of the warlike Querechos and Teyas, they were content to barter for enormous quantities of buffalo robes and meat, which seemed to be "more abundant" among them then than in later periods.[1]

The first known buffalo hunt of the Spaniards was also their most famous. In 1598, Juan de Oñate, the founder of New Mexico, sent Vicente de Zaldívar, his nephew and most trusted aide, with a detachment of sixty soldiers to the plains to see if the buffalo could be domesticated. Finding several large herds, Zaldívar followed the advice of the Teyas and built a cottonwood log corral so large and with "such long wings" that it could enclose ten thousand head. His expectations that the ungainly buffalo, lumbering around "as if they were hobbled," would be easy to capture

[1] Adolph F. Bandelier and Edgar L. Hewett, *Indians of the Rio Grand Valley*, 150.

were soon exploded, however, as he observed his soldiers vainly try "in a thousand ways" to drive the beasts inside the corral. After the "wild and fierce" animals, belying their awkward appearance, had killed three horses and wounded forty others, Zaldívar abandoned attempts to capture the adult buffalo and instead ordered a large number of the calves to be roped. His men started for the camp with these, but all of them died "within an hour." Zaldívar regretfully concluded that unless the buffalo "are caught soon after they are born and mothered by our cows and goats, they cannot be taken until [they] are tamer . . . than at present." The hunt was not a total loss, however, for Zaldívar enthusiastically proclaimed the meat of the buffalo that had been killed to be better than beef and the fat to be superior to lard.[2]

The Spanish documents of the seventeenth century contain very few references to buffalo hunting. Although both Pueblos and Spaniards probably obtained most of their buffalo meat and robes by barter, it also seems likely that they were familiar with buffalo-hunting techniques. One of the greatest buffalo slaughters on record was made in 1683 by the expedition which Juan Domínguez de Mendoza led into the Concho River region of western Texas. Mendoza stated that while he was camped among the Jumano Indians near present Ballinger, Texas, the Spaniards and Indians killed more than four thousand head for meat and left to rot on the prairie almost as many others, which were only skinned for the hides.[3] At no fewer than seven other campsites, Mendoza recorded buffalo killings that ranged from "only one" to "two hundred and fifty-five beeves."[4] Other expeditions onto the plains during this period must have made similar use of the great herds.

Eighteenth-century references, although infrequent, imply that buffalo hunting had become fairly common. In 1706, Ulibarrí noted that the natives of Picurís who were living at El Cuartelejo had gone on a buffalo hunt. In 1719, Governor Antonio de Val-

[2] Hammond and Rey, *Don Juan de Oñate*, I, 401–402.
[3] "Itinerary of Juan Domínguez de Mendoza, 1684," in Bolton, *Spanish Exploration*, 339.
[4] *Ibid.*, 329–43.

A History of New Mexican–Plains Indian Relations

verde, while leading his punitive expedition in search of the Comanches, encountered in eastern Colorado a great herd of buffalo. Mounting his horse, he "isolated a cow and ran it a good distance until he killed it with a spear."[5] His men then joined him in killing "many buffalo." This incident would seem to indicate that the Spaniards had had previous experience at buffalo hunting. In 1726, Governor Juan Domingo de Bustamante reported that a Pueblo chief and "others of his nation" had gone to hunt meat in the east,[6] but said nothing of the results. The matter-of-fact nature of this report suggests that hunting on the plains had become too common to be newsworthy.

The migration onto the plains of the warlike Comanches after 1725 probably reduced the number of *cibolero* hunts. In 1750, it is true, there was a cryptic report by a French trader that the Comanches "were spying upon the Indians of Pecos, who were hunting," but it is more likely that this statement pertained to the hunting of deer rather than buffalo. Moreover, Governor Tómas Vélez stated in 1752 that it was "very rare and risky for the Indians of these pueblos" to go far into the plains.[7] There are no more specific references to buffalo hunting until 1785, after Governor Juan Bautista de Anza's decisive victory over the Comanches, when "a party of Spaniards went buffalo hunting."[8] No details of the hunt are given; reference was made to it only because it led indirectly to the great peace conference between Anza and Ecueracapa.

The new patterns of New Mexican–Plains Indian relationships that grew out of the Comanche peace greatly stimulated buffalo hunting. The shifting of much of the Comanche trade to the plains diminished the quantity of meat and robes brought to the pueblos for barter. Traders who returned from the Indian camps told of massive concentrations of buffalo to the east of the province, and robes were needed in ever greater numbers to ex-

[5] "Diary of the Campaign of Governor Antonio de Valverde against the Ute and Comanche Indians, 1719," in Thomas, *After Coronado*, 129.
[6] Bustamente to Casa Fuerte, April 30, 1727, *ibid.*, 257.
[7] *Supra.*, p. 42.
[8] *Supra.*, p. 52.

change for manufactured goods in Chihuahua. In addition, the expanding population of New Mexico was putting greater pressure on the available food supply. These factors, plus the comparative safety with which expeditions could travel to the plains, combined to increase greatly the importance of buffalo hunting.

Although Spanish officials tried with some success to curtail the *Comanchero* trade, their few efforts to restrict the *ciboleros* had little effect. In 1811, the alcalde at Jémez threatened to arrest the natives of Santa Ana Pueblo who had gone to hunt without permission, and the alcalde at Taos reported in 1818 that a campaign against hostile Indians could not be undertaken because the Pueblos had taken all of the good horses on "an unauthorized buffalo hunt."[9]

Despite these minor complaints, the size and importance of the buffalo hunts increased steadily. A rapid growth during the second and third decades of the century can be inferred by contrasting the report of Don Pedro Bautista Pino in 1812 with that of Antonio Barreiro in 1832. Pino, an astute and thorough chronicler, did not mention buffalo hunting, but Barreiro included in his brief account detailed descriptions of the hunts. He estimated that the *ciboleros* were killing a minimum of ten to twelve thousand buffalo annually.[10]

Thus the day of the *cibolero* seems to have dawned in the first quarter of the nineteenth century. Rugged, daring, and picturesque, the *ciboleras* drew the attention of several Americans who visited New Mexico. An encounter with some hunters inspired Josiah Gregg to pen one of his most vivid descriptions of western life. The hunters, he wrote,

> usually wear leathern trousers and jackets, and flat straw hats; while, swung upon the shoulders of each hangs his *carcage* or quiver of bow and arrows. The long handle of their lance being set in a case, and suspended by the side with a strap from the pommel of the saddle, leaves the point waving high over the head, with a tassel

[9] Sánchez Vergara to Governor Manrique, January 6, 1811, MS, Document 2391, Spanish Archives of New Mexico.
[10] Carroll and Haggard, *op. cit.*, 102.

A History of New Mexican–Plains Indian Relations

of gay parti-colored stuffs dangling at the tip of the scabbard. Their fusil, if they happened to have one, is suspended in like manner at the other side, with a stopper in the muzzle fantastically tasselled.[11]

Governor W. W. H. Davis, a less enthralled observer, likened some hunters he met in 1853 to "a band of Gypsies" and recoiled from the homemade *aguardiente*, "as barbarous an alcoholic compound as was ever made,"[12] which the *ciboleros* hospitably offered him. Frederick Wislizenus, a German scientist-explorer, upon meeting a fierce-looking group of leather-jacketed *ciboleros*, asserted that they "were never hostile towards white men" and seemed to be afraid of Indians.[13]

Cibolero expeditions were commonly made in October. The crops had been harvested by then, the weather was not yet too severe for travel, the hides were in good condition, and meat was needed to sustain the sizable families during the winter. Furthermore, in October the buffalo were comparatively near at hand, for by then their annual migration southward from their summer haunts along the Arkansas River would have carried them into the Canadian Valley.

As the frost began to settle in the upland villages, caravans were formed under the leadership of veteran hunters known as *mayordomos*. Old and young, weak and strong participated. A few athletic young men called *cazadores* might suffice for the actual lancing, but many hands were needed to skin and prepare the meat. Occasionally, even women and children accompanied the expeditions. Wislizenus met a *cibolero* party in 1846 that included some women, and Frank Collinson, an Anglo buffalo hunter, in 1875 encountered a *cibolero* caravan that was made up of two hundred men and "half as many women and children and dogs."[14]

[11] Gregg, Commerce, 66.
[12] Davis, *op. cit.*, 44.
[13] Frederick A. Wislizenus, "Memoir of a Tour of Northern Mexico," 30 Cong., 1 Sess., Sen. Misc. Doc. No. 26, 12.
[14] *Ibid.*; Frank Collinson, "The Old Mexican Buffalo Hunters," MS, Panhandle-Plains Historical Museum Library, Canyon, Texas, 1936.

The Ciboleros

Many settlers also went on a short hunt after the crops had been safely planted in June. Preserving the summer kill was no problem, surprisingly enough, for "jerked" meat cured out rapidly under the hot sun. Since the buffalo had already shed their thick coats of hair, hides taken then were worthless for trade, but they could be used for rugs or bed covers or could be sliced into thin shreds for making ropes.[15]

On the hunt, the *cazadores* exercised skill and courage seldom equaled on the American frontier. Stealing as close as possible to a herd of buffalo, they dashed into the midst of the fleeing animals. Each hunter singled out a victim, shouldered his horse next to the brute, and drove his lance downward past the animal's left ribs into its heart. Wrenching the lance loose, the hunter swiftly turned on another lumbering beast. During the course of a single chase, which often covered two or three miles, an experienced lancer could kill from eight to twenty-five buffalo.[16]

A few hunters preferred the bow and arrow to the lance. Gregg, who went on a hunt with a Mexican archer, stated that as soon as they spied a herd of buffalo, the *cibolero* "put spurs to his horse" and started in hot pursuit. Before Gregg's mule could catch up, the hunter had killed and partially skinned a buffalo.[17]

The most extravagant testament to a *cibolero*'s skill was recorded by young Matt Field during a trip with a Santa Fe caravan. When the wagon train came into view of a herd of buffalo, a Mexican hunter named José Alexico set out to get fresh meat for the teamsters. Because it was a considerable distance to the next campsite, the wagon train could not wait for him, but if he killed the cow on the prairie, butchered her, and carried the meat after the caravan, he would not get to camp until after dark.

To solve his problem, Alexico, "with the coolest precision," separated a cow from the main herd and wounded her slightly. Then he worried her with torturing jabs of his lance to make her chase him. When the cow stumbled to her knees, he "beat her

[15] Carroll and Haggard, *op. cit.*, 102.
[16] Gregg, *Commerce*, 371; Fabiola Cabeza de Baca, *We Fed Them Cactus*, 42; John Cook, *The Border and the Buffalo*, 84.
[17] Gregg, *Commerce*, 371.

over the head . . . just as one might take a stick to drive away a sick dog" until she lunged suddenly at him and "passed her short curling horn within an inch of his horse's flank." In this manner, Alexico maneuvered the beast some three miles in advance of the wagons before completing the kill. As the animal fell, Alexico's companions closed in "with their knives, tearing away the reeking skin of the buffalo while she yet lay panting with life."[18]

Even before the lancers completed their work, the other members of the hunting expedition joined in. Men followed close behind the *cazadores* to slit the throats of the fallen animals to bleed them properly. Others brought up carts for carrying the carcasses to the camp, where the meat was prepared quickly to prevent spoilage.[19] On the night of the kill, every member of the party from the *mayordomo* to the lowliest novice worked at slicing the meat and hanging the thin strips up to dry. Among the Pueblos, "each man was given the same amount and the one who worked fastest went to bed first."[20]

It usually took only a few days for the prairie sun to cure the razor-thin slices; if by chance the weather was damp or cloudy, the meat was smoked over a fire of buffalo chips, which gave it a pungent, peppery taste. After the meat was jerked, the *ciboleros* packed their *carretas* by vigorously "beating or kneading the slices with their feet," which they also believed helped to preserve it.[21] At the village, the meat was pounded in large stone mortars up to three feet in diameter in order to break down its tough fibers. When some *ciboleros* in later years sold buffalo meat to Anglos, who had no taste for "jerky," they soaked it in brine and then smoked it much as pork was cured in the Mississippi Valley.[22]

The New Mexicans, like the Indians, used almost every part of the buffalo. After converting the flesh into jerky, they cut the

[18] Sunder, *op. cit.*, 301–302.
[19] Wesley Hurt, "Indian Influence at Manzano," *El Palacio*, XLVI (November, 1939), 353.
[20] Ruth Benedict, "Tales of the Cochití Indians," Bureau of American Ethnology *Bulletin 98*, 199.
[21] Gregg, *Commerce*, 67.
[22] Rex W. Strickland (ed.), "The Recollections of W. S. Glenn, Buffalo Hunter," *Panhandle-Plains Historical Review*, XXII (1949), 39.

fat into large chunks and rendered it into tallow for use in cooking and candlemaking. The crunchy cracklings *(chicharones)* which remained after the tallow was drained off were carefully hoarded to delight many a child's palate on long winter nights. The buffalo hides were tanned into highly valued robes and rugs by tediously scraping them and repeatedly kneading them with liberal applications of buffalo brains. Not even the long wool from the neck and shoulders was wasted; it was carted back to the settlements to be packed into mattresses or spun into coarse cloth.[23]

The successful hunters returned to their village in a triumphal procession, riding proudly through the intervening settlements as people gazed at them with envy and admiration. Occasionally, the less fortunate stood at the doors of their hovels and pleaded, "Buffalo hunter, give me some grease, give me some meat."[24] To show his great success, a *cibolero* might toss the beggar a small amount. The instant the hunters drew near their own village, they were sure to be spied by children, who would be craning anxiously from the rooftops. The returnees were honored the first night with a *fandango* (even as they had been bid *adios.*).[25] It was wonderful to be a successful *cibolero*.

The glamor of the hunt was somewhat offset by the dangers involved. The safety of the buffalo lancer rested directly upon the speed, agility, courage, and skill of his horse. The buffalo did not submit tamely; once wounded, it became enraged and often lunged desperately at its pursuer. An untrained horse could easily be "disembowelled," Gregg stated, but if "the steed understands his business, he will dodge the animal with the expertness of a fencer."[26]

Even the best of mounts was no guarantee of safety, however, for there was always the chance that a horse might trip in a prairie-dog hole or fall over some unexpected obstacle. A haunting

---

[23] Wesley Hurt, "Buffalo Hunters," *New Mexico Magazine*, XIX (November, 1941), 36; Cabeza de Baca, *op. cit.*, 42–43.
[24] Benedict, "Tales," *loc. cit.*, 201.
[25] Samuel Montoya, "A Buffalo Hunt," MS, New Mexico Historical Museum Library, Santa Fe, 1935.
[26] Gregg, *Commerce*, 372.

ballad of the New Mexico frontier, telling of a young hunter tragically impaled on his own lance when his horse tripped, is a grim reminder of the dangers faced by the *ciboleros*.

Caballo alazan tostado	Oh my sorrel colored horse
Que tu la muerta me dites	That you should be my death
En este llano estacado	On this Staked Plains
Vienes a hacer calavera	I will leave my skeleton[27]

Another dreaded danger encountered by the *ciboleros* was the late autumn blizzards which sometimes swept across the plains without warning. The perils of a blizzard are illustrated by a familiar story involving a *cibolero* who had become separated from his fellow hunters. When engulfed in a sudden storm, the hunter desperately scraped out the insides of a newly killed buffalo and took refuge in the warm carcass. To his dismay, the buffalo was soon frozen stiff, leaving him entrapped in an icy tomb. Luckily, the storm soon abated and his comrades, hearing his weakening cries, found him and thawed out the carcass. The hunter, who also "had to be thawed out," was afterward known as El Manco because he had lost an arm from the affair.[28] The bizarre imprisonment of a hunter inside a frozen buffalo either occurred more than once or else it was one of the favorite tall tales of old-time buffalo hunters. Colonel Henry Inman related a similar story about an Anglo hunter who was thus trapped in 1867.[29]

Because the *ciboleros* competed with the Indians in hunting buffalo, the red men harbored a resentment that sometimes flared into open hostilities. Indian groups frequently visited the *cibolero* camps and demanded flour, coffee, sugar, and any other provisions "that they took a fancy to." The hunters, thinking it "cheaper to buy peace than pay the consequences of a fight," generally complied.[30] They also kept on hand a supply of trade goods, including

[27] Lorin W. Brown (ed.), "Manuel Maes," MS, CL-1057, New Mexico Historical Museum Library, Santa Fe.

[28] Cabeza de Baca, *op. cit.*, 45.

[29] Inman, *op. cit.*, 206.

[30] Hurt, "Buffalo Hunters," *loc. cit.*, 35.

plenty of their oven-toasted hard bread, to use in soothing the Indians' passions.[31]

For added protection, the buffalo hunters traveled in large parties. In June, 1808, Don Francisco Amangual met 120 *ciboleros* near the Canadian River.[32] Josiah Gregg and Antonio Barreiro, writing during the Mexican period, agreed that the *ciboleros* went in "large parties or bands."[33] In 1846, Frederick Wislizenus recorded an encounter with a party of about 100 *ciboleros* in southwestern Kansas, and in 1853, W. W. H. Davis met a hunting party of 150 men who were employing 500 oxen and burros and 50 carts on a hunt in eastern New Mexico.[34]

Even the best of precautions did not always give the hunters security from the Indians. In December, 1801, some hunters from Santa Fe, well armed and bearing specific instructions to fight if they met the Apaches, turned back because some Comanches warned them that "the Nations of the North" were among the buffalo herds in great numbers.[35] In the winter of 1817, the Pawnees attacked a group of *ciboleros*, killing seven and capturing a ten-year-old boy whom they would have sacrificed had not Manuel Lisa, the noted Spanish trader, ransomed him.[36] In 1826, a party of Pawnees captured a group of buffalo hunters on the eastern side of the Sangre de Cristos, stripped them of their "mules, horses, meat, cloth, arms etc. & were seriously inclined to kill them all" until they recognized one of the *ciboleros* whom they had previously met in Kansas. They then released his party and returned his gun, but kept "everything else."[37]

With the decline in size of the buffalo herds, the Plains Indians became increasingly dangerous. In 1852, a large party of

[31] Gregg, *Commerce*, 67.
[32] Amangual, "Diary."
[33] Gregg, *Commerce*, 67; Carroll and Haggard, *op. cit.*, 101.
[34] Wislizenus, "Memoir," *loc. cit.*, 44; Davis, *op. cit.*, 44.
[35] "Extracto de las Novedades ocurridas en la Prov. del Nuevo Mexico desde 20 of Noviembre 1801 hasta 31 de Mayo de 1802." MS, Document 1594, Spanish Archives of New Mexico.
[36] George E. Hyde, *The Pawnee Indians*, 108–109; Richard E. Oglesby, *Manuel Lisa and the Opening of the Missouri Fur Trade*, 166.
[37] "General Sibley's Santa Fe Diary," in Hulbert, *op. cit.*, 168.

Mexicans and Pueblos hunting near Fort Atkinson, Kansas, evoked such loud protests from the Indians that the commander of the fort, ignoring the hunting permit the lancers had been given by the Indian superintendent in New Mexico, ordered them to abandon the hunting grounds.[38] In the autumn of the same year, some Santo Domingo hunters who were traveling toward the plains with their *carretas* were advised by a group of returning *ciboleros* that the Comanches had threatened to "take away all the animals and wagons" from hunting parties. The Santo Domingans prudently gave up the trip.[39] According to Colonel Philip St. George Cooke, the Indians in 1853 again warned the *ciboleros* not to bring to the plains more than a few pack animals.[40]

Failure to heed these warnings contributed to a short but violent war between the *ciboleros* and the Cheyennes. In the fall of 1853, a large party of New Mexicans who failed to find the buffalo herds along the Canadian River continued northeastward until they located them between the Cimarron and Arkansas rivers. During the hunt, two Cheyennes and a Mexican were killed in a skirmish. The New Mexicans claimed that the fight began when three Cheyennes attempted to steal some of their horses; the Cheyennes, that "the Mexicans caught two of our young men by themselves and killed them."[41]

Lieutenant J. E. Maxwell, who conducted an investigation of the matter, concluded from the testimony of a "Mr. Senecal, a gentleman of San Miguel," that the Indian version was the more accurate. After the buffalo hunters reached the hunting grounds, Maxwell reported, a small party led by a youth named Salazar— son of the Damasio Salazar who had brutally maltreated the members of the Texan–Santa Fe Expedition in 1841—split off from the main group and later attacked three visiting Cheyennes "to obtain their horses." Their treachery backfired, however, for young Salazar was killed and one of the Indians escaped. Salazar's com-

---

[38] Abel, "Journal of John Greiner," *loc. cit.*, 219.
[39] Abel, "Indian Affairs in New Mexico," *loc. cit.*, 229.
[40] Cooke to Maj. W. A. Nichols, January 29, 1854, C/10, Dept. of N. Mex., LR, Army Commands, RG 98, NA.
[41] David Meriwether to William Bent, March 11, 1854, N/246, N. Mex. Supt., OIA, LR, RG 75, NA.

rades then fled to New Mexico. They escaped, but the infuriated Cheyennes retaliated against the main body of *ciboleros,* who had known nothing of the altercation, by capturing between eighty and one hundred head of oxen and wrecking about twenty carts.[42]

The Indians were warmly supported by William Bent, powerful proprietor of Bent's Fort, and Thomas Fitzpatrick, the veteran Mountain Man who was now the agent for the Cheyennes. According to David Meriwether, governor and superintendent of Indian affairs in New Mexico, Fitzpatrick gave the Cheyennes permission "to take the property of the Mexican hunters," which the Indians sold to the traders about Bent's Fort.[43] After disposing of the *ciboleros'* stock, the Cheyennes had Bent pen a letter to Governor Meriwether, presenting their case against the New Mexicans. Claiming that hundreds of *ciboleros* had been roaming through their country in violation of their treaty rights, they demanded immediate compensation for their two slain tribesmen: "If the Mexicans will send us the pipe of peace and something to reward the parents of the two young men we will bury the tomahawk, but if not we will kill them when we see them." The missive was signed: "Your children the Cheyennes." In a personal postscript, Bent assured Meriwether that "from what I can learn ... the Mexicans were to blame in this case."[44]

Although the Cheyennes had promised not "to hurt one hair on the heads of our friends the Americans," Governor Meriwether was deeply alarmed. He asked Bent to tell the Indians that "any attack upon the Mexicans of New Mexico will ... be punished by me as though the same had been made upon the Americans." He also rejected the Cheyenne claim that the Mexicans were trespassing, pointing out that by the Treaty of Fort Laramie in 1851 the Cheyennes had been assigned the land between the Arkansas and North Platte rivers; the dispute with the *ciboleros*

---

[42] Lt. J. E. Maxwell to Cooke, January 28, 1854, enclosed with Cooke to Nichols, January 29, 1854, C/10, Dept. of N. Mex., LR, Army Commands, RG 98, NA.

[43] Meriwether to George W. Manypenny, March 15, 1854, N/246, N. Mex. Supt., OIA, LR, RG 75, NA.

[44] Bent to Meriwether, February 15, 1854, *ibid.*

had occurred south of the Arkansas. The "whole American people," he threatened, would punish the Cheyennes if they went to war.[45]

However, Meriwether did not have the support of the U.S. Army. Colonel John Garland, commander of the troops in New Mexico, felt that the Cheyennes were justified in their complaints. Since the *ciboleros* killed off the game upon which the Indians depended for subsistence, the latter, he argued, were forced to choose among breaking up the hunting parties, depredating upon the settlements, or starving to death.[46] The obvious solution was for the New Mexican hunters to stay away from the plains.

In the spring of 1854, the Cheyennes unleashed their threatened attacks on the New Mexican frontier. Although they harmed no Americans (as they had promised), according to Colonel Garland, they killed fourteen Mexicans in San Miguel County alone.[47] The American officers made little effort to punish the raiders because, as Colonel Cooke stated, it was "reasonably to be expected" that the

> Prairie Indians should commit depredations on this frontier, . . . in retaliation of serious depredations committed by the inhabitants of the Territory on them: Viz. the annual destruction of buffalo within their country (attended by occasional murder) in defiance of law and express treaty obligations; and I have information of repeated complaints and warnings by them to Americans passing through their country.[48]

In addition to the killings, the Cheyennes kidnaped eleven boys from the vicinity of Tecolote and Las Vegas. Governor Meri-

[45] Meriwether to Bent, March 11, 1854, *ibid.*
[46] Garland to Meriwether, January 18, 1854, Dept. of N. Mex., LS, Vol. 9, 115, Army Commands, RG 98, NA.
[47] Garland to Lorenzo Thomas, June 30, 1854, *ibid.*, 200.
[48] Cooke to Maj. W. R. Nichols, June 6, 1854, C/45, Dept. of N. Mex., LR, Army Commands, RG 98, NA. The American officials seem to have exaggerated the number of buffalo killed by the *ciboleros* when they justified the Cheyenne attacks on this score; they also ignored the fact that the territory south of the Arkansas River did not belong to the Cheyennes. Their lack of concern over the Indian raids may have been due in part to their anti-Mexican bias, but they were also engaged in a campaign against the Utes and Jicarilla Apaches, which may have left them with too few troops to risk hostilities with the Cheyennes.

The Ciboleros

wether, while en route to St. Louis during the summer of 1854, met a party of Cheyennes who openly boasted that they had committed the depredations and carried off the prisoners. Unable to carry out his threat to punish the Indians, Meriwether asked the new Cheyenne agent, J. W. Whitfield, to try to procure the release of the captives. Upon returning to Santa Fe, Meriwether perceived something of the pathetic impact of the raids when an old Mexican peon, "very poorly clad" and in "very bad health," walked sixty miles to inquire about his two sons, who had been among the kidnaped youths.[49]

Meanwhile, Agent Whitfield, with a "liberal present," had bribed the Cheyennes into releasing two of the Mexican captives, "very interesting children" who had aroused his sympathies. Despite this show of compassion, Whitfield realistically pointed out: "We cannot establish the precedent of buying Mexican prisoners, if we were . . . only to pay for what the Indians now have in my Agency it would Bankrupt your Treasury—I am certain the Comanches and Kiowas have one thousand."[50]

The last incident of the *cibolero* war occurred in November, 1854, when some Cheyennes ambushed twenty-five Taos Indians hunting near the Raton Mountains and killed twelve.[51] The enmity aroused between the *Taoseños* and the northern tribes by this attack did not end until 1858, when, at a peace conference called through the efforts of Kit Carson, Guatamo, an Arapaho chief who represented the Cheyennes and Arapahos, met with José María Cordova and Antonio José Suaso, the "war chiefs" of Taos, and entered into a "permanent treaty of peace and friendship" in which it was agreed that "parties may pass and repass through the country of each without molestation if on a peaceable mission."[52]

---

[49] Meriwether to Manypenny, October 25, 1854, N/339, N. Mex. Supt., OIA, LR, RG 75, NA.

[50] Whitfield to Meriwether, September 29, 1854, *ibid.*

[51] Christopher Carson to Meriwether, November 28, 1854, N/350, *ibid.*

[52] Carson to J. L. Collins, January 28, 1858, Y/26, N. Mex. Supt., Field Office Records, OIA, RG 75, NA.

In an ironic postscript to the trouble with the Cheyennes, Damasio Salazar, father of the good-for-nothing who had been largely responsible for the tragic war, unabashedly asked Judge W. W. H. Davis for five thousand dollars in damages for the death of his son—"it had cost a great deal of money to rear and educate him." To the old rogue's dismay, however, the Judge flatly refused to consider his request.[53]

After the hostilities with the Cheyennes, the *ciboleros* restricted their hunts mainly to the Comanche country east of New Mexico and thus avoided further Indian opposition until after the close of the Civil War. Protests resumed then, however, when the *ciboleros*, replacing the rickety *carretas* with larger wagons, each of which could hold the dried meat of thirty to forty-five buffalo,[54] began to make serious inroads on the buffalo herds. In 1866, Jesse Leavenworth, the agent for the Kiowas and Comanches, took note of this development:

> The Mexicans hitherfore have been in the habit of . . . killing large numbers of buffalo, drying the meat and taking it back to New Mexico as an article of traffic, selling it for thirty or forty cents a pound—This I am trying to put a stop to—have already stopped two or three parties, one party having escaped me, and had gone back with their large wagons, drawn by four or five yoke of cattle each, loaded with dried meat—I have adopted these measures to satisfy the Indians, who have complained, very justly I think, of these acts.[55]

When Leavenworth was unable to stop the encroachments by the *ciboleros*, some of the Indians again resorted to force. On January 13, 1868, a New Mexican from San José, Anirecha López, stumbled into Fort Bascom in eastern New Mexico with a tale of a tragic massacre. He had been with a party of forty-eight Mexican hunters on the "Agua Azul" about two hundred miles east of Fort Bascom. One morning, he and four other hunters from "a mesa about two miles from the camp" had seen an estimated

---

[53] Davis, *op. cit.*, 293.
[54] Hurt, "Buffalo Hunters," *loc. cit.*, 35.
[55] Leavenworth to D. N. Cooley, June 5, 1866, Kiowa Agency, OIA, LR, RG 75, NA.

The Ciboleros

two to three hundred Indians sweep down upon their unsuspecting comrades. The entire train of wagons and carts, thirty-three in number, was set afire and López presumed that all the *ciboleros* were killed.[56] A group of Pueblo hunters, attacked by about three hundred Kiowas in eastern New Mexico on May 26, 1872, were more fortunate. By chance they were able to reach a near-by cave in the side of a cliff and from its mouth beat off their attackers.[57]

By the late 1860's, the *ciboleros* also faced a serious threat from the military officials, who had become so highly upset by the illicit activities of the *Comancheros* that they were considering closing the plains to all New Mexicans. In early 1867, General James H. Carleton, commander of the District of New Mexico, described the problem:

> The citizens here claim the right from custom running back for at least two centuries to make an annual trip to the buffalo country for a supply of meat for their families, and as an article of trade. They claim this right as our eastern people claim the right to go off upon the New Foundland Banks to fish. Have the military any legal right to stop them? Now this going off after buffalo meat is without a doubt made a pretext when in reality the principal object of the voyage is to traffic for stock.[58]

Although the plains were never closed permanently to the *ciboleros*, there were sporadic interruptions of their vocation. During one of these in 1871, Vicente Garron, Indian governor of Isleta Pueblo, summed up the importance of the hunts to the New Mexicans when he pleaded simply but eloquently for his people's right to hunt the buffalo:

> Since this is the only food that we have here in order to be able to live through the winter, there would be many poor families that would have neither beef nor venison to eat in this season and they would die of hunger. For that reason, Señor, I with all the pueblo

---

[56] J. V. Dubois to the Asst. Adj. Gen., Dist. of N. Mex., January 15, 1868, Dist of N. Mex., Fort Bascom, LS, Book No. 82, 54, Army Commands, RG 98, NA.
[57] *Weekly New Mexican* (Santa Fe), June 18, 1872.
[58] Endorsement of Carleton on Maj. A. J. Alexander to Maj. Cyrus DeForrest, January 26, 1867, B/10, Dist. of N. Mex., LR, Army Commands, RG 98, NA.

ask for the license to be able to hunt the buffaloes in order to eat in the time of winter.[59]

Garron's people were soon allowed to return to the plains, only to encounter a menace far more ominous than either Indians or cavalry. Anglo buffalo hunters, armed with deadly repeating rifles and motivated by an unquenchable thirst for gore and money, would commit unceasing carnage on the teeming herds until, within the space of a few years, only rows of bleached bones would be left as grim reminders of the great beasts which had so admirably served the *ciboleros*.

[59] Vicente Garron to Nathaniel Pope, September 27, 1871, P/462, N. Mex. Supt., Field Office Records, OIA, RG 75, NA.

6
The Ascendancy of the Anglos, 1848–1861

NEITHER THE NEW MEXICAN FRONTIERSMEN nor the Comanches were greatly affected when the Americans first assumed control of the territory: the *Comancheros* continued to traverse the plains, the *ciboleros* to hunt the buffalo, and the Comanches to visit the little plazas along the Pecos. Although minor aggressions and chicaneries occasionally occurred, neither the New Mexicans nor the Indians, unlike the Americans, condemned the other race for the acts of individuals. As Kiowa Chief Dohasen strikingly summed up the unique situation: "The Spaniards and myself are men; we do bad things towards one another sometimes, stealing horses and taking scalps, but we do not get mad and act the fool."[1]

Not until June, 1851, did an American officer take notice of this strange alliance between the savage and the peon. A squadron of troops that had been dispatched to check an American merchant's complaint that the Comanches had entered the Pecos Valley in large numbers found "the inhabitants in their fields and everything quiet, no one having any fear of the Comanches." Colonel John Munroe, the troop commander, shrewdly recognized that since the residents at Antón Chico and the other settlements on the Pecos carried on a continual trade with the Comanches, it was to their interest to preserve peace with them.[2] But this harmonious coexistence, with its unique and colorful patterns of life, was soon to pass, for few of the incoming Anglo officials could understand or appreciate the fleeting glimpses they obtained of the compatible interplay of cultures.

---

[1] "Report of R. C. Miller, August 14, 1858," in *Annual Report of the Commissioner of Indian Affairs*, 1858, 451.
[2] Munroe to Adj. Gen. Jones, July 13, 1851, in Abel, *op. cit.*, 348.

A History of New Mexican–Plains Indian Relations

From the time of Anza's treaty with Ecueracapa, the New Mexican frontier had imperceptibly crept eastward, led by stolid *pastores* at the head of burgeoning flocks of sheep. By 1849, Captain Randolph Marcy found it difficult to find sufficient forage in the upper Canadian Valley because the *pastores* had recently made it a "pasture ground" for large flocks of sheep.[3] Four years later, Lieutenant A. W. Whipple, encamped on Plaza Larga Creek near present Tucumcari, reported that *rancheros* sometimes sent out large flocks of sheep to the valley.[4] Although the leading historians of the western sheep industry, Charles W. Towne and Edward H. Wentworth, state that by mid-century the *pastores* were driving their flocks as far down the Canadian as the central part of the Texas Panhandle,[5] this seems unlikely. Only one of the emigrants who crossed the Panhandle so much as hinted at an encounter with *pastores*. W. H. Chamberlain, a young Forty-niner, was startled to see striding into his camp northeast of present Amarillo three Mexicans, "rough looking fellows and the first we had seen," who said they lived at a "ranch" ten miles to the south.[6] They were quite likely *Comancheros* or *ciboleros* rather than sheepherders.

The expansion of the sheep frontier was especially remarkable because of the defenselessness of the *pastores*. An American officer described a typical *pastor* whom he met on the Gallinas River:

> A swarthy, copper-colored young Mexican, of eighteen or twenty years of age, most miserably clad, was driving them [sheep] slowly before him . . . Beside him was a gruff sheep dog, a couple of impudent puppies, and a most beautiful pet lamb. Moving correspondingly with and among the living mass was a whitish gray mule, which seemed to have imbibed the spirit of his master in meekness.[7]

Lieutenant J. W. Abert in 1846 similarly described some sheepherders as mere lads, "miserably clad in tattered blankets" and

[3] Capt. R. B. Marcy, "Report," 31 Cong., 1 Sess., *Sen. Exec. Doc. No. 64*, 189.
[4] "Whipple's Report upon a Route," *loc. cit.*, 39.
[5] Charles W. Towne and Edward H. Wentworth, *Shepherd's Empire*, 124.
[6] Bloom, "From Lewisburg to California," *loc. cit.*, 45.
[7] Lt. J. H. Simpson, "Report on the Route from Fort Smith to Santa Fe," 31 Cong., 1 Sess., *Sen. Exec. Doc. No. 12*, 18.

armed only with bows and arrows.⁸ Such helpless intruders maintained themselves on the fringes of the frontier only at the Comanches' sufferance.

The eastward advance of the *pastores* was temporarily checked by the bloodthirsty Apaches rather than by the Comanches. Sweeping down out of their mountain fastnesses, the Apaches raided on an unbelievable scale, stealing an estimated 450,000 sheep between 1846 and 1850.⁹ In a typically insolent foray, a party of Jicarilla Apaches in 1851 filed boldly into the Pecos Valley, seized a flock of one thousand sheep, and after slaughtering seven hundred, demanded pay for sparing the others.¹⁰ The eastward expansion, thus halted, did not resume until the late 1850s; then it was spearheaded by Anglos, who, unlike the *pastores*, would encounter determined Comanche resistance.

Until aroused by encroaching Anglo ranchers, the Comanches were so peaceful that the military officials in New Mexico seemed scarcely aware of their existence. In 1853, Captain John Pope, later to win fame in the Civil War, stated that the Comanches, except for some small groups who occasionally visited in the Pecos Valley, had "been little heard of in this Territory during the past two years, and have committed no depredations whatever within that period."¹¹

In contrast to the military's apparent lack of concern, the New Mexican Indian agents, who had acquired a considerable knowledge of the Comanches from Pueblo traders, were keenly aware of the importance of maintaining cordial relations between the tribe and the New Mexicans. Superintendent James Calhoun often plied his Pueblo visitors with sugar, coffee, and whisky to obtain information about the Comanches.¹² Don Carlos Vigil, the Indian governor of Tesuque Pueblo, was apparently the most responsive of the Pueblos, if such frequent entries in the agency

---

[8] Abert, "Report of Examination of New Mexico," *loc. cit.*, 443.
[9] Towne and Wentworth, *op. cit.*, 153.
[10] Calhoun to Lea, March 22, 1851, in Abel, *op. cit.*, 299.
[11] Robert M. Utley (ed.), "Captain John Pope's Plan of 1853 for the Frontier Defense of New Mexico," *Arizona and the West*, V (Summer, 1963), 156.
[12] Calhoun to Lea, April 29, 1851, in Abel, *op. cit.*, 339.

records as "Carlos, his wife, brother, and child, three meals each sugar and coffee—$3.43¾"[13] can be believed. In return for the agents' hospitality, Carlos, who reportedly understood the Comanche language and was "generally" admitted to their councils, served as an unofficial emissary to the Plains Indians. In June, 1850, Calhoun, upon hearing that the Comanches planned to hold a council on the Canadian at Sutton's Fort, "twelve days travel" from Santa Fe, sent Carlos to attend it,[14] but there is no recorded report by the Pueblo.

Calhoun, anxious to try his skill at personal diplomacy, in 1851 held a brief conference with the Comanches. Hearing in May that some of these people were gathering at the Bosque Redondo for a "grand council" with the Apaches, he dispatched a trader to ask their leaders to come to Santa Fe. In response to the invitation, Chief Pluma de Aguilar (Eagle Feather) and several warriors visited Calhoun on May 29, sold him a Mexican captive, and promised that "nothing but death" could prevent their return the following day. That night, however, the Indians, falsely warned by some "infamous individuals" that the Americans planned to kill them, slipped quietly out of the city, leaving behind their animals, robes, arms, and provisions.[15] Calhoun, mystified and dejected at the sudden departure, blamed it upon a plot by native New Mexicans to stir up enmity between the Americans and the Comanches. Although his conjecture may have been partially true, the Indians also may have feared a repetition of the massacre of their tribesmen in San Antonio in 1840 under similar circumstances. In an effort to alleviate the Comanches' distrust as much as possible, Calhoun inventoried and sent their abandoned property to them by Don Carlos.[16]

Before he had any chance of holding another conference with the Comanches, Calhoun had to surrender his duties to his sec-

[13] Abel, "Journal of John Greiner," *loc. cit.*, 192.
[14] Calhoun to Brown, June 15, 1850, in Abel, *op. cit.*, 212. Sutton's Fort may have referred to William Bent's old Adobe Fort (or Adobe Walls) northeast of present Borger, Texas.
[15] Calhoun to Lea, June 30, 1851, *ibid.*, 368.
[16] Calhoun to Lt. O. L. Chapman, June 9, 1851, *ibid.*, 356.

U. S. Signal Corps Photograph, The National Archives

Kit Carson, *circa* 1849.

U. S. Signal Corps Photograph (Brady Collection) The National Archives

Colonel John Irwin Gregg, commander of the District of New Mexico in 1871.

U. S. Signal Corps Photograph, The National Archives

Colonel Ranald Slidell MacKenzie, commander of the Fourth Cavalry.

The Ascendancy of the Anglos, 1848-1861

retary, John Greiner, and leave New Mexico in a vain attempt to reach his home in Georgia before death overtook him. Greiner, a political appointee whose most noteworthy accomplishment was writing the "famous log cabin campaign song in 1840,"[17] was haunted by the way in which a New Mexican mob had butchered Indian Superintendent Charles Bent in 1847. Ever on the alert for indications of a similar uprising,[18] he became greatly agitated in the spring of 1852 when Don Carlos of Tesuque reported that the celebrated Comanche chief Baja Sol and "the President of Mexico" had entered into an alliance against the United States. According to the rumor, Baja Sol also intended to invite the other roving tribes of the Southwest and the Pueblos to join the league.[19] Greiner immediately reported the plot to Colonel E. V. "Bull Head" Sumner, the military commander in New Mexico, but the Colonel discounted the possibility and asserted that he had enough troops to handle any emergency that might arise.[20]

[17] Obituary notice on Greiner, *Santa Fe Weekly Post*, May 27, 1871.

[18] On October 1, 1851, Greiner wrote to a friend: "Here I am in the Palace of Santa Fe . . . . If I succeed in getting safely back again among my friends under Providence I shall consider myself a highly favored man! Between the savage Indians, the treacherous Mexicans and the outlawed Americans a man has to run the gauntlet in this country. Three governors within twelve years have lost their heads (Pérez, Gonzales and Bent) and there are men here at present who talk so flippantly of taking Governor Calhoun's head as though it were of no consequence at all. . . . There is a great and deep gulf between the Americans and Mexicans . . . . There is hardly an American here that stirs abroad without being armed to the teeth." John Greiner, "Private Letters of a Government Official in the Southwest" (ed. by Tod Galloway), *Journal of American History*, III (July, 1909), 546.

[19] Abel, "Journal of John Greiner," *loc. cit.*, 192; Greiner to Sumner, April 4, 1852, in Abel, *op. cit.*, 521. The apparent basis for Don Carlos' story was an agreement between Baja Sol and the governor of Chihuahua in which the latter was to pay the Comanches for killing Mescalero Apaches. Ralph A. Smith, "The Scalp Hunter in the Borderlands, 1835-1850," *Arizona and the West*, VI (Spring, 1964), 19. William H. Emory, engaged in surveying the boundary between the United States and Mexico, also commented upon the negotiations between Chihuahua and Chief Baja Sol. At Presidio, Texas, on July 8, 1852, he learned that "Chihuahua, not receiving the protection it was entitled to from the central government of Mexico made an independent treaty with the Comanches, the practical effect of which was to aid and abet the Indians in their war upon Durango." William H. Emory, "Report on the United States and Mexican Boundary Survey," 34 Cong., 1 Sess., *House Exec. Doc. No. 135*, 86.

[20] Sumner to Asst. Adj. Gen. Jones, April 9, 1852, in Abel, *op. cit.*, 521.

Greiner, however, was not reassured. He spent an anxious summer admonishing his subordinates to remain alert: "*Talk around among the wild Indians and judge for yourself if there is any diplomacy carried on between them and other tribes. But say nothing—do nothing—to excite suspicion in the breast of anyone!*"[21] Greiner felt somewhat relieved when some Pueblos returned from the plains with word that the Comanches were "behaving well" and Pablo Romero, leader of Taos Pueblo, assured him that the traditional enmity of the Apaches and Utes toward the Comanches would preclude any alliance.[22] His optimism was dispelled in August, however, by a Pueblo report that the Comanches were moving toward the Bosque Redondo to hold a conference with the Mescalero Apaches and that they wished to make peace with the Navahos.[23] Upset more than ever over the possibility of an Indian alliance, Greiner sent a Pueblo trader to persuade the Comanches to see him before talking with the Navahos. Although nothing came of this endeavor, Greiner finally realized that his fears had been unjustified when he learned in September that the Comanches and Utes were at war.

The end of military indifference to the Comanches was foreshadowed by two mid-decade developments. Anglo ranchers began moving onto the eastern border of New Mexico: Lucien Maxwell and Samuel Watrous into the upper Canadian Valley and Alexander Hatch, James M. Giddings, and Preston Beck into the Pecos Valley below Antón Chico. Simultaneously, large numbers of Comanches were being forced to retire toward the New Mexican frontier. In 1855 Colonel John Garland, commander of the Department of New Mexico, complained that Comanches "driven from Texas" were hovering about the eastern border.[24] Later in the year, Governor David Meriwether was visited by some Comanches who claimed that they "had been driven from their homeland by the Osages" and stated that they wished to

[21] Greiner to Baird, April 7, 1852, *ibid.*, 520.
[22] Abel, "Journal of John Greiner," *loc. cit.*, 194–95.
[23] *Ibid.*, 234–41.
[24] Garland to Asst. Adj. Gen. Lorenzo Thomas, July 31, 1855, in *Annual Report of the Secretary of War*, 1855, 72.

The Ascendancy of the Anglos, 1848-1861

remain permanently in New Mexico.[25] Meriwether ordered them to return to Texas, but to no avail.

A rash of minor incidents accompanied the Comanche intrusion. In May, the Comanche bands of Chiefs Sanaco and Pahanca visited the Pecos settlements and voluntarily surrendered a prisoner, but on their departure they "broke up" the ranch of Beck and Giddings.[26] The following month, some three hundred Comanches stopped at the same ranch and proceeded to hold a barbecue, for which they "borrowed" two oxen, one calf, one "fine American boar hog," twenty-nine pigs, and sixteen chickens. One of the women at the ranch tried to stop them from killing the chickens, but they nonchalantly drove her away with two arrow shots and went ahead with their feast. Upon being asked about the incident later, the Comanche chiefs blamed it upon "bad Indians" whom they could not control.[27]

In July, a band of Buffalo Eaters (Kotsoteka Comanches) visited Lucien Maxwell's ranch on Rayado Creek and, according to Maxwell, killed two hundred sheep, stole a mule and all the loose ranch property, took several articles from his employees, and arrogantly promised to return when the "corn was ripe." Despite the apparent hostility of the Comanches, several things about the raid puzzled Governor Meriwether: Maxwell had voluntarily given the Comanches food and clothing, he had admitted trading horses with them *after* the occurrence of the alleged depredations, and the Indians, when intercepted by soldiers, had displayed a certificate of "good conduct" signed by Maxwell.[28] The Comanches did not consider these incidents as raids. For generations they had helped themselves to foodstuffs while visiting in New Mexico, and the native New Mexicans had learned to accept their dinner stops with grace. The Anglo ranchers, however, stridently demanded military protection.

[25] Meriwether to Manypenny, September 18, 1855, N/527, N. Mex. Supt., OIA, LR, RG 75, NA.
[26] Meriwether to Manypenny, May 28, 1855, N/439, *ibid*.
[27] Giddings to Meriwether, November 7, 1855, Indian Depredation Case No. 2653, Records of the U.S. Court of Claims, RG 123, NA.
[28] C. Carson to Meriwether, July 25, 1855, N/481, N. Mex. Supt., OIA, LR, RG 75, NA.

In response to the complaints, Colonel Garland in September dispatched Major J. H. Brooks and 150 soldiers to the eastern frontier with instructions to warn the Comanches against hovering around the borders of New Mexico and to attack them if they committed any act "worthy of chastisement." Although this order was temporarily suspended a week later because the troops were not "properly instructed and disciplined,"[29] the roles had been cast for the drama to be played during the balance of the decade. The Comanches would continue to visit the New Mexican frontier settlements, the American inhabitants to protest, and the military to oppose the Indian incursions. Silent onlookers at first, the native New Mexicans would gradually align with the Comanches.

Resuming their unwelcomed dinner visits in September, 1856, some Comanches under Chief Esaquipa camped on the Gallinas River and helped themselves to the corn on Alexander Hatch's newly established ranch. Hatch persuaded them to leave by giving them an ox and "some other staples,"[30] but then other parties, including some Kiowas on their way to fight the Navahos, stopped at the ranch and demanded food. As a result, Hatch "suffered much from the loss of corn, whole fields of which the Indians . . . destroyed."[31]

Besieged by both Hatch and James Giddings for protection, Garland sent Captain W. L. Elliott to survey the area for a suitable fort site. Elliott found that Giddings' ranch, located on the Pecos River twenty-five miles below Antón Chico, had little stock, few residents, and fewer signs of Indians. On the other hand, Hatch's ranch, located on the Gallinas River thirty-three miles southeast of Las Vegas and thirteen miles northeast of Antón Chico, offered an excellent site. Its buildings, Elliott reported, would afford "comfortable shelter" for a company of troops and their horses, there were ample water and firewood, and Hatch had

[29] Nichols to Brooks, September 29, 1855, Dept. of N. Mex., LS, Vol. 9, 403, Army Commands, RG 98, NA; Nichols to Brooks, October 4, 1855, *ibid.*, 413.
[30] Hatch to Garland, September 24, 1856, H/20, Dept. of N. Mex., LR, Army Commands, RG 98, NA.
[31] Stephen Baca to Garland, September 29, 1856, B/37, *ibid.*

The Ascendancy of the Anglos, 1848-1861

enough corn (despite the inroads of the Indians!) to supply the troops through the winter.[32] His recommendations accepted, Elliott in November established the new post, naming it Fort Biddle. The name, however, was disallowed by his superiors; consequently, the post, although occupied by as many as four companies of troops, was referred to simply as Hatch's Ranch until its abandonment during the Civil War.

The establishment of the new post was a boon both to Alexander Hatch personally and to the entire eastern frontier. The troops not only protected Hatch's corn fields and stock but, according to Lieutenant J. H. Beale, a young army engineer who visited the post in 1858, they furnished him with a lucrative market:

> Hatch settled a year or two since on the Gallinas, then an unsettled country, and by the fruitful product of the country has made himself independent. When we arrived he had already collected some ten thousand bushels of corn which he was selling at over one dollar a bushel *to the government* and others. . . . and being a shrewd man makes large profits by taking contracts for the delivery of grain or selling it at his house.[33]

Hatch profited further from his unique arrangement with the military by serving as sutler for the garrison.[34] Other Anglo ranchers, emboldened by the existence of the fort, moved to the Gallinas Valley, and soon an influx of Mexican settlers moved in to minister to the thirsts and appetites of off-duty soldiers. Pleasantly situated on the Gallinas three miles above Hatch's Ranch, the Mexican settlement, Chaparito, became one of the strongholds of the *Comancheros*.

Perhaps because of the presence of the garrison, the New Mexican frontier was relatively peaceful during 1857. A few "friendly" Kiowas stopped at Giddings' and Beck's ranch in early February,

---

[32] Elliott to Nichols, October 31, 1856, E/32, *ibid*.
[33] Lt. J. H. Beale, "Report on Construction of a Wagon Road," 36 Cong., 1 Sess., *House Exec. Doc. No. 42*, 30.
[34] Hatch to Col. E. R. S. Canby, December 3, 1861, H/39, Dept. of N. Mex., LR, Army Commands, RG 98, NA.

but they left after being given some beef.[35] J. L. Collins, the new superintendent of Indian affairs in New Mexico, was not entirely pleased when a few Comanches and Kiowas who visited the Mexican plazas treated the residents in a "menacing manner," but, he hastened to add, they complied peacefully when warned by the military to leave.[36] Later in the year, some Kiowas, questioned by Indian agent Robert Miller about a few depredations near Las Vegas, readily admitted committing the crimes and promised to "return in kind" what had been stolen.[37]

Underneath the apparent tranquility, the Comanches and their Kiowa allies were becoming increasingly resentful of the intruding Anglo ranchers. Years later, an old frontiersman recalled meeting in 1857 a grim-faced Comanche chief who declared that while he lived he would allow no settlements east of the Gallinas.[38] With the exception of one or two inconclusive encounters,[39] however, the eastern frontier remained calm until March, 1858, when the Comanches suddenly unleashed their pent-up fury on the encroachers. Samuel Watrous, lured by the deceptive quiet of the previous year, had sent his foreman, a Mr. Bunsham, to establish a ranch on the Canadian River about 130 miles below Fort Union. When Bunsham rejected their ultimatum to abandon the ranch, the Comanches decided to make an example of him. Three "Mexican captives" who had long lived among the Comanches secured jobs at the ranch; a few days later, four Indians arrived and pretended they wished to trade. After the renegade Mexicans lured

[35] *Santa Fe Weekly Gazette*, February 21, 1857.
[36] "Report of J. L. Collins, August 30, 1857," in *Annual Report of the Commissioner of Indian Affairs*, 1857, 545.
[37] "Report of R. C. Miller, October 14, 1857," *ibid.*, 431.
[38] Affidavit of John Odam, August 30, 1894, Indian Depredation Case No. 3252, Records of the U.S. Court of Claims, RG 123, NA.
[39] In early 1858, troops from Fort Craig surprised some Kiowas who, while returning from a raid on the Navahos, had stopped near Valverde to dine on borrowed cattle. The Americans killed several of the Kiowas and captured their wounded chief. After the Kiowas began to grow restless, the recovered chief was released with instructions to explain to his people that the army "neither knew nor cared to know" the identity of the Kiowas before the late attack and did not wish to have war with them. Any Kiowas found west of the Pecos, however, would be considered hostile. Nichols to Col. W. W. Loring, March 8, 1858, Dept. of N. Mex., LS, Vol. 10, 194, Army Commands, RG 98, NA.

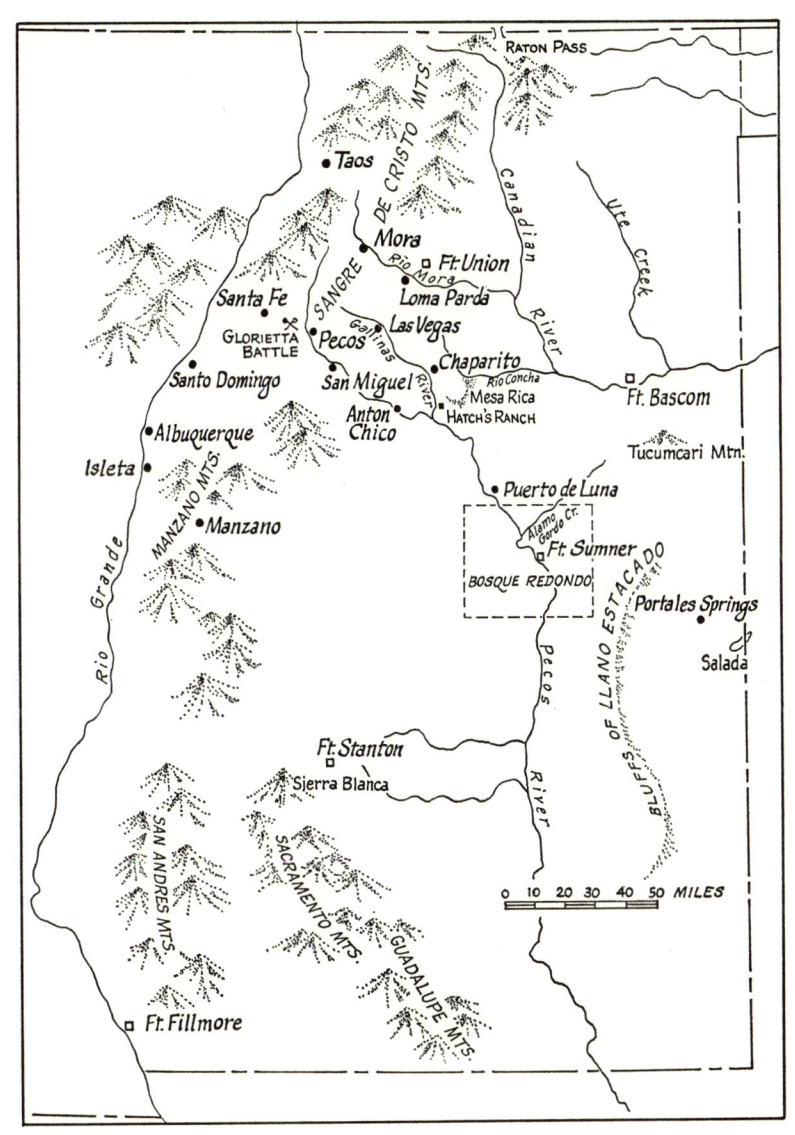

The Eastern New Mexican Frontier, 1850–1865.

Bunsham from his house unarmed, the Comanches speedily cut him down, burned the ranch buildings, and ran off the stock. They allowed the legitimate Mexican ranch hands to return unharmed to the settlements with instructions to tell the Americans that "they should not settle there, for the Comanches would kill any who attempted it."[40]

To emphasize that the raid was not the act of a few impetuous young braves, the Comanche leaders sent word to the American officers that the destruction of the ranch "had been resolved on in council beforehand" and that they were determined to prevent settlements east of Hatch's Ranch.[41] Although he responded to the raid by reinforcing the garrison at Hatch's Ranch, Colonel Garland's reaction was remarkably mild: the attack "was expected by many, and Mr. Watrous was advised not to undertake a settlement so distant from protection."[42]

The following year, when the Anglos undertook to survey the Canadian Valley, the Comanches dramatically re-emphasized their opposition to the eastward expansion of the settlements. R. E. Clements, the contractor for the survey, began the task in early July despite warnings not to proceed without military protection. The Comanches, understanding quite well that the surveyors' chains would be followed by settlers, immediately dispatched a war party which, without firing a shot, captured the government group. For four hours the Comanches debated the Americans' fate while Clements fervently promised to abandon the survey if spared and his Mexican employees (whose own safety was never in jeopardy) also pleaded for his life. After taking all the surveyors' property except their compass, chains, and animals and sternly warning them that he could call together five hundred warriors "by one smoke," the Comanche leader ordered their release.[43] With the army still unable to furnish an escort, Clem-

[40] Loring to Nichols, March 31, 1858, L/26, Dept. of N. Mex., LR, Army Commands, RG 98, NA; Lt. L. L. Baker to Nichols, April 28, 1858, B/28, *ibid*.
[41] *Ibid*.
[42] Garland to L. Thomas, May 1, 1858, in *Annual Report of the Secretary of War*, 1858, 288.
[43] Capt. Thomas Claiburn to Thomas Wilkens, July 4, 1859, C/16, Dept. of N. Mex., LR, Army Commands, RG 98, NA; Collins to Greenwood, July 10,

The Ascendancy of the Anglos, 1848-1861

ents, to the apparent disappointment of no one, called off the survey. Collins, who had been a veteran Santa Fe trader before his appointment as Indian superintendent, observed pointedly that no settlement could have been established in the Canadian Valley without the protection of a fort. When a fort was located there, he asserted, "it will be time enough to complete the surveys."[44]

Collins quite likely was irked at the surveyors because they had jeopardized his plan to hold a conference with the Comanches. The previous year, he had journeyed to Washington and in conjunction with Major J. S. Phelps, an influential congressman from Missouri, had persuaded Postmaster General Aaron Brown to approve a mail and stagecoach line from Neosho, Missouri, through Santa Fe to California.[45] Jacob Hall, who obtained the contract to carry the mail over the new route, had left Neosho on November 5, 1858, for the initial trip, only to be captured by Comanches who burned his wagon and the mail. Fortunately, Hall escaped and arrived in St. Louis in March, 1859, to tell of his misfortune;[46] but Collins and Phelps obviously had to placate the Comanches before the stage line could succeed. Congressman Phelps thereupon persuaded A. B. Greenwood, the Commissioner of Indian Affairs, to send Collins to treat with the Comanches and then hurried to New Mexico to participate in the negotiations.[47]

In preparing for the conference, Collins shrewdly used the capture of the surveyors to obtain the co-operation of Colonel B. L. E. Bonneville, the new military commander in New Mexico. Claiming that the incident indicated that the Comanches were "ready at any time to commence hostilities," he pointed out to

---

1859, C/41, New Mex. Supt., OIA, LR, RG 75, NA; "Report of the Commissioner of the General Land Office, November 30, 1859," in *Annual Report of the Secretary of the Interior, 1859,* 188.

[44] Collins to Greenwood, July 9, 1859, C/41, New Mex. Supt., OIA, LR, RG 75, NA.

[45] Phelps to Greenwood, March 1, 1858, P/754, *ibid.*

[46] LeRoy R. Hafen, *The Overland Mail, 1849-1869,* 118.

[47] Greenwood to Collins, May 18, 1859, N. Mex. Supt., LR, Field Office Records, OIA, RG 75, NA.

the Colonel that the province was ill prepared for a "rupture" with the Plains Indians.[48] Bonneville, readily convinced by the argument, agreed to accompany the negotiators.

On July 18, 1859, Collins, Bonneville, and Phelps left Santa Fe with an escort of 130 soldiers. At Hatch's Ranch, they were informed by Collins' Mexican scout that the Comanches had become alarmed upon learning of the expedition. Pressing on to the Comanche camp and finding that the Indians had fled toward the east "in great confusion," the Americans followed their trail down the Canadian to the mouth of Utah Creek before turning back.[49] The Comanches, afraid that the troops intended to punish them for the capture of the surveyors and painfully aware that no less than three of their tribesmen's villages had been destroyed by expeditions from Texas within the past year, had no intention of awaiting the approach of an armed column.

Their plans thwarted, Collins and Phelps parted company on July 27. Phelps, with an escort of thirty cavalrymen, returned to Missouri by way of the Antelope Hills, and Collins and Bonneville veered off to the south and returned to Santa Fe over the Fort Smith road. They met along the way thirty or forty Comanches, who were permitted to pass because there was "no chief" with them. At Hatch's Ranch, the officials learned, to their chagrin, that these Indians had killed one of the drovers with a herd of five hundred cattle that had recently been driven up the Canadian from the Creek Nation.[50]

In the autumn, the Comanches launched their most serious attacks yet on the New Mexican frontier, hitting for the first time the New Mexican *rancheros* as well as the Americans. Striking the ranch of Don Feliciano Guterous in the *Cañon de Quele* on November 20, they drove off the herders and butchered a large number of sheep. Four days later, they attacked the ranch of Don Féliz Chávez on the Río Conchas, "seized and stripped the herd-

[48] Collins to Bonneville, July 11, 1859, C/51, Dept. of N. Mex., LR, Army Commands, RG 98, NA.
[49] Collins to Greenwood, August 4, 1859, C/82, N. Mex. Supt., OIA, LR, RG 75, NA.
[50] Ibid.

ers," killed two head of cattle, and destroyed the ranch property. These were not isolated cases; all along the frontier the Comanches swarmed, killing cattle, stealing horses, and pillaging.[51] But out of respect for their traditional friendship with the New Mexicans, they did not kill a single herder. That would come if their warnings went unheeded.

Stepping up its efforts in response to the pleas of the frontiersmen, the military was seriously handicapped by false reports from New Mexican traders as to the whereabouts of the Indians. Many of the officers soon felt that the Mexicans, in the words of Lieutenant Colonel J. V. Reeve, were "a set of villainous vagabonds"[52] aiding the Indians. All efforts to intercept incoming Comanches were futile until June, 1860, when a force of fifty infantrymen surprised about one hundred Indians en route to trade at the Mexican towns on the Pecos. At a range of only 150 yards, the troopers fired a volley that killed three or four and wounded others, but the rest of the Indians escaped.[53] Levi Keithly, an Indian agent who was at Hatch's Ranch, later claimed that the Indians had not merited the punishment. The Comanches, he insisted, had come in with their families and pack animals to trade and when fired upon had run off "without making any hostile demonstration."[54]

Meanwhile, the New Mexican military forces had been assigned a key role in an ambitious three-pronged offensive against the Comanches and Kiowas. Three columns of six companies each (roughly 250 to 300 men) were to strike into *Comancheria* from different directions, hoping to catch the Indians between their converging forces. Major John Sedgwick was to lead an expedition southwestward from Fort Riley, Kansas; Captain S. D. Sturgis was to lead a force northwestward from Fort Arbuckle,

---

[51] Collins to Greenwood, December 5, 1859, C/255, *ibid.*
[52] Reeve to Lt. J. D. Wilkins, November 24, 1858, R/35, Dept. of N. Mex., LR, Army Commands, RG 98, NA.
[53] "Report of the Adjutant General, November 20, 1860," in *Annual Report of the Secretary of War*, 1860, 204.
[54] Michael Steck to General James H. Carleton, November 5, 1864, MS, Papers of Michael Steck, 1818-1883, Box 4.

Indian Territory; and Major C. F. Ruff was to push down the Canadian River from Hatch's Ranch. The commanders were ordered to hold no "intercourse" with the Indians: "make a fierce pursuit, overtake them, and attack them."[55] Such a campaign might have seriously crippled the Comanches and Kiowas, but the columns were poorly co-ordinated and severely hampered by the extremely dry weather. The two eastern columns, although marching hundreds of miles, fought only one battle: on August 6, Captain Sturgis's force engaged a party of Kiowas and Comanches on the Republican River in southern Nebraska, killing twenty-nine Indians and losing two troopers.[56]

From the inception of the campaign, the native New Mexicans, aware of the threat to their friendly relations and commerce with the Comanches, tried to sabotage the Canadian River expedition. A *Comanchero* told Major J. S. Simonson at Fort Union on June 7 that the Comanches and Kiowas were camped in great numbers on the Cimarron Ciba, ten or fifteen miles from Lucien Maxwell's ranch. Simonson, however, refused to believe the report and instead charged that there was "not a doubt" that the Indians were "well posted" by the New Mexicans on the movements of the troops and the strength of the garrisons in eastern New Mexico.[57]

Major Ruff, however, was less suspicious of the *Comancheros*. Having left Hatch's Ranch on June 1, he established a subdepot, naming it Camp Jackson, sixty miles to the east on the Canadian. Assured by "various sources" that six to twelve thousand Comanches were camped on the Pecos River below the Bosque Redondo, Ruff on June 8 altered his plans and led his force southwestward to the junction of the Pecos with the Río Hondo below present Roswell. He found neither Indians nor "Indian signs."

---

[55] General Order No. 6, March 15, 1860, Dept. of N. Mex., Orders, Vol. 39, 345, Army Commands, RG 98, NA; Col. E. V. Sumner to Major John Sedgwick, May 9, 1860, in LeRoy R. Hafen and Ann W. Hafen (eds.), *Relations with the Indians of the Plains, 1857–1861*, 194.

[56] Captain S. D. Sturgis to Capt. Jno. Withers, August 12, 1860, *ibid.*, 251–54.

[57] Maj. J. S. Simonson to Lt. D. H. Maury, June 7, 1860, S/60, Dept. of N. Mex., LR, Army Commands, RG 98, NA.

To add to his frustration, so many of his horses broke down because of a mysterious disease called "black-tongue" and the lack of forage that half his command had to walk back. Finally arriving at Camp Jackson on July 4, the duped commander vented his fury on the Mexicans who had led him astray:

> The representations were made by men who live by trading with the Comanche Indians, and who deprecate the loss of that trade ... more than they seek our friendship; lying Mexicans who never tell the truth, if a falsehood can possibly be made to answer the purpose.[58]

Lieutenant J. V. Dubois, one of Ruff's subordinates, was more lyrical and only slightly less impassioned in confiding his outraged feelings to his diary: "Alas for those who put their trust in Mexicans.... There is no truth in them. Their evident intention was to take us away from the Indians and they have succeeded."[59]

Major Ruff's troubles had only begun. Leaving the depot again on July 10, he proceeded down the Canadian with 225 cavalrymen and two highly unsatisfactory former *Comanchero* guides. The fourth day out, he encountered six Indians who raised a white flag and rode around in a small circle—the Comanche sign that they desired a peaceful talk. Ruff, however, having nothing of a "friendly character" to say to them, ignored their overtures and pressed on in search of their village. His Mexican guides led him almost directly to a large Comanche camp, which he destroyed, but the Comanches scattered in three directions. After exhausting his horses (which were still in poor shape and no match for the lean Indian ponies) in vain pursuit, Ruff, ever ready with an excuse, blamed his failure to surprise the village on the two *Comanchero* guides:

> It is a matter of keenest regret, to feel assured as I do, that our failure to capture, or destroy this entire body of Indians ... is solely to be attributed to a want of Guides, had I had with me, six good

---

[58] "Report of Major Ruff, July 3, 1860," in *Annual Report of the Secretary of War*, 1860, 58.
[59] George P. Hammond (ed.), *Campaigns in the West, 1856–1861*, 106.

Guides who knew the country, not afraid to proceed a mile or two in advance of my column, there could be no doubt whatever that the surprise and destruction of this large body of Indians would have been completed.[60]

Unwilling to concede defeat, Ruff followed doggedly after the elusive Indians, hoping to surprise them by a night attack. But his Mexican guides, he discovered to his disgust, could not trail at night and thus he lost another opportunity for "inflicting full and summary chastisement." After camping for a time at William Bent's old adobe fort,[61] about twenty miles east of present Stinnett, Texas, Ruff reluctantly turned back. With only 139 of 293 horses still serviceable, he dared not venture farther because of his lack of guides, grass, and water.

Upon returning to Hatch's Ranch, Ruff, his health temporarily broken by the arduous campaign,[62] relinquished his command to Lieutenant Colonel A. L. Porter, who energetically refitted the expedition and resumed the search for the Comanches. Taking a lesson from Ruff's unfortunate experience with *Comanchero* guides, Porter replaced them with "Old Leroux,"[63] a veteran Mountain Man who was confident that he could find the Indians. In an effort to surprise the Comanches, Porter moved in a sweeping circle northeastward to the Rabbit Ear Mountains, then southeastward into the Canadian Valley, and back to the New Mexican settlements—without seeing a single Comanche. Baffled by their repeated failures, the military leaders reluctantly called off the campaign.

[60] Ruff to Maury, July 30, 1860, R/21, Dept. of N. Mex., LR, Army Commands, RG 98, NA.

[61] *Ibid.* Ruff was one of the few to describe this obscure post. He reported that it was "a building of nine rooms, the walls of which are in good preservation, the west wall is 100 feet, and the north wall 180 feet long; nothing of the woodwork of this building remains." Ruff also noted that nine miles up the Canadian from the adobe fort, there were the "remains of another fort or trading post, called the 'wood fort' by the Mexicans."

[62] Hammond, *op. cit.*, 108.

[63] Antoine Leroux probably ranked next to Kit Carson as an army guide in the early Southwest. Since he died in 1861, this quite likely was his last assignment. See Grant Foreman, "Antoine Leroux, New Mexican Guide," *New Mexico Historical Review*, XVI (October, 1941), 367–78.

The Ascendancy of the Anglos, 1848–1861

Soon afterward, a band of Comanches, including many women and children, unwisely traveled to Chaparito to trade. The officer at Hatch's Ranch,[64] seeing his chance to avenge the humiliations of the preceding summer, dispatched a select body of troops, who found the Indians asleep in the courtyard of Don Féliz Ulibarrí, a local *rico*. Opening fire, the soldiers killed two and wounded one of the Indians before the survivors could take refuge in Ulibarrí's house. The troops then appropriated the horses and mules of the Comanches and reportedly sold them the next day in Las Vegas. The *Santa Fe Weekly Gazette*, in reporting this bizarre episode, vehemently denounced the action: "There is a culpability on those who ordered the attack that will not readily be cleared up. The Indians were among the whites on a peaceful trading expedition . . . the attack as made was unjustifiable and wanton . . . a miserable military exploit."[65]

In retaliation for this wanton attack, the Comanches struck anew at the frontier ranches. Within a few days, they had captured more than a thousand head of cattle in the Canadian Valley, including the entire government herd of 460 head.[66] When stealing the government's cattle, the Comanches, cognizant that their vendetta was with the Anglos, carefully refrained from harming the Mexican herdsmen, telling them that if they remained quiet they would not be injured but that if they interfered they would all be killed.[67] Despite a belated cavalry pursuit, the Indians escaped unscathed with the cattle.

At the beginning of 1861, the New Mexico military finally won a significant victory over the Comanches. Upon learning of a Comanche encampment on the Cimarron River, Lieutenant Colonel George B. Crittenden, commander at Fort Union, prepared to move against them "so quietly that none of the garrison knew his purpose" except the officers concerned.[68] Successfully

[64] The identity was not disclosed in the *Santa Fe Weekly Gazette*, November 3, 1860, which is the source for this account. The army records do not mention it.
[65] *Ibid.*
[66] Lt. D. H. Maury to Col. T. T. Fauntleroy, October 31, 1860, Dept. of N. Mex., LS, Vol. 10, 491–92, Army Commands, RG 98, NA.
[67] *Santa Fe Weekly Gazette*, November 3, 1860.
[68] Fauntleroy to L. Thomas, January 12, 1861, Dept. of N. Mex., LS, Vol. 10, 535, Army Commands, RG 98, NA.

eluding the watchful eyes of the *Comancheros*, Crittenden relentlessly pushed his picked force of sixty men through bitter cold and over a country "previously unknown to any but to the Indians" and the Mexican traders[69] until, eight days after leaving, he located a Comanche camp of 150 lodges. In a surprise dawn attack on January 4, Crittenden destroyed the village, killed ten Indians, and wounded many more. His own loss totaled three men "slightly wounded." Unsatisfied with the capture of forty Indian ponies, he lamented that if his force had been large enough to divide, he could have taken the entire herd.[70] Upon receiving the report of the engagement, Indian Superintendent Collins conjectured that the Indians had probably suffered more than the military realized. The loss of 150 lodges and a large number of robes just before the outbreak of cold weather, he stated, might cause many of them to perish.[71]

Temporarily subdued by Crittenden's attack, the Comanches sent peace offers by several *Comanchero* parties. Although the officers at Fort Union ignored the offers and pleaded for more troops, Colonel T. T. Fauntleroy, commander of the Department of New Mexico, was forced to concentrate his available strength at Fort Stanton to suppress a Mescalero Apache uprising. Consequently, he had to curb his warlike subordinates by informing them that peace was to be the new policy toward the Comanches.[72]

While Fauntleroy was considering the possibility of a peace conference, his junior officers became incensed at the Indian Department. In February, the troops at Hatch's Ranch apprehended a trading party en route to the plains that had passed "entirely beyond" any settlement. The traders, Santa Clara and Tesuque Pueblos led by Juan Vigil, brother of the highly respected Don Carlos, carried a pass from their agent authorizing them to visit

---

[69] Dabney H. Maury, *Recollections of a Virginian in the Mexican, Indian, and Civil Wars*, 118.

[70] Crittenden to Fauntleroy, January 9, 1861, C/7, Dept. of N. Mex., LR, Army Commands, RG 98, NA.

[71] Collins to Mix, January 27, 1861, C/4, New Mex. Supt., OIA, LR, RG 75, NA.

[72] Maury to Crittenden, February 23, 1861, Dept. of N. Mex., LS, Vol. 10, 551, Army Commands, RG 98, NA.

U. S. Signal Corps Photograph, The National Archives

View of Fort Sumner, New Mexico.

U. S. Signal Corps Photograph, The National Archives

General view of Fort Union, New Mexico, September, 1866.

the Comanches "unmolested."[73] The military officers, however, were infuriated that the agents would issue passes to "Mexicans" (they apparently had not learned to distinguish Pueblos from New Mexicans) to go to the plains and traffic with the Comanches, with whom the "government is at open war." By means of the trade, they charged, the Comanches received ammunition and information of troops movements in return for mules and horses stolen from Texas.[74] In their entire tirade, however, they failed to indicate that any contraband goods had been found on the accosted traders.

Despite their distrust of the *Comancheros*, the military officials had to use one to carry peace overtures to the Comanches. On April 5, Fauntleroy asked William B. Moore, a veteran army contractor living at Tecolote, to send a reliable Mexican trader to invite the Comanche chiefs to a conference. Fauntleroy issued a pass to the emissary ("so he will not be molested . . . by Troops") and instructed him to emphasize to the Indians that the proposal was in response to their many requests for peace.[75] Before the details for the conference could be worked out, Fauntleroy was replaced by Colonel W. W. Loring, a Confederate sympathizer who was seemingly just as concerned with protecting Texas from the Comanches as he was New Mexico.[76] While making his plans, Loring had to squelch an attempt by the settlers on the Pecos to make their own peace with the Comanches. Alexander Hatch, alarmed that Crittenden's attack might provoke retaliatory raids in the spring and doubtful that the secession-riven military could

---

[73] Pass issued to Juan D. Vigil, February 18, 1861, N. Mex. Supt., Field Office Records, Pueblo Agency, OIA, RG 75, NA.

[74] Lt. Col. B. S. Roberts to Maury, February 27, 1861, R/22, Dept. of N. Mex., LR, Army Commands, RG 98, NA; Fauntleroy to Thomas, March 3, 1861, Dept. of N. Mex., LS, Vol. 10, 562, Army Commands, RG 98, NA.

[75] Maury to Moore, April 5, 1861, *ibid.*, 563.

[76] Loring to Col. E. D. Townsend, April 22, 1861, *ibid.*, Vol. 11, 1. Loring reported that the Comanches "are very desirous of living in peace with the people of this Territory, and have sent in many messages to that effect. And as the Texans are not said to be treating with them, I have thought it best for the interests of this Department, to listen to their propositions and to suspend for the present, operations against them. In any agreement I shall make with these savages, *I shall stipulate for the exemption of the People of Texas from their incursions.*"

protect the frontier, sent word to the Comanches that neither he nor his neighboring settlers had had anything to do with the attack and invited them to his ranch for peace talks. Upon learning of Hatch's plan, Colonel Loring had a scouting party turn back the Comanches and went ahead with his own preparations.[77]

On May 10 and 11, the conference was held at Alamo Gordo Creek, a small tributary of the Pecos, with the government represented by Captain R. A. Wainwright and Superintendent Collins and the Indians by Chiefs Esaquipa, Pluma de Aguilar, and Paracasqua.[78] In return for an armistice, the Comanches, willing to pay almost any price for peace, promised to stop their depredations, to stay away from wagon trains on the Santa Fe Trail, to keep away from the settlements of eastern New Mexico, and to trade only at Fort Union or at "such places as shall be designated by proper authorities." Seeking to sever the intimate relations between them and the New Mexicans, Wainwright and Collins warned the Comanches that "if they listened to any other people" besides the military or acted upon their advice, they would "get in trouble."[79]

The truce thus established collapsed almost immediately. Failing to grasp the full implications of the treaty, Chief Esaquipa, only a few days after signing it, led a trading party to Chaparito. Captain Thomas Duncan, the commander at Hatch's Ranch, ordered the Comanches to return at once to the plains. Evidently they did not promptly oblige, for Duncan attacked as soon as he "got his men ready." Although the Indians fled wildly in all directions, the troops succeeded in killing one, wounding three, and capturing two.[80] This unwarranted attack once more alarmed the frontier settlers, who feared that the Indians would make reprisals against them. Levi Keithly, who was ranching on the

[77] Loring to Lt. A. R. McRae, April 25, 1861, *ibid.*, 3.
[78] *Santa Fe Weekly Gazette*, May 25, 1861.
[79] *Ibid.*; Maury to Wainwright, May 5, 1861, Dept. of N. Mex., LS, Vol. 11, 15, Army commands, RG 98, NA. The reports of the conference are missing from the files in the National Archives, but the account of it in the *Santa Fe Weekly Gazette* should be accurate, since Superintendent Collins, present at the conference, was also publisher and editor of the paper.
[80] *Santa Fe Weekly Gazette*, June 8, 1861.

Pecos, anxiously wrote that "one of my peons today saw Comanches not more than a mile from my house evidently acting as spies, one of them having come to him and inquired in regard to the soldiers, and as to how many persons were living in certain houses."[81] Fortunately, the Comanches chose to move to their summer hunting grounds on the Arkansas.

The American officials and the settlers differed sharply on the causes for the sudden collapse of the treaty. The Comanches would have remained away from the settlements, Superintendent Collins maintained, but for the intervention of some traders, "a lot of scoundrels who contribute more to the encouragement of Indian depredations than all other causes combined."[82] Rancher Keithly, realizing that the Comanches could not be expected to stay away from the New Mexican settlements, asserted that the unwise attacks by the troops were responsible for most of the Indian hostilities. Three times, he later wrote, he had seen peaceful Comanche trading parties fired upon: "They came with friendly intentions and it was my opinion at the time that they were badly treated."[83] The argument that the soldiers had provoked much of the trouble on the frontier was seemingly verified when the troops were withdrawn from the area at the outbreak of the Civil War. With the soldiers out of the way, the Mexicans and Comanches resumed their old-time trade relationships.

[81] *Ibid.*
[82] Collins to Samuel B. Watrous, October 26, 1861, L/69, 1863, N. Mex. Supt., Field Office Records, OIA, RG 75, NA.
[83] Levi Keithly to Michael Steck, October 8, 1864, MS, Steck Papers, Box 4.

7
The Civil War and the Adobe Walls Campaign

AS A RESULT OF THE MILITARY DEBACLE in New Mexico soon after the outbreak of the Civil War, New Mexican–Plains Indians relations underwent considerable modification. During 1861, the New Mexican troops, poorly trained and unimaginatively led, suffered a series of humiliating defeats at the hands of a force of Texans under the command of General H. H. Sibley. In quick succession, the Texans captured one Union column near Las Cruces, defeated another at Valverde and penned it up in Fort Craig, and occupied Albuquerque and Santa Fe. Sibley's troops then marched for Fort Union, hoping to capture its vast military stores, but in March, 1862, they were met by a Union force at Glorieta Pass, about twenty miles southeast of Santa Fe. While the Texans were carrying the main field of combat, their supply train was destroyed by a detachment of Colorado troops that had slipped unnoticed around their flank. Stripped of supplies and in danger of being trapped by an advancing column from California, the Texans began a disorderly retreat.

By summer they had evacuated the territory, but for the remainder of the war the Union commanders in New Mexico were fearful that the Texans might invade again, perhaps by way of the plains. To guard against a surprise attack, the Union officers changed their policy of screening the Plains Indians away from the settlements to one of cultivating their friendship and cooperation.

Already some steps had been taken to improve relations with the Plains Indians. On December 19, 1861, Colonel E. R. S. Canby, commander of the Department of New Mexico, reprimanded Colonel J. G. Gallegos, commanding at Hatch's Ranch,

The Civil War and the Adobe Walls Campaign

for capturing a Kiowa party visiting near Chaparito. Gallegos was ordered to release the Indians, to accept as genuine their "professions of friendship," and to treat them "with kindness" in order to encourage them to report any movement of Texans toward New Mexico.[1] The Kiowas left Hatch's Ranch "quite pleased," but there is no record that they afterward performed any significant amount of espionage for their newly found benefactors.

At the very outbreak of the war, the army officers began recruiting the heretofore despised *Comancheros* to serve as scouts. In June, 1861, forty New Mexican and Pueblo traders, stationed at Forts Union and Stanton, were assigned to patrol the Pecos and Canadian invasion routes.[2] Drawing food and ammunition from the army stores and allowed to trade freely with the Indians (to avoid suspicion from any Texans they might encounter), they were also paid quite liberally. Don Carlos of Tesuque, who with a group of his warriors in 1862 hired out to work at Fort Sumner "as spies and guides," was given $3.00 a day and "a ration"; his subordinates each received a daily wage of $1.75.[3]

Although the Texans never launched an attack by way of the plains, the New Mexican scouts, ranging past Horsehead Crossing on the Pecos and the Antelope Hills on the Canadian, occasionally reported that enemy forces were approaching. In December, 1862, an inaccurate report that six thousand Texans were preparing to march up the Pecos led General James H. Carleton, who had replaced Canby as commander in New Mexico, to prepare to fight a delaying action by burning the grass in front of the Texans, stampeding their stock, and firing into their camps at night.[4] Many of the inaccurate warnings were nothing more than rumors picked up from the Indians, but at times Texan scouting parties did follow Kiowa and Comanche raiders a considerable distance

[1] Lt. Hugh Nicodemus to Col. J. G. Gallegos, December 19, 1861, Dept. of N. Mex., LS, Vol. 11, 474, Army Commands, NA.
[2] Lt. A. L. Anderson to Lt. Col. Wm. Chapman, June 19, 1861, *War of the Rebellion, Official Records*, Series 1, IV, 36.
[3] Carleton to Capt. J. C. McFerran, November 13, 1862, Dept. of N. Mex., LS, Vol. 13, 156, Army Commands, RG 98, NA.
[4] Carleton to Capt. Joseph Updegraff, December 8, 1862, *ibid.*, 224.

A History of New Mexican–Plains Indian Relations

toward New Mexico. Such expeditions could easily have been mistaken for invasion forces.

Despite the earnest endeavors of the *Comancheros*, the army officers began to limit their use as spies and to restrict their commerce. In October, 1862, Superintendent Collins refused to license a *Comanchero* party from Picurís, and when the traders defiantly left for the plains, he informed Carleton. The General, suspecting the contrabandists would go down the Mora Valley and past Wagon Mound, a prominent landmark on the Santa Fe Trail, dispatched a patrol from Fort Union to capture the runaways and confine them to "public labor."[5] The *Comancheros*, however, eluded the troops. As an old trader from Cordova, a village near Picurís, later explained: "When we came close to Fort Union we would wait until night to slip by."[6] In February of the following year, Collins refused passes to several other trading parties because he feared that Texans might be approaching by way of the plains.[7] The efforts to restrict the *Comanchero* trade, however, were ineffective because the officers and enlisted men on the eastern frontier, all of whom were either native New Mexicans or long-time territorial residents, were sympathetic to the traders and thus were lax in carrying out the directives from headquarters. Even the official dispatches of the outpost commanders reflected little disapproval of the traffic; in 1864, for example, Captain E. H. Bergmann, commanding Fort Bascom in eastern New Mexico, casually mentioned the return from the plains of "an old Mexican trader, and as far as I know him, *a reliable man.*"[8]

Unwilling to depend upon the *Comancheros* for protection against a surprise attack from the east, Carleton in late 1862 resurrected an earlier plan to establish a military post in the Canadian Valley.[9] On October 31, he ordered Captain William H.

[5] Carleton to Capt. P. L. Plympton, October 30, 1862, *ibid.*, 129.
[6] Vicente Romero, interview with L. B. Brown, April 6, 1937, MS, New Mexico Historical Museum Library, Santa Fe.
[7] Collins to Carleton, February 14, 1863, C/62, Dept. of N. Mex., LR, Army Commands, RG 98, NA.
[8] Bergmann to Carleton, March 1, 1864, B/60, *ibid.*
[9] A fort on the Canadian (tentatively named Fort Butler) had originally been

Backus with one company of the Second Colorado Volunteers to establish a temporary post 120 miles east of the settlements.[10] After locating the outpost (subsequently known as Camp Easton) on the Canadian River fifteen miles above the mouth of Utah Creek, Captain Backus took up his lonely assignment of watching the approaches from Fort Smith and Texas for Confederates.

General Carleton, recognizing that the success of the small post depended upon the friendship of the Comanches, instructed Backus to try to establish a "good understanding with them in order to obtain information." To further this policy, Carleton asked his close friend Indian Superintendent Collins to establish a Comanche agency in eastern New Mexico. Collins, who had long advocated such a step,[11] immediately sent William B. Stapp, a former agent for the Mescalero Apaches, to care for the Comanches at Fort Bascom and then—almost as an afterthought—asked approval of Indian Commissioner William Dole.[12] Although Collins lauded Stapp as being "useful and efficient" and stressed the need for the agency, Dole vetoed the project. Like the rest of the Washington hierarchy, he could not understand that many of the Comanches could be dealt with effectively only through New Mexico.

Despite the Indian Department's refusal to co-operate, the army officers at Camp Easton managed to win the friendship of

---

authorized in 1860. Although the New Mexican press had lauded the proposal because it would open up "the rich soils of the Canadian to occupancy and settlement" and had printed glowing reports of the fertility of the region, the army officers were opposed because the new post was intended to replace Fort Union as the supply depot for New Mexico. Their delaying tactics held up establishment of the post until the outbreak of the Civil War caused the matter to be forgotten. For a detailed account of this affair, see Charles Leroy Kenner, "A History of New Mexican-Plains Indian Relations" (Ph.D. Dissertation, Texas Technological College, 1966), 215–18.

[10] General Order No. 94, October 31, 1862, Dept. of N. Mex., Orders, Vol. 37, 288–89, Army Commands, RG 98, NA.

[11] In June, 1860, Collins had recommended the establishment of an agency at Hatch's Ranch for the Comanches, who "occupy the country" on the Canadian and cause "some trouble and loss" for the frontier settlers. His request had been ignored. Collins to Charles Mix, June 3, 1860, C/87, N. Mex. Supt., OIA, LR, RG 75, NA.

[12] Collins to Dole, November 13, 1862, C/1921, *ibid.*

the Comanches. On November 3, 1862, a party of Chief Mow-way's warriors aided in the capture of some southern sympathizers fleeing down the Canadian. A few days later, Chiefs Mow-way and Little Buffalo visited Captain Backus and offered to help if he would "come down and fight the Texans." Backus was in no position to send them aid, but he promised to pay them for all information about Confederate troop movements they brought to Camp Easton.[13] Lured by the hope of reward, a group of Comanches led by Esaquipa, a frequent visitor to New Mexico in the 1850's and now "an old chief," visited the camp on May 6, 1863, to report that a body of Texas troops was moving across the plains between the Red River and the Butterfield Trail. Obviously exaggerating, Esaquipa stated that the Confederates had a large number of tents and five pieces of artillery and gravely assured the Federals that his warriors would "dispute every inch of soil" with the invaders. After staying overnight at the post and professing the "most friendly feelings," he and his followers departed.[14]

Although the alleged Confederate movement never materialized, the visits initiated a brief honeymoon between the Comanches and the garrison on the Canadian. On June 19, 1863, Captain Bergmann, commanding Camp Easton at the time, reported that the Comanches had promised to notify him if "anything should occur" on the plains. In accordance with the military's ardent courtship of the Comanches, he stated that he always greeted them cordially and had given "to one party some articles of old clothing and food" and to others some "Bread, Sheep, etc." He complained, however, that his stores had become depleted and requested additional supplies of flour and sheep for distribution among subsequent visitors. "They do not expect to get anything when they come here," he wrote, "but they will beg anyhow."[15] Upon receiving this report, General Carleton imme-

[13] Backus to the Asst. Adj. Gen., December 1, 1862, *War of the Rebellion*, Series 1, XV, 153–58.
[14] Lt. David Perry to Capt. B. C. Cutler, May 9, 1863, P/84, Dept. of N. Mex., LR, Army Commands, RG 98, NA.
[15] Bergmann to Cutler, June 19, 1863, B/81, *ibid.*

The Civil War and the Adobe Walls Campaign

diately ordered that some goods "intended for the Comanche Indians" be sent to Camp Easton by the next wagon train.[16]

In August, 1863, Camp Easton was converted into a permanent post and renamed Fort Bascom.[17] In addition to guarding against Texans, the new fort was intended to promote settlement. Carleton went out of his way to announce to the New Mexican press that the troops at Fort Bascom would prevent Indian raids upon any ranchers who desired to pasture the region between Utah Creek and the border settlements and would protect people who chose to settle in the Canadian Valley.[18] In October, he sent Major H. D. Wallen to survey the region around Fort Bascom. After a brief reconnaissance, Wallen reported that the soil in the Canadian Valley was arable and that fields there could be easily irrigated. Describing the climate as mild and pleasant with little, if any, snow during the winter, the Major assured potential settlers that there was plenty of cottonwood timber, game, fish, and "pleasant" drinking water. He also pointed out that settlers would be able to sell their grain, hay, and beef cattle at Fort Bascom— a statement which suggests that the need for supplies may have inspired the army's eagerness to get the region settled.[19]

Soon after the fort was established, the cordial relations with the Comanches were jeopardized by a petty feud between the military and the Indian Department. Captain P. L. Plympton, commander at Fort Bascom, complained that the Comanches were making "repeated visits" to beg for food and requested that an Indian agent be sent to care for them.[20] At the same time, Cap-

---

[16] Cutler to Craig, June 28, 1863, Dept. of N. Mex., LS, Vol. 13, 579, Army Commands, RG 98, NA.

[17] General Order No. 20, August 11, 1863, Dept. of N. Mex., Orders, Vol. 34, 368, Army Commands, RG 98, NA.

[18] *Rio Abajo Weekly Press* (Albuquerque), August 26, 1863.

[19] Wallen to Cutler, October 15, 1863, printed in the *Santa Fe Weekly Gazette*, November 21, 1863. The New Mexican newspapers, always anxious for territorial development, were jubilant over the establishment of the fort. The *Gazette* proclaimed on November 7 that a great number of families planned to move to the Canadian in the spring and declared that "every time there is a Fort Bascom established there is a blessing conferred upon New Mexico."

[20] Plympton to Cutler, October 10, 1863, P/144, Dept. of N. Mex., LR, Army Commands, RG 98, NA.

tain Bergmann, who upon Superintendent Collins' advice had spent $206.28 on the Comanches, presented his bill.

Carleton forwarded these matters to Collins' successor, Michael Steck, a Pennsylvania-born physician and former agent for the Mescalero Apaches, who referred them for approval to the Commissioner of Indian Affairs. Commissioner Dole refused either to reimburse Bergmann or to provide an agent at Fort Bascom; instead, he informed General Carleton that regulations specifically authorized frontier commanders to issue rations in order to conciliate potential hostiles. When he received Dole's refusal, Carleton sent it to Superintendent Steck with a curt threat that the commander at Fort Bascom would no longer be able to issue provisions to the Comanches.[21] In February, 1864, it became evident that Carleton was not bluffing when Esaquipa, reporting at Fort Bascom that he had seen "large bodies" of marching troops coming up the Canadian, was turned away without presents.[22] Esaquipa may have been lying but it was the wrong time to offend the Comanches.

Like the other Plains tribes, the Comanches had become agitated over the extension of settlement into their domain and were attracted toward the warpath by the shortage of troops on the frontier. Furthermore, *Comancheros* possibly were inciting them. In late 1863, Robert North, a squawman dispatched to ransom some white captives from the Plains Indians, reported that the Comanches had been visited by New Mexicans who were urging them to fight, "promising to help the Indians themselves, and that a great many Mexicans would come up from New Mexico for the purpose in the spring."[23]

The following year, the simmering discontent erupted into a major war, starting among the Cheyennes and spreading rapidly southward. By May, although General Carleton was still so un-

[21] All the correspondence in this episode is filed with Steck to Dole, October 22, 1863, S/219, N. Mex. Supt., OIA, LR, RG 75, NA.

[22] Bergmann to Carleton, March 1, 1864, B/14, Dept. of N. Mex., LR, Army Commands, RG 98, NA.

[23] Statement of Robert North, November 10, 1863, *War of the Rebellion*, Series 1, XXXIV, Part 4, 100.

The Civil War and the Adobe Walls Campaign

suspecting that he believed the Comanches would report any Texans who attempted to march across the plains,[24] small bands of Comanches and Kiowas had joined in the Cheyenne war. As the recalcitrants from the two tribes at first stole only a few mules and horses from unescorted wagon trains, they caused the New Mexican officials little concern until August, when they struck a small train at Lower Cimarron Springs on the Santa Fe Trail. The Comanches, seventy strong but "apparently friendly," entered the camp of the teamsters as if to trade, caught their hosts off guard, and killed and scalped the five Americans, "horribly" mutilating their bodies. Three New Mexican teamsters with the Americans were spared. Telling them they did not wish to kill Mexicans but "would kill every white man that came on the road," the Comanches gave them a wagon and oxen and sent them on their way.[25]

Although only a natural consequence of the long friendship between the Comanches and the New Mexicans, the sparing of the three teamsters was regarded by General Carleton as proof that the two peoples were united in an unholy league against the Anglos. He charged grimly that the discrimination which the Comanches frequently made in favor of the native New Mexicans and against Anglo-Americans was an insult to the "Government and to our people."[26]

In reaction to the massacre, Carleton proclaimed the Kiowas and Comanches to be hostile and ordered the frontier posts to take precautions against a surprise attack. From Fort Bascom a seven-man detachment was sent to the Tucumcari Mountain to "keep a vigilant lookout." The sentinels were to arrest any traders on their way to the plains, but returning *Comancheros,* unless of a "suspicious character," were not to be molested.[27] In addition to

[24] Carleton to Lt. Col. Wm. McMullen, June 4, 1864, Dept. of N. Mex., LS, Vol. 14, 489, Army Commands, RG 98, NA.
[25] Capt. Nicholas Davis to Carleton, October 30, 1864, *War of the Rebellion,* Series 1, XLI, Part 1, 212–13. Another account, which differs somewhat, was printed in the *Weekly New Mexican* on August 19, 1864, and is quoted in Oliver LeFarge, *Santa Fe,* 26–27.
[26] Carleton to Steck, October 31, 1864, in Steck Papers, Box 4.
[27] Special Order No. 47, August 30, 1864, Dept. of N. Mex., Fort Bascom, Orders, Book 84, Army Commands, RG 98, NA.

such defensive measures, the General began mobilizing his slender resources for an all-out attack on the Plains Indians.

Thoroughly alarmed when some *Comancheros* informed them of Carleton's war preparations, ten Kiowa and Comanche chiefs headed by "F. M. Bears" went to Fort Bascom under a flag of truce on September 22. They admitted that they had committed depredations, but promised that if peace were made, they would instruct their tribesmen to cease hostilities immediately.[28] Summarily rejecting the peace overture, Carleton ordered Captain Charles Deus, the commander at Fort Bascom, to remind the chiefs of their many atrocities and to tell them that "their hearts are bad and that they talk with a forked tongue." Deus was also to inform them that there would be no further negotiations until the Indians had returned all the stock stolen during the year and surrendered the perpetrators of the massacre at Lower Cimarron Springs.[29]

The *Comancheros*, working desperately to prevent Carleton's punitive campaign, found a passionate supporter in Michael Steck, the Indian superintendent. On October 26, Steck asked Carleton to reconsider because "several respectable citizens" who had recently returned from a trading trip had assured him that the Comanches had never been more peaceably disposed. These Indians, he reminded Carleton, had for about eighty years acted in good faith toward the people of New Mexico, and a war with them would be disastrous to the settlers on the eastern frontier as well as to transportation routes across the plains.[30] Steck maintained—somewhat lamely in view of the Lower Cimarron Springs massacre—that the hostilities of the past

[28] Capt. Charles Deus to Capt. Cyrus H. DeForrest, September 24, 1864, C/119, Dept. of N. Mex., LR, Army Commands, RG 98, NA. "F. M. Bears" quite likely was the noted Comanche chief and orator, Ten Bears, who achieved fame at the Medicine Lodge conference in 1867.

[29] DeForrest to Deus, September 27, 1864, Dept. of N. Mex., LS, Vol. 16, 59, Army Commands, RG 98, NA.

[30] Steck to Carleton, October 16, 1864, Steck Papers, Box 4. Copies of the extensive correspondence between Steck and Carleton concerning the Comanche campaign of 1864 can also be found in the National Archives.

The Civil War and the Adobe Walls Campaign

summer had been entirely the work of the Kiowas, who thus should be the only tribe punished.

Carleton refused to accept Steck's argument. The *Comancheros*' statements were untrustworthy, he declared, because they favored the Indians out of gratitude for past favors and in order to continue their trade. In defense of his own position, he recalled a long list of Comanche forays, of which most had occurred in the 1850's and were quite petty. He admitted that he knew of no Comanche attacks upon the settlements since 1861.[31]

On November 5, Steck, desiring to rid himself of "all responsibility" for the disasters which would be incurred by a Comanche war, appealed once more for Carleton to revise his campaign plans. Saying he spoke for the frontier residents, he argued that the Comanches should not be attacked but the Kiowas, on the other hand, should be severely chastised: "I hope the Government will be able to inflict the punishment they so richly deserve."[32] Seeing that Carleton was determined to go on with the campaign, Steck dejectedly complained to the Commissioner of Indian Affairs that the Comanches had been at peace with the people of New Mexico for many years and that war with them was "entirely uncalled for."[33]

Carleton, meanwhile, was finding it difficult to gather enough troops for the expedition. To lead the command, he chose Colonel Christopher (Kit) Carson, who had recently won new acclaim for the conquest of the Navahos. In October, Carleton instructed Carson to recruit some Utes and Jicarillas, hereditary foes of the Plains Indians, and for a time considered the use of Navahos (despite the recent war with them). He asked General James G. Blunt, the commander at Fort Larned, Kansas, to send a supporting expedition against the Kiowas and Comanches, but Blunt, distracted by General Sterling Price's unexpected invasion of Missouri, could not oblige.[34] Carleton also requested the use of

[31] Carleton to Steck, October 31, 1864, *ibid.*
[32] Steck to Carleton, November 5, 1864, *ibid.*
[33] Steck to William Dole, November 16, 1864, *ibid.*
[34] Carleton to Blunt, October 22, 1864, Dept. of N. Mex., LS, Vol. 16, 98, Army Commands, RG 98, NA.

the territorial militia, but Governor Henry Connelly refused to call it out, reportedly stating that the Comanches were "at peace with the people of New Mexico and that it was impolitic to stir up this powerful tribe without a cause."[35] Consequently, Carleton was able to provide Carson with only 335 cavalrymen (most of whom were native New Mexicans of the First New Mexico Volunteers) and 75 Indians—a force far too small for the job at hand.

To prevent the *Comancheros* from warning the Indians, Carleton asked Steck and Governor Connelly on October 22 to grant no more trade permits and ordered the commanding officer at Fort Bascom to turn back all New Mexicans going east.[36] To the General's chagrin, however, Steck ignored his request and issued passes to two groups of traders, and the troops at Fort Bascom allowed one party to bluff its way past and were unsuccessful in apprehending others. Thus Carson's force was preceded into the Texas Panhandle by traders who not only warned the Indians of the impending attack but also delivered to them a quantity of arms and munitions.

After being informed of the location of the Comanches and Kiowas by (of all people) a party of *Comancheros*, Carleton ordered Carson to march as quickly as possible. Leaving Fort Bascom on November 12 along a road well worn by generations of traders and Comanches, Carson made excellent time, despite two severe but short snowstorms. Locating the Indian camps near Adobe Walls on November 25, he quickly captured a Kiowa village of 150 lodges but was then assailed by an estimated 1,000 warriors from camps farther downstream. In the long day of bitter, confused fighting that followed, Carson's force escaped annihilation only by the adroit management of two mountain howitzers. When dusk closed over the battlefield, the Colonel withdrew, flattering himself that he had "taught these Indians a severe lesson." The casualties had been surprisingly light: Carson

---

[35] Steck to Dole, November 16, 1864, Steck Papers, Box 4; *Weekly New Mexican*, April 7, 1865.

[36] Carleton to the Asst. Adj. Gen., January 29, 1865, Dept. of N. Mex., LS, Vol. 16, 194, Army Commands, RG 98, NA.

The Civil War and the Adobe Walls Campaign

reported that he had 3 killed and estimated that the enemy had 60 killed or wounded.[37]

Upon returning to Fort Bascom, Carson learned that Jesús Amalla and José Castillo, two *Comancheros* apprehended while returning with cattle obtained from the Indians, had carried a pass signed by Superintendent Steck on October 27, five days after Carleton had asked that no more passes be issued. Carson thereupon penned a supplementary campaign report and blamed his failure to win a decisive victory upon Steck and the *Comancheros*. Asserting that his losses had been inflicted by ammunition supplied the Indians by the New Mexican traders, he bitterly declaimed:

> I blame the Mexicans not half as much as I do Mr. Steck ... who gave them the pass to go and trade, he knowing perfectly well at the time that we were at war with the Indians, and that the Mexicans would take what they could sell best, which was powder, lead, and caps.[38]

General Carleton later took advantage of this incident to obtain Steck's removal. On January 29, 1865, he sent to Washington a packet of letters and documents intended to incriminate Steck and complained that the military could never defeat the Indians as long as a "high civil functionary gives passports to men to carry on a nefarious traffic, when he knows in reason that those men will give information of the movements of troops."[39] On May 1, 1865, Steck was asked to resign "for the good of the service."[40] Quite ironically, Felipe Delgado, the veteran New Mexi-

---

[37] Carson to Carleton, November 29, 1864, *War of the Rebellion*, Series 1, XLI, Part 1, 939-43. For an excellent account of the Adobe Walls battle, see Captain George H. Pettis, "Kit Carson's Fight with the Comanche and Kiowa Indians," Historical Society of New Mexico, *Personal Narratives of the Battles of the Rebellion* (1908), 7-35. Pettis, who had been in charge of the two howitzers during the battle, supplemented the documentary sources by drawing on his personal recollections.

[38] Carson to Carleton, December 16, 1864, *War of the Rebellion*, Series 1, XLI, Part 1, 943.

[39] Carleton to the Adj. Gen., January 29, 1865, Dept. of N. Mex., LS, Vol. 16, 197, Army Commands, RG 98, NA.

[40] William Keleher, *Turmoil in New Mexico*, 506, n. 134.

can politician named to replace him, was far more sympathetic to the *Comancheros* than Steck had ever been.

Impelled by Carson's report to strengthen the restrictions previously imposed on the traders, on November 30, 1864, Carleton ordered the arrest of all parties attempting to visit the Comanches to barter, no matter *"from what source"* they had derived their authority.[41] Although Captain Bergmann at Fort Bascom was able to intercept a few traders, not one was ever brought to trial.

The failure of the Adobe Walls campaign to crush the Comanches and Kiowas led to fears of a possible counterattack. On January 21, 1865, however, Sheer-kee-na-kwaugh, optimistically called by Bergmann "the principal chief of the whole Comanche nation," visited Fort Bascom and stated that he wished to "live in good faith" with the Americans. In return for peace, he promised to do everything within his power to prevent further Comanche raids and to inform the Americans if any were planned by the Kiowas or Apaches. Although Sheer-kee-na-kwaugh refused to remain at the fort until Bergmann could receive instructions from Santa Fe, he promised to return the following month to hear General Carleton's answer.[42]

Since the fear of Comanche reprisals had become a major issue in a hot race for territorial delegate to Congress, Carleton and Collins, who were actively backing Colonel Francisco Perea, used Sheer-kee-na-kwaugh's visit to prove that the Adobe Walls campaign had been effective. Collins' *Santa Fe Weekly Gazette*, under the heading "Comanches and Peace," editorialized that Carson's victory had made the Indians feel "the white man's power," predicted that the Comanches would now "become our permanent friends and allies," and assured its readers that Carleton was quite willing to negotiate a peace treaty.[43]

Retorting through the *Weekly New Mexican*, the anti-Carleton forces claimed that the visit proved that the southern Co-

---

[41] Cutler to Bergmann, November 30, 1864, Dept. of N. Mex., LS, Vol. 16, 127, Army Commands, RG 98, NA.

[42] Bergmann to Cutler, January 21, 1865, *War of the Rebellion*, Series 1, XLVIII, Part 1, 611.

[43] *Santa Fe Weekly Gazette*, February 4, 1865.

The Civil War and the Adobe Walls Campaign

manches should not have been attacked, that the war with them was a blunder, and that Carleton, realizing his mistake, was trying to "patch the matter up as best he can."[44] The *Weekly New Mexican* also challenged the contention that the Indians had been defeated at Adobe Walls. The troops had been so "badly whipped," it asserted, that they had been unable to prevent the Indians from retaking their captured horses.[45] Carleton's sudden willingness to negotiate was due to his recognition that the unpopular Comanche war, unless ended, would cause the loss to his candidate, Perea, of the counties of San Miguel and Mora.[46]

Meanwhile, Carleton, encouraged by Sheer-kee-na-kwaugh's peaceful visit, had relaxed his restrictions on the *Comanchero* trade. As soon as peace with the Comanches was restored, he promised, unlimited trade would be allowed; until then, traders whose passes were countersigned at his headquarters could go to the plains.[47] When Carleton soon afterward endorsed passes for some of his political allies, ostensibly to ransom captives from the Indians, the native New Mexicans hotly charged him with favoritism. On March 20, 1865, a resident of Las Vegas wrote to the editor of the *Weekly New Mexican* that he marveled to see so many traders on their way to the Comanche country, "especially so soon after some of our worthy citizens" had been detained at Fort Bascom. He complained that it was unfair to allow a few privileged parties to trade in return for their promise to liberate captives when it was known they were interested only in making a profit.[48] A week later, the *Weekly New Mexican* noted that another party licensed by Carleton had started for the plains and demanded sarcastically that the General "inform us . . . whether the Comanches are at peace or war."[49]

---

[44] *Weekly New Mexican*, March 24, 1865.
[45] *Ibid.*, February 24, 1865.
[46] *Ibid.* Perea, a candidate for congressional delegate, was defeated by Colonel Francisco Cháves, who as an army officer had deliberately evaded having anything to do with the Kiowa-Comanche campaign.
[47] General Order No. 2, January 31, 1865, Dept. of N. Mex., Orders, Vol. 30, 185–86, Army Commands, RG 98, NA.
[48] *Weekly New Mexican*, March 24, 1865.
[49] *Ibid.*, March 31, 1865.

The prospects of peace with the Comanches waned as rapidly as they had appeared. After Sheer-kee-na-kwaugh failed to return to Fort Bascom, there were renewed rumors of Indian hostility. In early April, Lorenzo Váldez, one of the traders licensed by Carleton, reported that the Kiowas and most of the Comanches had made an alliance with the Texans. Claiming that he had been held prisoner for two days by Comanches and spared only because he was personally acquainted with their leader, Váldez warned that "almost all" of the Plains Indians had combined to commit depredations upon trains crossing the plains during the forthcoming summer.[50]

Making no mention in the press of this or other disturbing reports, Carleton and his aides professed to hope that the ominous allegations might be "devoid of truth" because they had been made by Mexicans, who had purposely shaped them to "serve their purpose." The failure of the Comanches to return to Fort Bascom for a peace conference, they thought, might be due to the *Comancheros'* having "abundantly replenished" the Indians' wants.[51]

Upon hearing the rumors, the editor of the *Weekly New Mexican* stated that the renewal of hostilities was "the fruit" of the Comanche war, for which there had existed "not the least necessity." He also declared that Carleton, fearing the indignation of the people whom he had exposed to the "ravages of their former friends," was suppressing the gravity of the situation. He taunted sardonically: "Where is Sheer-kee-na-kwaugh and his peace makers?"[52]

Any hope that the rumors were unfounded vanished on May 10 when Arthur Morrison, Carleton's former military aide, returned from the plains with indisputable news of Comanche hostility. Morrison, hoping to reap large trade profits when he left Fort Bascom on March 18, had followed the Canadian to a point one hundred miles below Adobe Walls without contacting the

[50] Váldez to Carleton, April 11, 1865, enclosed with Bergmann to Carleton, April 18, 1865, B/135, Dept. of N. Mex., LR, Army Commands, RG 98, NA.
[51] Bergmann to Carleton, April 18, 1865, *ibid.*
[52] *Weekly New Mexican*, April 28, 1865.

The Civil War and the Adobe Walls Campaign

Comanches. Then two of his Mexican scouts were captured by thirty-eight Comanche warriors and robbed of their pistols and saddles. Before being released, the two captives were told that the Comanches, Kiowas, "and twelve more nations"[53] had concluded a treaty with Texas by which they would receive ammunition, clothing, and foodstuffs in return for their aid in an expedition against New Mexico. Morrison also met a party of Mexican traders, licensed by Carleton, who had had their goods taken by the Comanches and had been told to warn other traders that they would be killed if they came to the plains. Considering himself lucky to escape unharmed and without the loss of his trade goods, Morrison hastily returned home. The Indians were "very much aggrieved" by Carson's attack, he reported, and in their passion for revenge were boasting that they and the Texans would destroy Fort Bascom.[54]

Morrison had sized up the situation quite well. The southern Plains Indians were now infuriated, not only at the Anglos in New Mexico, but at the Spanish element as well, because so many native New Mexicans had served with Carson at Adobe Walls. In May, 1865, for example, the Kiowas told their agent that they had robbed "some Mexicans that came to trade" and had warned them "they must not come again, as the Mexicans with Kit Carson were fighting them."[55]

To secure help against New Mexico, the Comanches turned to their traditional enemies, the Texans. The Confederate leaders in the Trans-Mississippi Department were sufficiently impressed by the overtures to appoint as emissaries to treat with the Indians Brigadier General James W. Throckmorton, later to be governor

---

[53] This number coincides with the total number of tribes that were represented at the Camp Napoleon, Indian Territory, conference on May 26, 1865. The "twelve more nations" were the Cherokees, Choctaws, Creeks, Chickasaws, Seminoles, Caddos, Osages, Cheyennes, Arapahos, Lipans, Northern Caddos, and Anadarkos. W. P. Adair to Brig. Gen. J. C. Veatch, July 20, 1865, *War of the Rebellion*, Series 1, XLVIII, Part 2, 1102–1103.

[54] Morrison to Carleton, May 10, 1865, M/58, Dept. of N. Mex., LR, Army Commands, RG 98, NA.

[55] Jessie Leavenworth to Brig. Gen. J. H. Ford, May 30, 1865, *War of the Rebellion*, Series 1, XLVIII, Part 2, 688.

of Texas, and Albert Pike, the Arkansas poet and journalist who in 1861 had negotiated a compact with the Comanches. The Plains Indians had waited too long before seeking new allies, however, for the sudden collapse of the Confederacy doomed their effort. Throckmorton attended a conference between the Five Civilized Tribes and the Plains Indians at Camp Napoleon on the Washita River on May 26, 1865, not to formulate an alliance, but to persuade the Indians to stay away from the Texas settlements.[56]

Left without support, the Comanches were soon ready to resume friendly relations with New Mexico. José Ulibarrí, a trader from Chaparito, stated on his return from the plains in June that the Comanches were "desirous of remaining at peace."[57] General Carleton immediately sent Ulibarrí back to the plains to bring the Indians to Fort Union for a conference. The Comanches, however, were unwilling to trust the pledge of safe passage and refused to accept the invitation. Farther north, Jesse Leavenworth, the agent for the southern Plains tribes, had better success. In October, 1865, he signed with these Indians the Treaty of the Little Arkansas, which temporarily restored peace and confirmed the Comanches' claim to much of northwestern Texas, a right no Union agent legally could grant. The final disposition of the Comanche problem, however, had to await a new treaty and the end of another war on the plains.

[56] Of the considerable correspondence in *War of the Rebellion* concerning the proposed council, see especially Gen. E. Kirby Smith to Albert Pike, April 8, 1865, LXVIII, Part 2, 1266–69, and Brig. Gen. Douglas Cooper to Brig. Gen. J. W. Throckmorton, May 16, 1865, *ibid.*, 1309. Throckmorton recovered nine prisoners from the Comanches and was convinced that "with proper management," the Indians could be kept at peace with his state. *Dallas Herald*, July 1, 1865. As soon as the Comanches resumed friendly relations with the New Mexicans, however, they reverted to their traditional pattern of hostility toward Texas.

[57] *Santa Fe Weekly Gazette*, June 17, 1865; Ulibarrí to Carleton, July 1, 1865, U/4, Dept. of N. Mex., LR, Army Commands, RG 98, NA.

8
The Great Comanchero Cattle Trade

THE CHARACTER OF THE *Comanchero* TRADE changed for the worse during the early 1860's. In addition to biscuits, flour, and corn meal, the traders carried to the plains powder, lead, guns, and whisky—to be exchanged for cattle that had been stolen in Texas and trailed hundreds of miles across the barren Llano Estacado. Moreover, the nefarious trade enabled the Comanches and Kiowas to wreak a gruesome toll on the advancing Texans before surrendering control of the South Plains. The traders were rarely seen by their Anglo victims, but this very elusiveness added to their notoriety. Once their commerce had been described as harmless by such men as Josiah Gregg and Lieutenants Abert and Whipple; now the very term *Comanchero* was synonymous with evil.

It is not clear just when the illicit cattle trade began. It may have been shortly before the Civil War,[1] but the commerce most likely grew out of the chaos and confusion created by that conflict. William J. Wilson, a Texas cowman who learned much about the *Comancheros* during a sojourn in New Mexico in the 1870's, stated that toward the end of the Civil War the Comanches began gathering and selling cattle to the New Mexicans because so many untended animals were "running at large" on the frontier.[2] At first, the Indians merely drove off the unbranded

[1] J. Evetts Haley, "The Comanchero Trade," *Southwestern Historical Quarterly*, XXXVIII (January, 1935), 163. The only contemporary evidence for this, however, is found in two rather casual statements: in 1871, some New Mexicans, indignant at efforts to suppress the trade, asserted that it had been going on for fifty years (*Santa Fe Weekly Post*, June 17, 1871); in 1873, John Hittson estimated that the trade had been in progress for twenty years (*Daily New Mexican*, March 21, 1873).

[2] Deposition of William J. Wilson, June 26, 1893, Indian Depredation Case

155

mavericks, but after the war, when Texas stockmen with hard-bitten crews and fast branding irons moved into the mesquite thickets and carved out cattle empires for themselves, the Comanches began to seize beeves by force.

There are some inconclusive indications that Union encouragement during the war abetted the early raids. Early in the conflict, Oliver Loving, a Texas cattleman who had made a drive to Denver, excitedly wrote back to his home state that the Comanches were being paid by the Union troops in Colorado for all the "scalps taken in Texas."[3] Although this report may have been exaggerated, the Comanches in 1867 told Lorenzo Labadi, a veteran New Mexico Indian agent, that some Union officers had encouraged them to raid in Texas.[4]

Whether or not it originated then, the cattle trade expanded rapidly during the latter part of the Civil War. In April, 1864, H. T. Ketcham, a pioneer physician detailed by the Indian Department to vaccinate the southern Plains Indians for smallpox, reported that the Kiowas and Comanches had large herds of cattle and were preparing for another excursion to the Texas ranges.[5] A few months later, Robert North, a white squawman, accused the Mexicans of helping the Plains Indians by driving their stolen stock to New Mexico.[6] In October, a corporal at Fort Bascom encountered on the Fort Smith road a party of westbound Mexican traders with a "lot of cattle,"[7] and the following month, Captain Bergmann, commander at Fort Bascom, apprehended

---

No. 9133, *Charles Goodnight and John Sheeks vs. The United States and Comanche Indians*, Records of the U.S. Court of Claims, RG 123, NA.

[3] Oliver Loving to F. R. Lubbock, 1862, in James M. Day and Dorman Winfrey (eds.), *Texas Indian Papers, 1825–1916*, IV, 67.

[4] "Report of Lorenzo Labadi, August 23, 1867," in *Annual Report of the Commissioner of Indian Affairs*, 1867, 214.

[5] "Report of H. T. Ketcham, April 10, 1864," in *Annual Report of the Commissioner of Indian Affairs*, 1864, 253.

[6] Statement of Robert North, June 15, 1864, in *War of the Rebellion*, Series 1, XXXIV, Part 4, 422.

[7] Lt. Col. Francisco Abreau to Capt. B. C. Cutler, October 10, 1864, *ibid.*, XLI, Part 3, 771.

The Great Comanchero Cattle Trade

some New Mexicans who had purchased 250 head of cattle from the Indians.[8]

Bergmann and his fellow officers, however, have been charged with being more interested in profiting from the *Comanchero* trade than in stopping it. José Tafoya, an old *Comanchero*, later testified that in 1864 Bergmann had furnished him with supplies and goods to barter to the Plains Indians for livestock.[9] Mrs. Marian Russell, the bride of a young lieutenant at the fort in 1865, recalled some sixty-seven years later that "most all the folks" at Fort Bascom supplied themselves with cattle; she vividly remembered sending a "copper kettle and a small Navajo blanket" to the plains by a *Comanchero* and receiving in exchange twelve head of cattle.[10]

Although time may have clouded the memories of Tafoya and Mrs. Russell, Captain Bergmann can be linked to the Indian trade by his own words. After resigning from the U.S. Army, he established a "farm" on the Canadian below Fort Bascom and in 1868 applied to the Commissioner of Indian Affairs for a license to trade with the Comanches, "to keep up the friendly relationship" with them and to prevent depredations upon the settlements in "this part of the country." In his application, he stated that while commanding Fort Bascom he had had "frequent intercourse" with the Comanches. "Having served my country for many years," he reminded the Commissioner, "I think it justice that my request be granted."[11] As to whether Bergmann received a license, the records are silent, but concerning his involvement in the Indian trade there appears to be little doubt.

Captain Bergmann was not the only military figure to engage in the Indian trade. Mrs. Russell, in her memoirs (which made

[8] Cutler to Bergmann, November 30, 1864, Dept. of N. Mex., LS, Vol. 16, 108, Army Commands, RG 98, NA.
[9] Deposition of José Pieda Tafoya, June 26, 1893, Indian Depredation Case No. 9133, Records of the U.S. Court of Claims, RG 123, NA.
[10] Marian Russell to J. Evetts Haley, August 25, 1932, cited in Haley, "Comanchero Trade," *loc. cit.*, 166.
[11] Bergmann to N. G. Taylor, September 9, 1868, enclosed with Charles Mix to L. E. Webb, October 14, 1868, N. Mex. Supt., Field Office Records, LR, OIA, RG 75, NA.

as charming a book as ever concerned a woman of the Old West), unconsciously revealed the respectability of the cattle trade and indicated the ease with which an enterprising entrepreneur could build up a stake. Her husband, Richard, upon being discharged from the army in 1866, established a trading post at Tecolote. Since he had always longed to be a cattle rancher, he invested "every extra penny" in Texas longhorns. By buying corn cheaply from the New Mexicans and trading it to the Indians for cattle, he was able, at the end of five years, to sell the trading post and move to a Colorado ranch to which he had been sending "herds of cattle."[12]

Lieutenant Russell's involvement in the trade was minuscule, however, compared to that of four of his fellow officers: Patrick Henry Healy, Charles J. Jennings, E. W. Wood, and R. C. Vose. This audacious quartet, with chicanery in their hearts and larceny in their eyes, calmly set out in 1866 to monopolize the *Comanchero* commerce. In their quest for riches, they hoodwinked successively the Commissioner of Indian Affairs, the agent for the Comanches, and the superintendent of Indian affairs in New Mexico, only to lose in the end to the lowly *Comancheros*. The cupidity of these officers was undoubtedly aroused by the vigorous manner in which the *Comanchero* trade had rebounded from the setback given it in 1865 by General Carleton. The General had issued several permits, upon each of which, according to Indian Superintendent A. B. Norton, as many as fifty New Mexicans would trade, "claiming they are doing business" for the recipient.[13] Soon *Comancheros* were arriving in the settlements "almost daily" with "large numbers of cattle."[14]

An opportunity for Healy and his fellow officers to enter the lucrative commerce arose unexpectedly in mid-1866 with the arrival of Norton to replace Superintendent Felipe Delgado. Norton, while en route to New Mexico, had been informed by Comanche Agent Jesse Leavenworth in Kansas that the Plains

[12] Mrs. Hal Russell (ed.), *Land of Enchantment*, 117-25.
[13] "Report of A. B. Norton, July 31, 1866," in *Annual Report of the Commissioner of Indian Affairs, 1866*, 151.
[14] *Santa Fe Weekly Gazette*, July 28, 1866.

The Great Comanchero Cattle Trade

Indians were supplied with guns and ammunition by New Mexican traders and were thereby induced to steal stock and children in Texas. Deeply incensed by this disclosure, Norton promised Leavenworth that he would "use the extent of his power" to end the illicit traffic.[15] After arriving in Santa Fe and conferring with General Carleton, he announced that all passes then in effect were revoked and that subsequent ones must have the personal approval of the Commissioner of Indian Affairs.[16] Messrs. Healy, Jennings, Wood, and Vose, assuming that the Mexican traders would be forced out of business, immediately applied for permits.

Healy, the spokesman for the group, resigned from the army on August 4, 1866, and rushed to Washington. Using his six years of military service in New Mexico as a source of authority, he regaled D. N. Cooley, the Commissioner of Indian Affairs, with a misleading description of the situation on the southwestern frontier. The Comanches were very peaceable, he stated, and in their Canadian Valley homeland, well wooded and watered and covered with a "luxuriant growth of grass," raised large numbers of cattle and horses. Since they were well adapted and deeply "attached" to their country, it would be cruel to remove them; but they were in dire need of trade goods! Why, therefore, Healy pleaded, should "honest, loyal American citizens" be deprived of the benefits of this trade?[17] Since Healy and his colleagues had obtained the endorsement of Agent Leavenworth (by holding out the prospect that they could break up the malevolent influence of the *Comancheros* upon the Indians),[18] Cooley allowed himself to be duped into granting the licenses.

Upon arriving in New Mexico in January, 1867, Healy, Jennings, Wood, and Vose gaudily flashed their permits and indignantly demanded that Carleton and Norton stop "the illicit trade by citizens of this country." Although Norton's order of the pre-

---

[15] Leavenworth to D. N. Cooley, June 5, 1866, L/54, Kiowa Agency, OIA, LR, RG 75, NA.
[16] *Santa Fe Weekly Gazette*, July 28, 1866.
[17] Healy to Cooley, October 15, 1866, H/394, Kiowa Agency, OIA, LR, RG 75, NA.
[18] Leavenworth to G. W. Todd, December 24, 1866, L/88, *ibid*.

A History of New Mexican–Plains Indian Relations

vious summer had supposedly ended the traffic, both he and Carleton had been hesitant to enforce it. Carleton now professed to doubt that the military had any legal rights to stop New Mexicans "from going east . . . to buy things of the Comanches," but after his superior, General Winfield Scott Hancock, advised him to the contrary, he and Norton jointly proclaimed a new ban.[19] Thus supported by both the army and the Indian Office, Healy and his partners plunged into the *Comanchero* trade.

To their misfortune, however, they had underestimated the persistence and ingenuity of the *Comancheros*. John D. Henderson, the veteran agent for the Pueblos, was persuaded by his charges to issue them permits upon which, Healy complained, "at least seven hundred men from various parts of the Territory" began to trade. Unable to cope with this unexpected competition, the Anglos quickly incurred heavy losses. As Healy lamented,

> I sent a party to the Indian country to trade for furs and ponies, my men returned in fifty days losing nearly all their goods ($1,000 worth) . . . they informed me that there was more than four hundred men in the Indian camp having goods of every description to the amount of $20,000 and that it was impossible to make any kind of an average trade . . . if a man bought a good horse the Indians would take the same away from him.[20]

Withdrawing from personal participation in the commerce, the Americans sought to profit by subletting their licenses to *Comancheros*, anxious to evade a military crackdown on unauthorized trade.[21] Jennings established a trading post at Hatch's Ranch and began selling impressively worded permits "under authority of the license granted him by the Commissioner of Indian Affairs."[22] José Tafoya later recalled that he had traded supplies

---

[19] Healy to the Asst. Adj. Gen., January 22, 1867, N. Mex. Supt., Field Office Records, LR, OIA, RG 75, NA. The comments of Carleton and Hancock are in the form of endorsements on the letter.

[20] Healy to the Commissioner of Indian Affairs, July 31, 1867, N/142, N. Mex. Supt., OIA, LR, RG 75, NA.

[21] *Infra*, p. 177.

[22] Norton to Taylor, September 10, N/151, N. Mex. Supt., OIA, LR, RG 75, NA; Letterman to DeForrest, August 31, 1867, L/128, Dist. of N. Mex., LR, Army Commands, RG 98, NA.

furnished by Jennings to the Indians for cattle and "sometimes some horses." Upon returning from the plains, Tafoya paid Jennings "with stock" and kept the balance for himself.[23] Healy also sublet licenses to the natives, while Vose sold his license outright to Manuel Chávez, an ambitious *Comanchero*, who in turn franchised many of his countrymen. Of the four Americans, Norton reported, only Wood (Carleton's former adjutant) had not as yet "been complained of."

Upon realizing that the activities of the quartet had reopened the *Comanchero* trade on "a more extensive scale" than ever, Norton asked Nathaniel Taylor, the new Commissioner of Indian Affairs, to revoke their licenses.[24] Although the Commissioner agreed that the four had forfeited all right to their permits, he observed that it was not necessary to revoke them because they would expire within a few days.[25] With his refusal to renew the licenses, the bizarre attempt of four Anglo officers to obtain control of the *Comanchero* trade collapsed.

Although the Anglos had been forced out of the Plains Indian trade, the *Comancheros*, in the face of persistent regulatory efforts, sustained their thriving commerce for another decade. In making their lonely excursions, the traders normally followed a similar routine. At the outset, they had to evade the troops, who sometimes seized their goods without reporting the action. W. F. M. Arny, Pueblo agent and former acting governor of New Mexico, charged in 1871 that some soldiers had stopped a Pueblo party and appropriated for their own use "a good private horse, several silver-mounted bridles, saddles, and other articles."[26] Jim Duncan, a trooper with the Eighth Cavalry, recalled capturing a burro train loaded with ammunition, whisky, and about fifty bolts of

---

[23] Deposition of José Tafoya, June 26, 1893, Indian Depredation Case No. 9133, Records of the U.S. Court of Claims, RG 123, NA.

[24] Norton to Taylor, September 10, 1867, N/151, N. Mex. Supt., OIA, LR, RG 75, NA.

[25] Mix to Norton, October 4, 1867, N. Mex. Supt., Field Office Records, LR, OIA, RG 75, NA.

[26] "Report of W. F. M. Arny, August 18, 1871," in *Annual Report of the Commissioner of Indian Affairs*, 1871, 804.

red and blue cloth. It was sold to a merchant, and the troopers used the proceeds to get "a couple of extra shirts apiece."[27]

At one time, complaints about seizures were so widespread that Captain George F. Letterman, commanding at Fort Bascom, instructed his officers to inventory accurately all stock and trade goods taken so that the "whole matter" could be fully investigated and articles wrongfully withheld returned "to their proper owners."[28]

In addition to the military, trading parties occasionally had to contend with hostile Indians, especially the Navahos and Kiowas. While the Navahos were confined at the Bosque Redondo Reservation on the Pecos from 1864 to 1868, they were in position to strike swiftly at the *Comanchero* routes to the plains. In February, 1866, Manuel Olona of Valencia County was returning from the Comanche country with a herd of cattle when his party was attacked by about thirty Navahos at a place called the "Pintadea." With the loss of only one man wounded, however, the New Mexicans repulsed the Navahos and saved the entire herd of stock.[29]

Trouble also sometimes occurred with the Kiowas, often friendly but never dependable. In 1868, some Kiowas opened fire on a party of ten Mexicans taking provisions to trade at a Cheyenne village in the present Oklahoma Panhandle. With their opening volley, the Kiowas killed three of the New Mexicans and forced the others to abandon their wagons and flee for their lives. The Indians then looted the wagons and appropriated the draft animals.[30]

After evading these dangers, the traders faced the task of making contact with friendly Indians. Often a rendezvous in one of the canyons which indented the rugged eastern escarpment of the Staked Plains was agreed upon in advance. Clandestine trysts were held in a dozen secluded valleys beneath the Caprock, rang-

[27] Haley, "Comanchero Trade," loc. cit., 171.
[28] Letterman to Sergeant James Rieves, September 15, 1867, Dist. of N. Mex., Fort Bascom, LS, Book 82, 21, Army Commands, RG 98, NA.
[29] *Santa Fe Weekly Gazette*, March 3, 1866.
[30] John S. Smith to Col. Thomas Murphy, February 16, 1868, enclosed with Murphy to Taylor, March 10, 1868, M/13, Kiowa Agency, OIA, LR, RG 75, NA.

ing from Blanca Cita (a branch of Palo Duro Canyon) and Quitaque on the north to Mucha Que (near the present town of Gail) on the south.[31] While waiting for the Indians to arrive with cattle, traders sometimes built surprisingly elaborate living quarters. During the 1871 campaign of Colonel Ranald S. Mackenzie, the troops came across on Duck Creek the

> trading stations of the Mexicans with the Indians, consisting of curiously built caves in the high banks or bluffs, the earth propped up or kept in place by a framework of poles, giving these subterranean abodes the appearance of grated prison doors or windows, reminding us of the cave dwellers of Arizona and New Mexico.[32]

Although most trade occurred on the plains, some daring *Comancheros* slipped onto the reservations in western Oklahoma and "corrupted" the agency dwellers. In 1870, Lawrie Tatum, the Quaker agent on the Comanche-Kiowa Reservation, charged that his wards were well supplied with guns and ammunition by New Mexican traders who encouraged them to "steal from Texas."[33] The following year, a *Comanchero* party visited a Kiowa camp northwest of the Wichita Mountains, bartered arms, ammunition, whisky, and sugar for "stock and robes," and then urged the Kiowas "to go to Texas and steal cattle." Although the New Mexicans offered to pay liberally, the Kiowas, in an unprecedented display of virtue, rejected the proposal.[34]

Other traders, in the absence of a prearranged rendezvous, depended entirely upon chance and their skill as plainsmen to locate their nomadic customers. Vicente Romero, reflecting on his days as a young trader from Cordova, stated that because the Indians were always following the buffalo, "we never knew where we could

---

[31] Other trading sites were in the *Cañon del Rescate* (Yellowhouse Canyon) above present Lubbock, *Las Lenguas* Creek (the Pease River), *Las Tecovas* (a spring northwest of Amarillo), and McClellan Creek. Haley, "Comanchero Trade," *loc. cit.*, 164.

[32] Robert G. Carter, *On the Border with Mackenzie*, 161.

[33] "Report of Lawrie Tatum, July 20, 1870," in *Annual Report of the Commissioner of Indian Affairs*, 1870, 264.

[34] George H. Smith to Enoch Hoag, February 3, 1871, enclosed with Hoag to the Commissioner of Indian Affairs, February 20, 1871, H/249, Kiowa Agency, OIA, LR, RG 75, NA.

find them." On one trip, his party had to go "here or there" over the plains looking for Indian signs until they found a fresh trail. After tracing it to the vicinity of the Indian village, the traders set up camp at a convenient water supply, unpacked their trade goods, and sent up "a smoke signal" to announce their presence. When they awoke the next morning, they were "surrounded by a large group" of Comanches busily making camp.[35] Not all traders found the Indians: in June, 1871, the *Daily New Mexican* reported that some parties which had gone to the plains to trade had returned without "effecting their object."[36]

Once among the Indians, the traders might remain for several days or even weeks before completing their transactions. According to Romero, a *Comanchero* at the age of eighteen, the trading was preceded by a "sort of feast" and athletic contests such as archery matches, wrestling bouts, and horse races, all accompanied by vigorous wagering. With his favorite hunting horse, Romero added "considerably" to his "store of goods" by winning "six out of about nine races."[37] Herman Lehmann, a white captive who for many years was a full-fledged Comanche warrior, recounted the Indian side of the meetings: "we traded, horse-raced, gambled and had a good time while they got all we had, and then we left them, to rob the palefaces."[38]

After the festivities, the bartering began in earnest, with the *Comancheros* usually getting the better of the transactions. Clinton Smith, another white captive of the Comanches, recalled that "those fool Indians would let the Mexicans pick their mules for a keg of whiskey; ten pounds of coffee was accepted for a pack horse, five pounds of tobacco would get a mule, and a buffalo robe would be exchanged for little or nothing."[39] Cattle were equally as cheap. The *Daily New Mexican* reported in 1871 that a "burro

[35] Vicente Romero to L. B. Brown, interview, April 6, 1937, MS, New Mexico Historical Museum Library, Santa Fe.
[36] *Daily New Mexican*, June 6, 1871.
[37] Romero to Brown, interview, April 6, 1937.
[38] Jonathan H. Jones, *A Condensed History of the Apache and Comanche Indians Prepared from the General Conversation of Herman Lehmann, Willie Lehmann, Mrs. Mina Keyser, Mrs. A. J. Buchmeyer and Others*, 165.
[39] Hunter, *op. cit.*, 58.

load" of powder, caps, lead, and biscuits would secure quite a herd of cattle, and Superintendent Norton stated that a man from Santa Fe had taken goods worth about $150 to the plains and returned with one hundred head of Texas cattle.[40]

Pueblo traders, whose "biscuits made for that purpose" were still in great demand as trade goods, competed vigorously for Texas cattle. According to Herman Lehmann, the Pueblos were especially esteemed by the Comanches because they paid "a good price" for cattle and were completely trustworthy. "We could send by these fellows" for whatever was needed, he said, and they were always "faithful to their promises."[41]

Although whisky, for which Indians would reportedly "give the robes off their backs . . . on the coldest winter day,"[42] enabled traders to get cattle even cheaper, taking it to an Indian camp created an explosive situation. Lehmann matter-of-factly recalled that while his party was trading three thousand head of cattle to some New Mexicans, a fight broke out in which the Comanches killed two traders and "raised their scalps on a pole." After that, the Indians "drank all the whiskey, ran off the Mexicans," and kept all their trinkets, guns, and ammunition.[43]

To avoid similar incidents and to guard against an unpleasant Comanche penchant for retaking cattle already sold, one group of *Comancheros* promised the Indians kegs of whisky hidden several miles away as a bonus for good behavior. After the purchased cattle were well on the road to New Mexico, a trader who

---

[40] *Daily New Mexican*, April 20, 1871; "Report of A. B. Norton, July 31, 1866," *loc. cit.*, 191. In another oft-quoted observation on the trade, Norton stated that "when no cattle or horses are found in the Comanche camp by the Mexican traders, they lend the Indians their horses and pistols and remain at camp until the Comanches have time to go to Texas and return, and get the stock they desire." *Annual Report of the Commissioner of Indian Affairs*, 1867, 191. This statement, however, is unreliable because it was lifted almost verbatim from a report by P. H. Healy, who was deliberately seeking to discredit his New Mexican competitors. Healy to the Commissioner of Indian Affairs, July 31, 1867, N/142, N. Mex. Supt., OIA, LR, RG 75, NA.

[41] Jones, *op. cit.*, 198-99.

[42] "Report of H. T. Ketcham, April 10, 1864," *loc. cit.*, 401.

[43] Jones, *op. cit.*, 41.

had remained behind pointed out the liquor and raced swiftly away before his hosts had drunk enough to become vicious.[44]

While carrying on their illicit barter, the *Comancheros* on rare occasions ran afoul of vengeful Texans. In the summer of 1870, a party of traders arriving from the plains reported that a body of "Texan rangers" had trailed a stolen cattle herd to a Comanche camp in which there were some New Mexicans. Surprising the village, the Texans killed all the Indians and traders except a Pueblo native from San Juan, "who mounted a swift horse and dashed through the Texan line" to safety. In announcing this massacre, the *Daily New Mexican* admonished the *Comancheros* that if they continued to encourage the Comanches "to kill the Texans and steal their stock," they should expect no mercy when caught by the embattled ranchers.[45]

The traders needed no reminder, however, to be on the alert. One aged veteran recalled that "we rounded up the cattle at night by the light of the moon and we drove them on a fast run," leaving behind the animals too weak to keep up. Sometimes, he added, a party of Comanches would stay behind to repulse any *Tejano* pursuers.[46] Two other traders, José Medina and Vicente Romero, independently stated that the Comanches provided two- or three-day escorts for cattle en route to New Mexico.[47]

Much of the trouble with the Texans undoubtedly stemmed from *Comanchero* participation in the cattle raids. Texas rancher John Hittson stated in 1873 that the Comanche marauders "not infrequently" were accompanied by Mexican traders who were "much more savage and expert than the Indians themselves."[48] About one hundred "Comanches" who charged through a trail

---

[44] James East, "Recollections," MS, Panhandle-Plains Historical Museum Library, Canyon, Texas, 1926.
[45] *Daily New Mexican*, July 30, 1870. The "Texan rangers" in question were probably a party of Texas cowmen, for the Texas Rangers had not yet been reorganized after the Civil War.
[46] Cabeza de Baca, *op. cit.*, 49.
[47] Deposition of José Medina, June 26, 1893, Indian Depredation Case No. 9133, Records of the U.S. Court of Claims, RG 123, NA; Romero to Brown, interview, April 6, 1937.
[48] *Rocky Mountain News* (Denver), April 29, 1873.

The Great Comanchero Cattle Trade

camp northwest of Fort Bascom in 1866 were shouting to one another in such good Spanish that the herders were positive that many of them were Mexicans.[49] Herman Lehmann remembered a raid in which a party of 60 New Mexicans and 140 Comanches captured a cattle herd west of Fort Griffin and beat off a counterattack by 40 whites.[50] About ten or twelve "Mexicans in Indian disguise" captured a few miles north of Fort Stockton in 1868 were held for some time before being released.[51]

In the best-known case involving New Mexican cattle thieves, troops from Fort Concho on a routine patrol in 1872 discovered that some apparent Indian thieves were New Mexicans. Polonio Ortiz, who was captured in this encounter, revealed that he was one of fifteen New Mexicans regularly employed to steal cattle in Texas.[52] Numerous other parties probably made similar trips to the Texas cattle ranges.

Most of the raids, however, were the work of the Comanches, who arrogantly denuded the Texas frontier with incredible ease. One of the depredators boasted to Captain Bergmann in 1866 that "it will not pay to go any longer to Texas for those people have already been robbed poor."[53] Instead of slackening off, however, the Indians stepped up their pillaging. After a visit to the Comanche camps in 1867, Lorenzo Labadi reported that the Indians had Texas cattle "without number" and that at the time no less than eighteen parties were out on forays along the frontier.[54]

A favorite target of the raiders was the Pecos Trail. In 1867, A. M. Adams, a beef contractor for the military garrison at Fort Sumner, lost three separate herds along the trail. His herds, he complained, were attacked "before they had crossed the state

[49] Major H. B. Bristol to Lt. Charles Porter, July 14, 1866, printed in the *Santa Fe Weekly Gazette*, July 28, 1866.
[50] Jones, *op. cit.*, 41.
[51] Testimony of Louis Johnson, December 4, 1877, in "Texas Border Troubles," 45 Cong., 2 Sess., *House Misc. Doc. No. 64*, 136.
[52] Post Medical Records, Fort Concho, Vol. 401, 259, Adjutant General's Office (cited hereafter as AGO), RG 94, NA.
[53] Bergmann to DeForrest, August 11, 1866, Dist. of N. Mex., Fort Bascom, LS, Book 82, 103, Army Commands, RG 98, NA.
[54] "Report of Lorenzo Labadi, August 23, 1867," in *Annual Report of the Commissioner of Indian Affairs*, 1867, 215.

A History of New Mexican–Plains Indian Relations

line" by armed bands of Kiowa and Comanche Indians, the herdsmen killed or driven away, and 2,449 head of cattle captured. Government officials presented Adams' claim for damages to the Comanches "in council," and they, quite surprisingly (for any recompense he received would be deducted from their annuity allotments), admitted their guilt.[55]

A single band of 75 Comanches on June 30, 1868, captured 900 cattle at Independence Springs, just below the New Mexico line; on the following day, at the same place, they took 1,100 head from "Thomas & Slater" and 1,000 more from "another party." In addition, they were assumed to be the same group which a few days earlier had escaped with John Chisum's herd of 1,100 head farther down the Pecos Trail.[56] Thus within a week this band alone had netted approximately 4,100 cattle, an average of more than 50 per person.

The Comanches were equally adept at seizing stock on the open range. The *San Antonio Express* in 1871, under the heading "More Raids—Indians in Force—What Texas is Coming to," reported an encounter twelve miles from Fort Concho between some Texas cowboys and a party of Comanches who had been discovered with a herd of eight hundred cattle. The cattlemen "let in upon the savages and a fierce fight ensued on the spot known as the Devils-court-house," but—outnumbered thirty to nine—they were driven off. Shocked by the boldness of the Indians, the *Express* complained:

> Instead of coming in, in twos or threes, and skulking through the country, stealing under cover of night, the reds come boldly in, in force.... The stockraisers and cow hunters are not safe from them unless they band together and hunt their stock in large parties.[57]

Although the military officers at Fort Concho strove desperately to protect the cattle herds in their vicinity and along the

---

[55] A. M. Adams, "Memorial to Senate Committee on Appropriations Concerning His Claim Against Comanches and Kiowas" (n.d.), A/966/1873, Kiowa Agency, OIA, RG 75, NA.
[56] *Daily New Mexican*, July 20, 1868.
[57] *San Antonio Express*, April 8, 1871.

Pecos Trail, they were handicapped by a lack of manpower. After a small detachment of cavalry had safely escorted a herd of 1,500 to Horsehead Crossing in July, 1872, the Indians captured it twenty-three miles upstream, killing three of the drovers. Four days later, on July 13, another band, after stampeding a herd of 2,600 head twelve miles west of Fort Concho, eluded a pursuit by forty-five cavalrymen. Major John Hatch, commanding the fort, reported on July 15 that because of the troop shortage, several thousand cattle were there awaiting escort and that within a few days there would be 10,000 more.[58] Ironically, Colonel Mackenzie at the time had most of the post's garrison in Blanco Canyon two hundred miles to the north—looking for cattle thieves.

While these raids were occurring on the Pecos Trail, a band of forty Comanches attacked Jesse Hittson, the seventeen-year-old son of John Hittson, and his ten-man roundup crew near present Ballinger. Although the cowboys stood off the Indians in a four-hour battle, the marauders escaped with seven hundred cattle, all of the herd except one lone heifer. Young Hittson, with a slightly embittered sense of humor, promptly branded the survivor: "7-11-72 Indians Thick as Hell J. H."[59]

For every herd taken by force on the sparsely settled Texas frontier, the Indians probably escaped undetected with a dozen. John Hittson stated that it was "comparatively easy" for the Comanches to steal cattle unobserved and that it was not uncommon to strike a trail made by herds being driven toward the Staked Plains.[60] The Texans learned by costly experience that the Comanches were adept *vaqueros*.

Unfortunately, the Comanches did not limit their crimes against the Texans to cattle rustling. At times their uninhibited tastes led them to steal things verging on the ridiculous: a party raiding a ranch above Fredericksburg in 1869 took a mare, the

[58] Major John Hatch to the Asst. Adj. Gen., Dept. of Texas, July 15, 1872, filed under M/350, Dist. of N. Mex., LR, Army Commands, RG 98, NA.
[59] Testimony of Jesse Hittson, November 2, 1899, Indian Depredation Case No. 6501, R. F. Tankersly v. U.S. and Kiowa and Comanche Indians, Records of the U.S. Court of Claims, RG 123, NA.
[60] *Rocky Mountain News*, April 29, 1873.

clothes from the clothesline, and "one of the bee hives."[61] More often, however, the raiders left a trail of murders, rapes, and kidnapings. A brief notice in the *San Antonio Express* hints at the heart-rending tragedies that occurred in scores of Texas communities:

> Taken from my house by the Indians in Legion valley, Llano County, Texas, on Wednesday, Feb. 5, 1868, my son Lee Temple Friend, aged eight years, black eyes, light hair and fair complexion: also my neighbor's daughter, Malinda Caudle, aged seven, blue eyes, fair complexion and light hair. All Indian agents or traders or any person having an opportunity, are requested to rescue the above named children; and delivering them to me or notifying me of their whereabouts will be liberally remunerated.
>
> Jno S. Friend.[62]

Friend had been absent during the attack in which the Indians, in addition to kidnaping the two children, had brutally killed a three-month-old infant, a sixteen-year-old girl, and two neighbor women. The sole survivor of the massacre was Mrs. Friend, who in a desperate hand-to-hand struggle was slashed across one hand, wounded in the arm, pierced with an arrow through the breast, and scalped. Before leaving her for dead, an Indian pushed the arrow in her breast "up and down" several times. She did not flinch. Despite having to wait two days for a doctor, the victim recovered and five years later greeted her son Lee Temple when, "completely Indianized," he was finally rescued.[63] Most families were not so fortunate.

Deeply moved by these atrocities, the New Mexican papers vied with one another in denouncing the *Comancheros* for instigating the raids. In 1870, the *Daily New Mexican* charged that the traders were the "strongest incentives" for the marauding and murdering expeditions and that they must share the responsibility for the bloodshed and misery inflicted on the Texans.[64] In

[61] *San Antonio Express*, January 18, 1869.
[62] *Ibid.*, March 24, 1868.
[63] Joseph C. McConnell, *The West Texas Frontier*, II, 217-18; Carl C. Rister, *Border Captives*, 143-47.
[64] *Daily New Mexican*, July 18, 1870.

similar fashion, the *Republican Review* described the trade as "pandering to red murderers and thieves."[65] Even more violent, the *Santa Fe Weekly Post* proclaimed that the *Comancheros* should "be shot down like so many dangerous dogs." They are worse, it declared, "than the savages whom they aid."[66]

The native New Mexicans, however, were little bothered by the outrages which horrified the Anglo press. Living in a society where life was cheap and the very term *Tejano* was so odious that mothers hushed their little ones with the threat "I'll give you to the Tejanos,"[67] few even thought about the distant depredations. The *Daily New Mexican*, despite its hostility toward the *Comancheros*, recognized that the typical trader, "thoughtless and ignorant," did not

> consider or realize the terrible character of his trade, or the misery, suffering or death produced by his course. In other cases, long familiarity with such scenes and such thoughts has blunted his sensibilities and . . . he is thoughtless or reckless of the fact that he is in a great measure responsible for the deaths of the slain owners of the scalps, and the captivity of those to whom death were preferable.[68]

[65] *Republican Review* (Albuquerque), July 30, 1870.
[66] *Santa Fe Weekly Post*, June 17, 1871.
[67] Miguel Otero, *My Life on the Frontier, 1864-1882*, 63.
[68] *Daily New Mexican*, July 18, 1870. The contemporary press was inaccurate in blaming the *Comancheros* exclusively for gun and liquor running and for instigating the Comanche raids. Anglo traders, based in Kansas and the Chickasaw Nation, introduced large quantities of whisky to the Indians and sold them guns and ammunition. In 1867, for example, General Sherman complained that Charles Rath, operating out of Fort Zarah, Kansas, had armed the Kiowas with revolvers and had "completely overstocked" them with powder. Sherman to Grant, January 26, 1867, quoted in Carl C. Rister, *The Southwestern Frontier, 1865-1881*, 81. At the outset of the Red River War of 1874, Thomas C. Battey, a gentle Quaker schoolmaster, observed that the licensed traders for the Cheyennes were selling pistols and ammunition to all of the southern Plains Indians. Thomas C. Battey, *The Life and Adventures of a Quaker Among the Indians*, 260-61. In making their raids on Texas, the Comanches, although stimulated by their desire to obtain cattle for the New Mexican market, were also motivated by their passion for horses, glory, status, scalps, and revenge. They also stole cattle for food. Those who took A. M. Adams' cattle in 1867 admitted the following year that from the time of the raid they had been living on the captured stock and still had a "few in their possession." Adams, "Memorial to Senate Committee on Appropriations," (n.d.), A/966/1873, Kiowa Agency, OIA, LR, RG 75, NA.

A History of New Mexican–Plains Indian Relations

Most *Comancheros*, however, reflected not at all on such abstract matters as the degree of their guilt. They simply saw nothing wrong in the trade, as Julian Baca, an old contrabandist testifying in one of Charles Goodnight's claims cases, exemplified in a disconcerting courtroom confrontation with a government attorney:

> *Attorney:* Do you mean to say you bought stolen cattle?
> *Baca:* Didn't matter to us whether they were stolen or not, we were buying cattle.
> *Attorney:* Did you belong to a church at that time?
> *Baca:* Yes sir, I was a Catholic and am now.
> *Attorney:* Did you think it right to deal in stolen cattle?
> *Baca:* For me it was right because I gave my money for it.[69]

The attorney changed the subject. The few *Comancheros* who rationalized their vocation claimed that the Comanches stole cattle primarily "as a means of revenge against the Texan cattle owners who were moving into their lands."[70] This statement, not entirely devoid of truth, suggests that the common dislike of Texans may have strengthened the traditionally friendly ties between the Comanches and New Mexicans.

The successful *Comanchero* returned to his village to receive unabashedly the acclaims of his townsmen. According to the *Daily New Mexican*, he was regarded as "a good citizen," respected, and trusted by his neighbors.[71] Vicente Romero stated that traders returning to Cordova proudly discharged their firearms at the crest of the ridge overlooking the hamlet to salute its patron saint and to announce their arrival. Longingly, the old *Comanchero's* mind drifted back through the years:

> The closer we got to our homes the more we pushed our poor horses ... Soon we were firing our firearms in the Salvo to San Antonio. We could see the people on the roof-tops counting us as we rode down into the village to see who were missing. My poor mother cried with joy to see me back safe. The next few days were filled

---

[69] Testimony of Julian Baca, June 26, 1893, Indian Depredation Case No. 9133, Records of the U.S. Court of Claims, RG 123, NA.
[70] Cabeza de Baca, *op. cit.*, 47.
[71] *Daily New Mexican*, July 18, 1870.

with feasting and the nights with dancing. Blessed be God; those were the times.[72]

Less colorful than the *Comancheros* but equally indispensable to the success of the cattle trade were the merchants who backed them. Although these profiteers were at times castigated by the authorities, they were never subjected to effective punitive action. In 1870, Captain Horace Jewett, the last and the most ingenious commander at Fort Bascom, charged that the chief instigators of the cattle trade were "wealthy and prominent" Mexicans who furnished the supplies, "taking no risks themselves of apprehension, but the lion's share of the profit."[73] Like Jewett, Texas rancher John Hittson firmly believed that those most responsible for the depredations were merchants "who occupy prominent and responsible" positions in the government.[74]

Few of the financiers can be identified, but it is likely that a large proportion of the merchants of northeastern New Mexico, including the Anglos, dabbled in the lucrative trade. Although perhaps not a typical case, John Watts in 1867, one year before he was appointed to the Territorial Supreme Court, received a conditional license to trade with the Comanches.[75]

The merchants evidently paid the *Comancheros* comparatively little for the stolen cattle. Although Manuel Gonzales, who bought cattle for many years, testified in a claims case that he paid the *Comancheros* as much as twenty dollars a head,[76] he may have deliberately exaggerated the figure to help the claimant obtain a better settlement from the government. One old trader vehemently complained that "we gained little from the trade, as the Americans to whom we sold the cattle paid us low prices for them."[77] John Hittson, who on his many cattle drives through

[72] Romero to Brown, interview, April 6, 1937.
[73] Jewett to the Asst. Adj. Gen., August 25, 1870, Dist. of N. Mex., Fort Bascom, LS, Book 144, 139, Army Commands, RG 98, NA.
[74] *Rocky Mountain News*, April 29, 1873.
[75] A. B. Norton to N. G. Taylor, February 20, 1867, N/20, N. Mex. Supt., OIA, LR, RG 75, NA.
[76] Deposition of Manuel Gonzales, June 26, 1893, Indian Depredation Case No. 9133, Records of the U.S. Court of Claims, RG 123, NA.
[77] Cabeza de Baca, *op. cit.*, 48.

New Mexico had ample occasion to observe the trade, estimated in 1873 that the traders turned their cattle over to the merchants "at a total cost of say two dollars a head."[78] As a result of these low prices, the merchants in 1866 were able to sell dressed beef at ten cents a pound, an all-time low.[79]

The size of the trade is also hard to judge. Charles Goodnight was positive that more than 300,000 head of Texas cattle had been run off between 1860 and 1867, yet Hittson, equally familiar with the commerce, estimated in 1873 that only 100,000 head had been stolen during the preceding twenty years.[80] The larger estimate probably was more accurate. In 1871, the *Daily New Mexican* stated that its "informant" reported that more than 30,000 cattle had been brought into New Mexico by the Comanche traders during the *last three months*. Charging that more than 1,000 persons were currently engaged in the trade, the paper predicted that since the "people on the Pecos have almost entirely neglected their ranches for this more profitable traffic, . . . the consequence will be a scarcity of bread stuffs this year."[81]

Despite the condemnation heaped upon the great *Comanchero* cattle trade, it received a few indirect plaudits. The United States Census of 1880, for example, contained a terse and unusual description of the commerce:

> The Indians east and northeast of the Llano Estacado were killing the western pioneer stockmen of Texas and stealing their herds. Stockmen from New Mexico fitted out expeditions into the dangerous country and purchased the herds. Many thousand cattle were thus secured for New Mexico, especially for the northeastern section. This constituted an *important advance* in the New Mexican stock occupation.[82]

---

[78] *Rocky Mountain News*, April 29, 1873.
[79] *Daily New Mexican*, July 14, 1866.
[80] J. Evetts Haley, *Charles Goodnight, Cowman & Plainsman*, 194; Hittson to Veale, February 23, 1873, printed in the *Daily New Mexican*, March 21, 1873.
[81] *Daily New Mexican*, May 24, 1871.
[82] Clarence Gordon, "Report on Cattle, Sheep, and Swine," in *Tenth Census of the United States*, 1880, III, 989.

The Great Comanchero Cattle Trade

Apparently, this was the way the *Comancheros* and their customers wished to see their trade remembered.

While encouraging the Comanches to steal Texas cattle, the *Comancheros* were also bolstering their resistance to the Americans. J. R. Mead, an official interpreter, reported in 1866 that the Kwahadi Comanches, living on the eastern borders of the Staked Plains, were under the influence of New Mexican traders. The Kwahadis "don't care anything about goods or presents," he complained, "because they can get all they want from the Mexicans." He also pointed out that the refusal of the Kwahadis to make peace had "a bad effect on the young men of the other tribes who see with what impunity these fellows escape."[83] Comanche Agent Leavenworth also observed that the Kwahadis, who were the only "ones who are giving . . . the whites any trouble," would be obliged to "come in and make peace" if the New Mexicans could be stopped from trading with them.[84] But the *Comancheros* could not be stopped, and the Kwahadis would not submit until their power was finally crushed in the Red River War of 1874.

[83] Mead to Thomas Murphy, September 7, 1866, M/724, Kiowa Agency, OIA, LR, RG 75, NA.
[84] Leavenworth to Cooley, June 5, 1866, L/54, *ibid.*

9
The Suppression of the Comanchero Cattle Trade, 1867–1872

FOR TWO YEARS FOLLOWING THE CIVIL WAR, almost nothing was done to combat the *Comanchero* commerce. General Carleton soon lifted his restrictions of early 1865, and both he and Indian Superintendent Felipe Delgado issued permits on a generous scale. Moreover, some frontier military officers, as has already been noted, were quite likely engaged in the traffic. Even Superintendent Norton's well-publicized revocation of all extant trading licenses in mid-1866 had little effect because Pueblo Agent John D. Henderson obstinately continued to issue permits.

Henderson's actions went unchallenged until January, 1867, when Major A. J. Alexander, upon replacing Captain Bergmann as commander at Fort Bascom, complained that Pueblo Indians bearing permits signed by the agent were "constantly passing" and asked for instructions on dealing with them.[1] Seven weeks and many conferences later, Lieutenant General William Tecumseh Sherman, head of the Division of the Missouri, belatedly advised the New Mexican officers to confiscate all livestock obtained illicitly by traders. "Have all parties traveling to and from the plains report at Fort Bascom," he suggested, and if "new horses" are found with returning traders, "presumption can be made they were... bought of thieves."[2]

Upon receiving Sherman's "solution," Carleton dourly commented that he lacked sufficient troops to force traders to report at Fort Bascom and that, in the absence of a specific statute authorizing his action, an officer who confiscated cattle from the

[1] Alexander to DeForrest, January 26, 1867, B/10, Dist. of N. Mex., LR, Army Commands, RG 98, NA.
[2] *Ibid.*, The endorsements of Carleton and the other officers completely cover the letter.

The Suppression of the Comanchero Cattle Trade, 1867-1872

traders "could be sued in every court in New Mexico."[3] This unduly cautious attitude perhaps explains why so little was done to stop the trade while Carleton commanded the District of New Mexico.

The controversy stirred up by Alexander's request, however, did lead to an end of the practice of licensing *Comancheros*. Upon learning of Henderson's actions, the military officials in Washington lodged a formal protest with the Office of Indian Affairs. Soon afterward, Indian Commissioner Nathaniel Taylor ordered Superintendent Norton to recall all outstanding permits and to forbid Henderson's issuing others "under any circumstances."[4] No longer able to obtain passes, many *Comancheros* attempted to keep their commerce legal by purchasing bogus permits from Charles Jennings and his cronies. Upon the strength of these, they traded at a brisk pace throughout the summer of 1867.

The garrison at Fort Bascom, almost as if intimidated by the forbidding wastes which surrounded it, paid little attention to the trade. Early in the year, a patrol led by a guide "who knew nothing of the country" lost its way on the Llano Estacado and wandered aimlessly for fifty-two waterless hours before reaching safety.[5] As a result, subsequent detachments usually steered clear of the trackless expanses over which the *Comancheros* were moving their illicit cattle.

Despite their feeble attempts at patroling, the troops managed to catch a handful of liquor runners who passed too near the post. The *Comancheros* were immediately turned over to the civil authorities, but United States District Attorney Stephen B. Elkins, later to serve West Virginia as a United States senator for nineteen years, was unable to secure an indictment. The district judge ordered that the traders be released and their confiscated whisky returned, doubtlessly with an apology for the inconvenience caused them.[6] This lack of judicial co-operation was to be a han-

[3] *Ibid.*
[4] Taylor to Norton, April 13, 1867, OIA, LS, Vol. 82, 566, RG 75, NA.
[5] Alexander to DeForrest, January 12, 1867, B/5, Dist. of N. Mex., LR, Army Commands, RG 98, NA.
[6] Maj. Gen. George Sykes to Elkins, April 28, 1867, Dist. of N. Mex., LS, Vol.

dicap which the military would never completely overcome in its efforts to stop cattle smuggling.

A speedup in patrol activities was presaged in July by the replacement of Carleton as district commander by Colonel George Washington Getty. Soon after his arrival, Getty established "picket posts" at Hubbell's Ranch and at the intersection of the Fort Smith Road and the trail connecting Forts Bascom and Sumner.[7] His innovation brought quick results, for the detachment at the crossroads almost immediately intercepted several New Mexican traders "on their way to the Comanche Indians," confiscated their improperly endorsed permits, and forced them to return to the settlements.[8] A few days later, a patrol from Fort Bascom overtook another caravan of traders about sixty miles below the post. Although the New Mexicans lacked a permit of any type, they tried to escape arrest by asserting that "others of their band on before had the legal papers." The troops, however, escorted them to the fort, where Captain George L. Letterman, the commander, inventoried their trade goods:

> About 200 pounds of corn meal—500 of Mex. Hard Bread, 35 or 40 butcher knives—9 files—Vermillion—a lot of shirts, Some red and white flannel—one vest—Some iron hoops, Ducking and Calico—shelled corn—tea—sugar—flour—*letter paper*—candy—one regalia—one box of army caps (100), about 400 percussion caps (small)—

43, 156, Army Commands, RG 98, NA; Elkins to DeForrest, May 18, 1867, E/8, Dist. of N. Mex., LR, *ibid.*

[7] DeForrest to DuBois, August 16, 1867, Dist. of N. Mex., LS, Vol. 43, 253, Army Commands, RG 98, NA. The crossroads was about twenty-five miles southwest of Fort Bascom; Hubbell's Ranch was twenty-five miles farther south on the edge of the Llano. It had been established in 1865 by Charles Hubbell, another of the motley collection of officers who served in eastern New Mexico near the close of the war. Hubbell, perhaps buying beef of the *Comancheros*, was a leading contractor for the military until April, 1867, when some cattle stolen from Fort Bascom were tracked to his ranch. Since he thereupon fled the country, his ranch quarters were available for use as an army subdepot. Letterman to DeForrest, April 24, 1867, Dist. of N. Mex., Fort Bascom, LS, Book 82, p. 21, Army Commands, RG 98, NA.

[8] Hilderbun to DuBois, August 22, 1867, B/121, LR, *ibid.*

The Suppression of the Comanchero Cattle Trade, 1867-1872

several pounds of lead—about 5 pounds of powder—16 elongated balls calab. 58[9]

This was not such a sinister lot of merchandise—no whisky, no arms, and a surprisingly small quantity of munitions. Captain Letterman released the traders in order to avoid having "to supply them rations," but he kept their trade goods pending further instructions.

A few days later, two soldiers from the picket on the Fort Smith Road arrived at the fort with eighty-two head of cattle taken from another party of *Comancheros* who had been released because they carried "papers" issued by Charles Jennings. After carefully recording their brands, Letterman impounded the animals. Other captures followed, so that by September 11 the troops were holding more than eight hundred head of stock.[10]

The disposition of the captured cattle posed a ticklish problem. Superintendent Norton and Colonel Getty decided the animals should be returned to their legal owners "upon the presentation of satisfactory proof." Although they went so far as to publicize the brands in the "best advertising medium" in Texas,[11] few, if any, of the animals were returned to their owners. Charles Goodnight, en route to Colorado with a cattle herd, visited Fort Bascom and estimated that 250 head there had been stolen from him, but the officers, Goodnight stated years later, refused to surrender his cattle because he lacked "legal authority to receive them."[12]

Any chance that the cattle would be returned was soon demolished by a crushing judicial setback. At the fall session of

---

[9] Letterman to DeForrest, August 31, 1867, Dist. of N. Mex., Fort Bascom, LS, Book 82, pp. 12-13, Army Commands, RG 98, NA.

[10] Letterman to DeForrest, September 7, 1867, *ibid.*, p. 21.

[11] Charles Mix to Evans, October 3, 1867, OIA, LS, Vol. 84, 379, RG 75, NA; Mix to Norton, October 4, 1867, N. Mex. Supt., LR, OIA, RG 75, NA.

[12] Haley, *op. cit.*, 194. Apparently relying upon Goodnight's memory, Haley states that the troops had captured "seventy-three hundred" head of cattle, as compared to the eight hundred which the military records report. Goodnight also recalled that he went into court at Las Vegas to recover six hundred of his cattle which he had located on the Gallinas River. Although he was confident that he had proved his case, he was defeated, had to pay the court costs, and "felt lucky to get out of the place alive."

the United States District Court in Las Vegas, charges were brought against several *Comancheros* for "trading with the Comanche Indians without a license." The lawyers for the defendants blandly contended that New Mexico was completely exempt from the federal trade regulations because they had been passed before it became a part of the United States and no subsequent legislation had ever specifically extended coverage to it. Readily accepting this specious line of reasoning, Judge J. P. Slough ruled that there was *"no Indian Country* in New Mexico within the meaning of the act of 1834," quashed the charges against the *Comancheros,* and ordered the return to them of the confiscated cattle.[13] United States Attorney General Henry Stanberry, angered at this highhanded negation of the Indian trade laws, hastily instructed Elkins to appeal the case to the Territorial Supreme Court, and, if necessary, to the United States Supreme Court.[14] Fortunately, the obnoxious ruling was reversed and the trade laws were applied to New Mexico without question.

Despite the judicial difficulties, the energetic actions of the military brought about a temporary decline in the *Comanchero* trade. In withdrawing his pickets on October 24, Captain Letterman stated that the "Comanche trade has entirely ceased."[15] José Tafoya later testified that he and several others stopped trading in 1867 because the troops "got after" them,[16] and Phillip McCusker, Comanche squawman and highly respected government interpreter, reported in early 1868 that the vigorous patrolling had "entirely broken up" the cattle trade. Because the New Mexicans had ceased trading with the Comanches, McCusker added, the Indians lacked a market for Texas cattle and consequently stole only "such as they needed for subsistence."[17] Cor-

[13] S. B. Elkins to Henry Stanberry, October 1, 1867, Records of the Attorney General's Office, LR, New Mexico, RG 60, NA.

[14] Stanberry to Elkins, November 23, 1867, in *Annual Report of the Commissioner of Indian Affairs,* 1867, 222.

[15] Letterman to Lt. Edwin Hunter, October 24, 1867, Dist. of N. Mex., Fort Bascom, LS, Book 82, pp. 33-34, Army Commands, RG 98, NA.

[16] Deposition of José Tafoya, June 26, 1893, Indian Depredation Case No. 9133, Records of the U.S. Court of Claims, RG 123, NA.

[17] McCusker to Leavenworth, April 6, 1868, Kiowa Agency, OIA, LR, RG 75, NA.

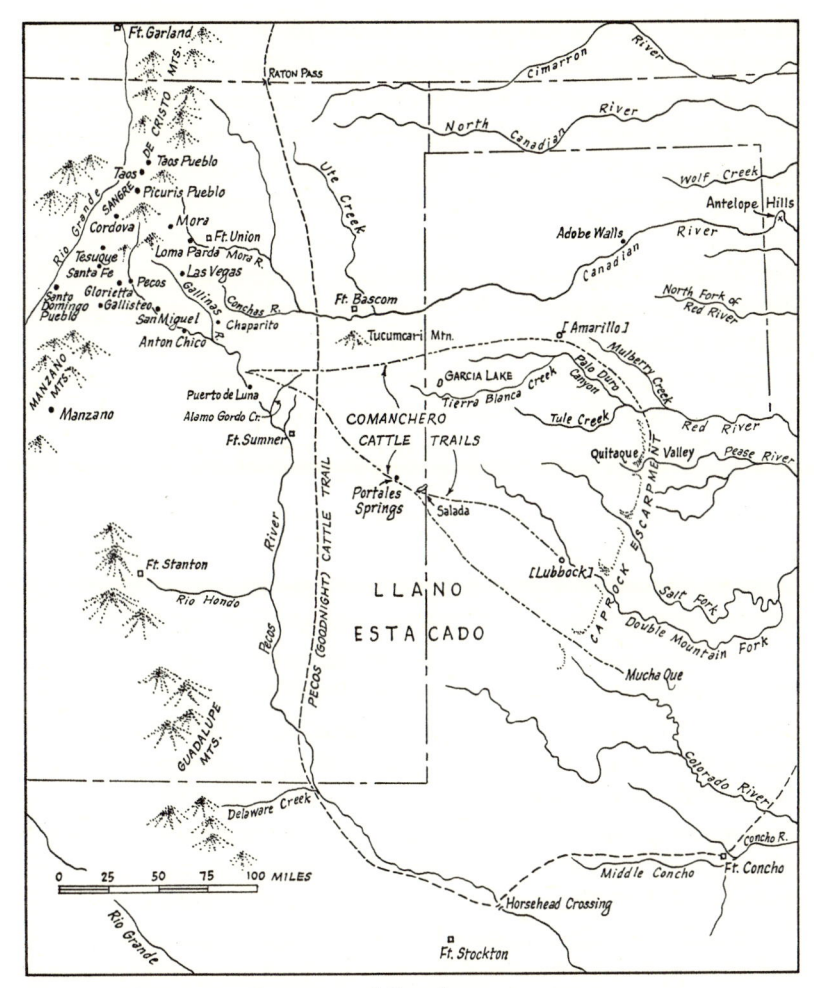

The Southwestern Frontier, 1865–1875.

roborating these statements was the military's failure to apprehend any contrabandists during the following two years.[18]

Not even General Philip Sheridan's extensive, three-pronged winter campaign of 1868–69 unearthed any signs of the *Comancheros*. Major A. W. Evans, in command of a column from Fort Bascom, marched down the Canadian to Monument Creek, near present Canadian, Texas, and then continued southeastward to the Wichita Mountains without encountering any traders. He did meet several parties of *ciboleros*, but found no indication that they had been trading with the Indians.[19]

Although Sheridan's campaign forced many of the Comanches to move onto the reservation in southwestern Oklahoma, the Kwahadis and part of the Kotsotekas clung tenaciously to their old haunts and to their ties with New Mexico. Apparently hoping to receive a reservation on the New Mexican frontier, they sent word to Fort Bascom in early 1869 that they would surrender to Colonel Getty.[20] However, Getty instructed them to follow Sheridan's orders and report to Fort Cobb in Indian Territory. Despite this rebuff, Mow-way, the leading Kotsoteka chief, and a number of other Comanche leaders traveled to Fort Bascom to press their case. The commander there sent them to Santa Fe, where on March 6 they conferred with Colonel Getty and Superintendent Norton. Becoming apprehensive during the night, the chiefs stole out of Santa Fe but were captured before they could reach the safety of the plains. After being held as prisoners for a few days at Fort Union, they were transported to Fort Cobb.[21] In this

[18] Some trade, however, undoubtedly continued. Some *Comancheros* probably used more southerly trade routes that were still unknown to the military. Others conceivably were able to slip undetected past the pickets. In 1868, for example, Captain Louis Morris, upset that a picket south of Fort Bascom had failed to detect a party of Comanche raiders, stated that the Indians "soon know where the picket is stationed and always go around it, and the picket knows nothing about them." This also probably held true for *Comancheros*. Morris to Hunter, September 26, 1868, Dist. of N. Mex., Fort Bascom, LS, Book 82, p. 104, Army Commands, RG 98, NA.

[19] Carl C. Rister (ed.), "Evans' Christmas Day Indian Fight," *Chronicles of Oklahoma*, XVI (September, 1938), 284.

[20] Major William Kobbe to Lt. Col. A. W. Evans, January 10, 1869, Dist. of N. Mex., LS, Vol. 46, 160, Army Commands, RG 98, NA.

[21] Getty to Brig. Gen. C. McKeever, March 13, 1869, *ibid.*, p. 213.

The Suppression of the Comanchero Cattle Trade, 1867-1872

ignominious way, another Comanche attempt to remain legally on the New Mexican frontier went for naught.

Well aware that the detention of the chiefs could provoke an Indian war, the frontier residents panicked when they learned that an Anglo and three New Mexicans had been killed at a saline east of Fort Bascom.[22] Fortunately, the assumption that the murders had been committed by a Comanche retaliatory party proved inaccurate. On March 16, the *Daily New Mexican* announced that the killings had been the work of Navahos seen "headed in that direction, intending, no doubt, to make their semi-occasional raid on the Comanche stock."[23] This assurance, however, did not dispel the anxiety of the frontiersmen. Vincent Colyer, who made an inspection tour of the region for the Indian Department in May, reported that the officers at Fort Bascom were still "considerably" upset about Getty's arrest of the chiefs and that the settlers on the frontier had "quite numerously signed" a petition for their release.[24]

Meanwhile, General Sheridan, apparently blaming the New Mexicans for the Kwahadis' refusal to move to the reservation, had authorized Colonel Getty to

> make every effort to break up and punish the bands of New Mexico traders who have been and are still trading for captured stock with hostile Indians: and if hereafter such traders are found at any point east of the eastern line of New Mexico their *goods will be burned and their stock killed*.[25]

By publishing copies of this order in the territorial newspapers and distributing Spanish translations at the settlements of eastern New Mexico, Getty may have kept many *Comancheros* from going to the plains. At any rate, none were apprehended during the remainder of the year.

[22] Capt. L. T. Morris to Hunter, March 11, 1869, Dist. of N. Mex., Fort Bascom, LS, Book 82, p. 194, Army Commands, RG 98, NA.
[23] *Daily New Mexican*, March 16, 1869.
[24] Vincent Colyer, "Report on Indians in Indian Territory, New Mexico, and Arizona, October 20, 1869," in *Annual Report of the Commissioner of Indian Affairs*, 1869, 88.
[25] Printed in the *Republican Review*, July 30, 1869.

By the spring of 1870, however, traders were again going to the east. In March, Captain Horace Jewett, the outspoken commander of Fort Bascom, noted that about twenty Mexicans and six Pueblos, posing as buffalo hunters, had been sighted about fifty miles east of the fort. Although convinced that the New Mexicans were illicit traders, Jewett did not send a patrol in pursuit because they had too much of a start.[26] Never slow to volunteer advice, he suggested that the *Comanchero* traffic could be stopped by commissioning private citizens to seize traders in return for their trade goods. With the aid of these vigilantes, he asserted, the trade could be made "too risky" to attempt.[27] Colonel Getty, however, was unwilling to entrust the enforcement of the trade laws to bounty hunters.

Dispatching instead an additional company of cavalry to the frontier, Getty in July ordered Jewett to reoccupy the intersection of the Fort Smith and Fort Sumner roads and advised him he was expected to "diminish if not break up" the illegal traffic.[28] An eighteen-man force stationed at the crossroads by Jewett captured two traders on August 19 and slaughtered their small herd of cattle. The following day, the patrol encountered a lone fugitive, a "colored man," who claimed he was a trooper who had been captured by the Indians in Texas and rescued by the two traders.[29] The patrol leader, however, suspected that he was a deserter in league with the two *Comancheros* and sent all three to Fort Bascom. From there, Jewett sent them to Santa Fe, where they were immediately freed.

In response to growing complaints from the military about the lack of civil co-operation, Governor William Pile on August 29 issued a proclamation ordering the officials of the eastern counties to "exercise their full authority" against the *Comanchero*

---

[26] Jewett to Kobbe, March 15, 1870, Dist. of N. Mex., Fort Bascom, LS, Book 144, p. 89, Army Commands, RG 98, NA.

[27] *Ibid.*

[28] Kobbe to Jewett, July 2, 1870, Dist. of N. Mex., LS, Vol. 45, 2, Army Commands, RG 98, NA.

[29] Jewett to Getty, August 25, 1870, Dist. of N. Mex., Fort Bascom, LS, Book 144, p. 39, *ibid.*

The Suppression of the Comanchero Cattle Trade, 1867-1872

traffic. Citizens were to co-operate by giving information to the officers at Fort Bascom and on the picket lines.[30] Publishing this proclamation with its full endorsement, the *Daily New Mexican* charged that the traders "knowingly and intentionally" promoted murder and robbery. Such men, it continued, "ought to be safely enclosed within the walls of a penitentiary."

In an economy move that greatly encouraged the traders, Fort Bascom was abandoned as a permanent fort in October, 1870. But just as the fort had been in existence under the name Camp Easton before its formal creation in 1863, it remained occupied for four years after its announced dismantling. Seven months a year, a noncommissioned officer and a handful of enlisted men took care of the buildings; each summer, however, under the designation "Summer Camp on the Canadian," its quarters reverberated with milling troops assigned to suppress the *Comancheros*.

In many respects, 1871 was the Indian Summer of the *Comanchero* commerce as traders, heartened by the evacuation of Fort Bascom, once again flocked to the plains. Soon after assuming his post as commander of the District of New Mexico, Colonel J. I. Gregg, taking note of the renewed interest in the trade, had Sheridan's order of 1869 relative to the burning of traders' supplies and the killing of their cattle read at each of the pueblos. He also pleaded with the Pueblo leaders to use their "influence and authority" to keep their young warriors from trading.[31]

Gregg's efforts were unavailing. By February, 1871, he was receiving reports that traders were moving toward the plains with large quantities of goods. At first the accounts were rather vague, but on March 15, Gregg learned from Major D. R. Clendenin, commander at Fort Union, that the caretaking detachment at Fort Bascom had reported burros and *carretas* passing "towards the Comanche Territory in considerable numbers every day." The eleven men at the fort, apprehensive for their own safety, did not dare to interfere. Numerous moccasin tracks, they stated, indi-

---

[30] *Daily New Mexican*, September 1, 1870.
[31] "Report of Nathaniel Pope, August 31, 1871," in *Annual Report of the Commissioner of Indian Affairs*, 1871, 802.

cated that Indians were constantly prowling around their post and even entering its buildings at night.[32]

In response to these developments, Gregg on March 29 ordered Major Clendenin to dispatch two companies of the Eighth Cavalry to patrol a long arc from Fort Union past Bascom to Fort Sumner. Frequent detachments moving along the route were to "pursue all Indian trails leading towards or from" the frontier settlements and to arrest and seize the property of any traders they discovered.[33] In mid-April, Gregg posted Captain James F. Randlett at Fort Bascom with a sizable detachment and stridently demanded results. When one of Randlett's directives failed to stress the importance of apprehending illicit traders, Gregg caustically upbraided him and again exhorted him to keep frequent patrols moving in different directions throughout the region.[34]

Having established the first comprehensive and effective patrol line, Gregg did not have to wait long for results. In early May, while Lieutenant Andrew Caraher was leading a large scout across the Llano south of Fort Bascom, an eleven-man patrol sent to "scour the country on his flank" spotted some traders with a large herd of cattle. With a surprising show of resistance, the *Comancheros* repulsed the small patrol and held off the main command for several minutes before being overpowered. They proved to be twenty-one Isleta Pueblos, armed with bows, muskets, and a demeanor so fierce that it shocked their captors: "They do not look like any Pueblos I ever saw."[35] Caraher had netted 10 ponies, 57 burros, and more than 700 head of cattle. In accordance with instructions, he began to shoot the cattle but, because of an ammunition shortage, stopped after only 250 head had been killed. He then took the prisoners and the remaining livestock to Fort Bascom.

[32] Clendenin to Gregg, March 15, 1871, U/23, Dist. of N. Mex., LR, Army Commands, RG 98, NA.

[33] Gregg to Clendenin, March 29, 1871, Dist. of N. Mex., LS, Vol. 45, 180, Army Commands, RG, 98, NA.

[34] Gregg to Randlett, April 18, 1871, *ibid.*, pp. 139–40.

[35] Clendenin to Lt. J. W. Pullman, May 13, 1871, U/48, Dist. of N. Mex., LR, Army Commands, RG 98, NA; *Daily New Mexican*, May 14, 1871.

The Suppression of the Comanchero *Cattle Trade, 1867-1872*

Before the *Comancheros* had time to recover from this blow, Captain Randlett, leading a patrol some fifty miles southwest of Hubbell's Ranch, overhauled a trading party en route to the plains and without a fight took 12 prisoners (11 New Mexicans and a Comanche woman who was serving as their guide) and 20 burros loaded with powder, lead, cloth, trinkets, and "fancy articles." After killing the burros, destroying the trade goods, and sending the prisoners to Fort Bascom, Randlett continued his scout. Discovering another party coming from the plains the next day, he captured only one of the *Comanchero* herdsmen but recovered 510 head of cattle, which, in accordance with the most recent instructions, he drove to the fort.[36]

In the wake of these captures, which foretold the impending end of the trade, wild stories of organized *Comanchero* resistance spread rapidly along the frontier. A rumor reached Fort Bascom that a large party of traders was driving three thousand cattle "up from the Comanche country" and was prepared to fight the troops. Another report claimed that some *Comancheros* had fortified themselves at Portales Springs and were making "every preparation to fight."[37] Alarmed by this rumor, Gregg ordered Clendenin to take "not less than one hundred mounted men" and to find, subdue, and arrest the traders "at all hazards." In support of the operation, he instructed the commander at Fort Stanton to patrol the Pecos south of the Bosque Redondo to prevent traders from slipping into New Mexico by that route.[38] Clendenin's scout to Portales Springs, however, failed to discover any *Comancheros*, and the whole episode may simply have been a plot to lead the Anglo soldiers astray. Although the troops continued their patrols for the remainder of the summer, no more traders were found.

Meanwhile, the officers at Fort Bascom were discovering that

[36] Clendenin to Gregg, May 31, 1871, U/60, Dist. of N. Mex., LR, Army Commands, RG 98, NA.

[37] *Ibid.*; *Daily New Mexican*, May 24, 1871.

[38] Gregg to Clendenin, June 3, 1871, Dist. of N. Mex., LS, Vol. 45, 174, Army Commands, RG 98, NA; Gregg to the Commanding Officer, Fort Stanton, June 7, 1871, *ibid.*

A History of New Mexican–Plains Indian Relations

capturing cattle was much easier than holding them. On May 13, Lieutenant Caraher delivered to Lieutenant A. G. Hennissee the 435 cattle he had seized. While driving the animals to Fort Union, Hennissee lost all but 212 head. In accounting for the large loss, he stated that some had strayed in a storm, others had sickened and died, and all stragglers had been killed "to prevent their falling into the hands of the Mexicans." More than 100 head, he admitted, "must have been disposed of" by his soldiers to the New Mexicans.[39] The remaining cattle and the 21 captured Isletans were delivered to Nathaniel Pope, the superintendent of Indian affairs. Pope released the Isletans on bond and, having no way of caring for the herd, put them in charge of it until its legal status could be determined.[40] There is, however, no record that the animals were ever reclaimed. The ludicrous circle was complete.

Captain Randlett fared just as poorly with the cattle he had taken. While he held them at Fort Bascom during the summer, their number dwindled from 510 to 384. Court-martialed for negligence, Randlett maintained in his defense that it was impossible to recover cows which strayed or were scattered by the summer thunderstorms because the near-by settlers gathered up all "stray cattle" and put them in their own herds. Randlett admitted that none of his command could recognize cattle thus appropriated and recommended therefore that animals captured thereafter be branded "U.S."[41]

The proper venue for the trial of the captured traders presented another troublesome question for the military commanders. General John Pope, head of the Department of the Missouri,

---

[39] Hennissee to Pullman, June 14, 1871, U/68, Dist. of N. Mex., LR, Army Commands, RG 98, NA.

[40] Gregg to Pope, June 1, 1871, Dist. of N. Mex., LS, Vol. 45, 171, *ibid.*; *Daily New Mexican*, June 12, 1871, June 27, 1871, and July 1, 1871.

[41] Randlett to Gregg, June 30, 1871, R/6, Dist. of N. Mex., LR, Army Commands, RG 98, NA. Randlett was charged specifically with appropriating two cows for his personal use and allowing his men to retain the New Mexicans' personal ponies. In defending himself, he charged that the court-martial charges were fabrications trumped up by Colonel Gregg and Lieutenant Caraher to discredit him. He was acquitted. File 1605, AGO, 1872, RG 94, NA.

The Suppression of the Comanchero Cattle Trade, *1867-1872*

recommended that they be tried in Texas. New Mexicans who knew they would go before a *Tejano* jury if captured, he asserted, would hesitate to engage in the unlawful traffic. Furthermore, he thought it only "proper" that the stock stolen in Texas and the individuals who traded for it should be "disposed of" by the Texas courts.[42] General Sherman, however, disagreed and ordered the prisoners to be delivered to the civil authorities in New Mexico.[43] Ten Mexicans and three Pueblos were accordingly bound over for the October session of the Las Vegas District Court.

From the beginning, there was little hope of securing a conviction. On August 18, six weeks before the court convened, W. F. M. Arny, a veteran New Mexico politician and the Pueblo Indian agent, predicted that the prisoners would go "scot free" because of the inefficiency of S. M. Ashenfelter, the United States district attorney.[44] Ashenfelter, a 28-year-old political appointee from Reading, Pennsylvania, had more than upheld the reputation of the Grant Administration for incompetency. Earlier in 1871, B. J. Waters, chief justice of the New Mexico Supreme Court, had complained about Ashenfelter to President Grant himself:

> There were *fifty-one* cases on the criminal docket. . . . Case after case was called and tried by jury, and *not a conviction* had during the term.
>
> He knows nothing about the practice of law and appears perfectly ignorant of every principle of law in the examination of witnesses and the trial of a case. . . . His incompetency and ignorance of the law and practice has become a matter of universal remark, not only by the members of the bar, but by the people generally.[45]

Ashenfelter did not disappoint his detractors. The cases of the accused *Comancheros* were thrown out of court because he drew

---

[42] Pope to Col. G. L. Hartstuff, June 22, 1871, Dept. of the Missouri, LS, No. 57, Army Commands, RG 98, NA.
[43] Sherman to Sheridan, June 27, 1872, File 2196, AGO, 1872, RG 94, NA.
[44] "Report of W. F. M. Arny, August 18, 1871," in *Annual Report of the Commissioner of Indian Affairs,* 1871, 804.
[45] Waters to Grant, February 20, 1871, Chronological Files, New Mexico, No. 53, Department of Justice, RG 60, NA.

up defective indictments. Vigorous complaints of his conduct were made to Attorney General A. G. Akerman, but Ashenfelter defended himself by arguing that Congress should enact simpler, more direct laws "providing fine and imprisonment" for both the *Comancheros* and their customers. He also maintained unabashedly that his legal efforts had caused several traders to leave the country in "hot haste" and had curtailed the activities of those still "in the business."[46] The *Daily New Mexican* also noticed a reduction in the trade, but it was credited to the vigilant patroling of the Eighth Cavalry rather than to the inept district attorney.[47]

After the military had ceased its patroling for the year, a disgruntled observer at Fort Bascom, perhaps reflecting Anglo opinion of the traders, prescribed his own remedy for the traffic. Noting that buffalo would provide beef cheaper—"if anything could be cheaper"—than buying cattle from the *Comancheros*, he proposed (with tongue in cheek) to break up the trade by having

> the buffalo herded up this way—for . . . such is the fondness of the Mexican appetite for dried buffalo meat and chile that I know they wouldn't pass a buffalo herd to buy the longest horned Texas steer that ever roamed over Maverick's land, even if they could get him for a jack knife and two beads.[48]

During the winter's brief respite, the Kwahadi Comanches, desiring vainly to return to the time when New Mexico could be relied upon as a haven of trade, told former Indian Agent Lorenzo Labadi they wanted to make peace with the Territory. Although Labadi faithfully relayed the proposal to the authorities, the army officials refused to consider it and the *Daily New Mexican* sternly warned that the Comanches must be taught that "peace with us in New Mexico means peace with the people of Texas."[49]

The end of the period of calm was presaged in February, 1872, when a band of fifteen New Mexicans gathered at Puerto de Luna

[46] Ashenfelter to Akerman, October 9, 1871, *ibid.*, No. 276.
[47] *Daily New Mexican*, April 18, 1872.
[48] *Santa Fe Weekly Post*, November 25, 1871.
[49] *Daily New Mexican*, April 1, 1872.

The Suppression of the Comanchero *Cattle Trade, 1867-1872*

and slipped onto the Llano Estacado on a venture that would set off the most vigorous campaigning yet against their trade. Following a trail known only to themselves and the Comanches, they crossed the Alamo Gordo and Las Truchas (pigmy streams which flowed off the Llano into the Pecos), climbed the western escarpment of the Staked Plains, then moved southeastward past a series of watering places—Tule Lake, Tierra Blanca Lake, and Portales Springs—to the Salada, a large salt lake just west of the Texas line where New Mexican cattle buyers had formerly bargained with "the men who deal directly with the Indians." The trail branched at the Salada, with one fork running east toward the *Cañon del Rescate*, but the *Comancheros* followed the other fork southeastward to the Mucha Que Valley. Here the traders had often bartered for thousands of cattle, but on this occasion the Indians had no stolen stock. While waiting for a Comanche party to make a quick visit to the Texas ranges, the New Mexicans unfortunately grew impatient and went on a scavenging expedition of their own.[50]

Unknown to them, Sergeant William Wilson and a small detachment of the Fourth Cavalry from Fort Concho were trailing some stolen horses in the vicinity. The soldiers had often followed similar trails without success, but this time they accidentally encountered the *Comancheros*, who were unsurely feeling their way through the alien brakes of the Colorado. Although the New Mexicans fled, the pursuing cavalrymen, in a "brisk little fight," killed two and captured a youth from La Cuesta named Polonio Ortiz.[51]

When Ortiz sought to shield himself and his friends by giving incorrect names and information, Major John Hatch, commanding Fort Concho, threatened that only by the "most faithful service" could he ever expect to receive a pardon. Ortiz, finally breaking, named his home town, his fellow traders, and the merchants who backed them; described the method of trading and

[50] Major John Hatch to Col. Gordon Granger, April 15, 1872, C/36, Dist. of N. Mex., LR, Army Commands, RG 98, NA.
[51] Post Medical Records, Fort Concho, Vol. 401, 259, AGO, RG 94, NA.

the trails across the Llano Estacado; and agreed to serve the military as a guide. To verify his story, Hatch on April 29 dispatched Captain N. B. McLaughlin to reconnoiter the Mucha Que Valley. Led by Ortiz, McLaughlin arrived at Mucha Que after a five-day march, only to find that the Indians had deserted it the preceding day. The many cattle tracks, however, confirmed Ortiz's account.[52]

These disclosures prompted General C. C. Augur, head of the Department of Texas, to order Colonel Ranald S. Mackenzie of the Fourth Cavalry to establish a base near the head of the Brazos River in order to suppress the "thieving marauders." Wasting no time, Mackenzie had by July 2 established a supply camp near the mouth of Blanco Canyon on the Freshwater Fork of the Brazos about eleven miles southeast of present Crosbyton.

After three weeks of fruitless patroling, one of Mackenzie's scouts discovered a large cattle trail leading west. Anxious to catch the thieves, Mackenzie followed the rain-beaten trace up the Double Mountain Fork of the Brazos and across the plains to the Salada. From there he tracked the *Comancheros* northwestward, hoping to arrest them and two Puerto de Luna merchants, Hughes and Church, who had been named by Ortiz as the chief suppliers of the traders. Mackenzie discovered, however, that the trail broke up on Alamo Gordo Creek and that the merchants had left the country "to escape capture by a party of citizens who are arresting cattle thieves and taking possession of stolen cattle."[53]

Foiled in his efforts to surprise the cattle traders, Mackenzie informed Colonel Gordon Granger, the new commander of the District of New Mexico, that there had been an immense number of stolen cattle driven by the trail he had followed.[54] After

[52] Hatch to Granger, March 31, 1872, C/31, Dist. of N. Mex., LR, Army Commands, RG 98, NA; Ernest Wallace, "Colonel Ranald S. Mackenzie's Expedition of 1872 Across the South Plains," *West Texas Historical Association Year Book*, XXXVIII (October, 1962), 7.
[53] Mackenzie to the Asst. Adj. Gen., Dept. of Texas, August 15, 1872, Dept. of Texas, LR, Army Commands, RG 98, NA; Henry W. Strong, *My Frontier Days and Indian Fights on the Plains of Texas*, 34.
[54] Mackenzie to Granger, August 15, 1872, M/361, Dist. of N. Mex., LR, Army Commands, RG 98, NA.

The Suppression of the Comanchero Cattle Trade, 1867-1872

replenishing his supplies at Forts Sumner and Bascom, Mackenzie recrossed the Staked Plains by way of Tierra Blanca Creek, the head of Tule Canyon and Quitaque, still searching in vain for traders and Indians.[55]

Although he had not caught the thieves, his expedition had been of great significance. According to General Augur, it was

> the first instance . . . where troops have been successfully taken across the Staked Plains. This fact, that troops can be so moved, and the general knowledge of the country, and the specific knowledge of the routes and *modus operandi* of the cattle thieves, obtained by Colonel Mackenzie, I regard as very important and well worth the summer's labor.[56]

Meanwhile, the "citizens" whose actions had thwarted Mackenzie's hope of capturing the traders at Puerto de Luna were giving the cattle trade some of its worst moments. John Hittson, deciding to retrieve at least part of his stolen cattle and obtaining from many of his fellow ranchers powers of attorney to recover their animals also, raised a force of ninety gunmen and in July moved into New Mexico. During the next three months, Hittson's forces roamed over the Territory, rounded up some six thousand cattle, and drove them north into Colorado.[57]

In operating against the traders, Hittson had the full consent of the New Mexican military officials. Colonel Granger even ordered Colonel Gregg at Fort Union to lend him some "surplus arms." Granger also ordered his subordinates to co-operate with Hittson in recovering his stolen cattle and in arresting cattle thieves, but on August 1, he instructed them to confine their activities to preventing bloodshed, "if possible," and enforcing the laws when "application is made by the proper civil authorities."[58]

---

[55] Ernest Wallace, *Ranald S. Mackenzie on the Texas Frontier*, 72-73.

[56] *Annual Report of the Secretary of War, 1872*, 56.

[57] For a more complete study of Hittson's raid, see Charles Leroy Kenner, "The Great New Mexico Cattle Raid, 1872," *New Mexico Historical Review*, XXXVII (October, 1962), 243-59.

[58] Granger to Gregg, July 18, 1872, Dist. of N. Mex., LS, Vol. 45, 522, Army Commands, RG 98, NA; Granger to Commanding Officer, Fort Bascom, August 1, 1872, *ibid.*, p. 542.

To avoid violence, Hittson deliberately operated in such force that no one would dare oppose him. As Governor Marsh Giddings explained to Secretary of State Hamilton Fish, "he goes with such numbers that he generally acquires the property quite peaceably, as it is well understood that this large force for peace carry the means of securing it by force."[59]

Despite the precautions, clashes between Hittson's men and the New Mexicans were inevitable. At Las Vegas a delegation of townsmen petitioned Don Miguel Otero, their former delegate to Congress, to use his influence to halt the activities of the Texans. Reluctantly agreeing, Otero, accompanied by his two teen-age sons, went to the Texans' camp and urged their leader "to have greater regard" for the New Mexicans' property. The Texan, remembered by young Miguel Otero, Jr., future territorial governor of New Mexico, only as a "large, red-headed man with chin whiskers, weighing fully two hundred and twenty-five pounds," answered the urbane New Mexican with a burst of profanity:

> These God damn greasers have been stealing our horses and cattle for the past fifty years, and we got together and thought we would come up this way and have a grand round-up, and that is why we are here. What is more we intend to take all the horses and cattle we come across and drive them back to Texas where they belong. My advice to your fellows is: Don't attempt to interfere with what we are doing unless you are looking for trouble.[60]

With that, the conversation ended.

As weeks passed and Hittson's men continued their methodical search for stolen cattle, rumors of gunfights spread across the Territory. An old *Comanchero* later remembered, not too unhappily, that the *Tejanos* had whipped a band of *Americanos* in a gun battle and then had lynched one of them "from a pine tree

---

[59] Giddings to Fish, October 28, 1872, Territorial Papers, New Mexico, Records of the State Department, RG 59, NA.

[60] Miguel Otero, *op. cit.*, 62–63. The Texan in question may or may not have been Hittson. He had a light complexion and beard, but he was also frequently absent from his men while attending business in Santa Fe or Las Vegas.

The Suppression of the Comanchero Cattle Trade, 1867-1872

close to the house." Jim Duncan, just out of the army and into the ranching business, recalled that an Anglo named Simpson who sought to stop the Texans by blocking the entry to his corral was coldly shot down and the herd driven out over his lifeless form.[61] Although such stories, recalled fifty to sixty years after the raid, may or may not have been accurate, a sensational clash at Loma Parda, a small hamlet just outside the Fort Union Military Reservation, shocked the entire Territory.

It was not surprising that the Loma Pardans, accused by the officers at Fort Union of being a gang of "thieves and cut-throats" who lived by preying on off-duty soldiers,[62] were the first (and the last) to oppose the Texans with force. Led by Edward Seaman, their police chief and postmaster, they twice prevented parties of Texans from inspecting their herds for stolen cattle. On September 10, however, Hittson's men, sixty strong and ready for a showdown, swept into the little village. In a wild, terrifying melee that broke out within a few minutes of their arrival, the Texans killed two Loma Pardans, including Police Chief Seaman, pistol-whipped another into insensibility, shot the town alcalde through both legs, and left the stunned townspeople huddling helplessly in their adobe huts while they gathered up their cattle.[63] Although this episode marked the end of armed opposition, it solidified the New Mexican ranks against the intruders.

The Texans' protestation that they had acted only in self-defense did little to calm the storm of outrage and resentment which mounted around them. The *New Mexico Union* bitterly condemned Hittson's men for entering the Territory with "braggadocio, swaggering, and offers of violence" and taking cattle

---

[61] Cabeza de Baca, *op. cit.*, 60; Haley, "Comanchero Trade," *loc. cit.*, 173.
[62] Chris Emmett, *Fort Union and the Winning of the Southwest*, 316.
[63] *Weekly New Mexican*, September 24, 1872. In Hittson's absence during this affray, the Texans were led by one of his lieutenants, H. M. Childress, a notable frontier character in his own right. According to Joseph G. McCoy, Childress had "a nerve of iron," was "cool and collected" under fire, and was a "deadly pistol shot." According to his enemies, moreover, he had the "peculiar characteristic of smiling demoniacally whilst he is plainly and openly maneuvering to shoot them through the heart." Joseph G. McCoy, *Historic Sketches of the Cattle Trade of the West and Southwest*, 132.

where they pleased under the "pretense" that the animals had once been unlawfully taken from Texas. Complaining that the authorities had allowed "these blowing bullies" to succeed with their pretensions, it warned the New Mexicans that there was no safety but in their "own hands."[64]

The New Mexicans, however, preferred to resort to legal measures rather than physical combat with Hittson. In the Texan's own words, some of the parties from whom he had reclaimed cattle secured indictments against him "to the number of about a dozen."[65] Probst and Kirchner, one of the leading New Mexican ranching firms, obtained writs of replevin forbidding Hittson to drive cattle out of the Territory until the courts had determined their ownership.[66] According to Governor Giddings, "a few of these cattle takers" were placed under heavy bond.[67] In San Miguel County alone, Hittson and his associates were charged (according to a court docket, which is the sole surviving county court record of the era) with no less than twenty-one offenses, such as stealing cows, "assault in a menacing manner," carrying arms, and "rioting." These charges, moreover, did not include the Loma Parda affray, which had occurred in Mora County.[68]

With his activities thus circumscribed, Hittson decided to return to Texas and left Santa Fe by stage on October 26. Although he put James Patterson and Thomas Stockton in charge of gathering his cattle, the great raid, for all practical purposes, was over. In December, the last of Hittson's men in New Mexico were arrested for the murders at Loma Parda, but they broke out of jail and fled for "parts unknown."[69]

During the winter, Hittson reported to the Committee on Indian Affairs of the Texas Legislature that he had only partially accomplished his goals of putting "a stop to the Indian depreda-

[64] *New Mexico Union* (Santa Fe), October 1, 1872.
[65] *Rocky Mountain News*, April 29, 1873.
[66] *Daily New Mexican*, October 4, 1872.
[67] Giddings to Fish, October 28, 1872, Territorial Papers, New Mexico, Records of the State Department, RG 59, NA.
[68] Court Docket for San Miguel County, 1871–1876, Special Collections Division, University of New Mexico Library, Albuquerque.
[69] *Daily New Mexican*, December 28, 1872.

tions" and recovering his stolen property. Although he had regained almost six thousand cattle, their recapture had incurred "enormous expense, nearly equal" to their value.[70] Despite his pessimism, his flamboyant raid, which brought him sudden fame as far east as New York,[71] had hit the *Comanchero* trade at one of its most vulnerable links: the purchasers of the traders' cattle.

In addition to Hittson and Mackenzie, the cattle buyers and *Comancheros* during 1872 had to contend with the New Mexican military officials, anxious to repeat their successes of the previous year. Armed with instructions from General Pope to send all prisoners and captured stock to Fort Sill for delivery to the Texas authorities,[72] Granger kept his troops on patrol all summer, continually spurring them to "break up" the camps of illicit traders and to take their cattle. On July 11, he dispatched a company from Fort Bascom to Las Truchas to capture a gang of cattle thieves allegedly led by "Celco Baca and Labadie,"[73] but the New Mexicans escaped. Although Granger had troops patroling the eastern frontier from the Canadian to the junction of the Pecos with the Río Hondo, neither stolen cattle nor *Comancheros* were discovered. If the traders had not suspended operations for the time being, they were having phenomenal success in avoiding the patrols.

In the most ambitious project of the summer, Granger ordered Colonel Gregg to lead a large expedition to the Quitaque trading grounds. Gregg, after a number of delays which brought sharp rebukes from Granger, left Fort Bascom on August 7 with 214 enlisted men and 11 officers. After following the Fort Smith Road

---

[70] *The Daily Statesman* (Austin), February 2, 1873.

[71] *The Colorado Chieftain* (Pueblo), January 16, 1873, quoted a glowing account published in the *New York Evening Post* under the eye-catching headline "Cattle Jack—A Modern Hercules to the Rescue!" and the *Rocky Mountain News*, January 5, 1873, stated: "John Hittson's operations against the border thieves seem to have attracted general attention; and our bold, honest and wealthy stockman has gained a national reputation by the effectiveness of his operations and its entire lack of 'red tape!'"

[72] Pope to Granger, August 6, 1872, Dept. of the Missouri, LS, No. 130, Army Commands, RG 98, NA.

[73] Lt. W. J. Lorile to Commanding officer, Camp on the Canadian, July 11, 1872, Dist. of N. Mex., LS, Vol. 45, 532, *ibid.*

for a few miles, he turned off to the southeast on a trail described by Polonio Ortiz as the Quitaque Trail. Ascending the bluffs of the Llano Estacado at their intersection with the western boundary of Texas, Gregg passed by Garcia Lake in southwestern Deaf Smith County and then followed Tierra Blanca Creek northeastward to its junction with Palo Duro Creek. While encamped near the present site of Canyon on the night of August 15, his command was attacked by about 40 Kiowas, who stampeded the cattle being driven along for food. Other than the beef herd, Gregg lost only one enlisted man wounded and 3 horses killed. The Kiowas, he learned later, lost 4 killed and 8 wounded.[74]

Gregg then moved southeastward along the northern rim of Palo Duro Canyon, which he admiringly reported was "unsurpassed in rarity of color and beauty of outlines." On the eighteenth, his *Comanchero* guide lost the Quitaque Trail amidst the tracks of a large buffalo herd. Two days later, however, when a stream of clear water flowing over a "white sand bed . . . fully one hundred yards wide" was discovered, the guide proclaimed it to be Cibola Creek (Mulberry Creek today) and asserted that Quitaque was a short distance to the northeast.

Leaving most of his troops in camp, Gregg wandered for several hours through broken country until he came upon a circular valley enclosed by a "high ridge" that afforded "an outlook from which the surrounding country can be seen for many miles in every direction."[75] Mistakenly, he concluded that this was Quitaque, which in reality lay about forty miles to his south on the other side of the Red River. Gregg's guide, who had taken him into Donley County southwest of present Clarendon, was either incredibly ignorant of the trading grounds or had deliberately led the Anglo military expedition astray.

Finding neither Indians nor cattle, Gregg moved south to the junction of Mulberry Creek and the Red River. Exploring the base of the Caprock southwest of the Red on the twenty-sixth

---

[74] Gregg, "Report of a Scout to the Vicinity of Quitta Que, September 17, 1872," File 4548, AGO, 1872, RG 94, NA.
[75] Ibid.

U. S. Signal Corps Photograph, The National Archives

Mow-wies' village near Wichita Mountains, Indian Territory.

*U. S. Signal Corps Photograph,
The National Archives*

Mow-wi (Mow-way), war chief of the Kwahadis.

*Courtesy of the Smithsonian Office of
Anthropology, Bureau of American
Ethnology Collection*

Quirts-quip, or Chewing Elk, a Comanche tribal chief. Born, 1827; died, 1880. By Alexander Gardner, Washington, D.C., 1872.

*Courtesy of the Smithsonian Office of Anthropology,
Bureau of American Ethnology Collection*

Big Bow, Kiowa tribe. By John K. Hillers, 1894.

U. S. Signal Corps Photograph, The National Archives
Kiowa hunting camp, showing buffalo meat drying on frames.

*Courtesy of the Smithsonian Office of Anthropology,
Bureau of American Ethnology Collection*

Taos men, left to right: Antonio Jose Atencio; Juan Jesus Leo (standing); Antonio Al Churleta. All former governors.
Photograph made prior to 1877.

*Courtesy of the Smithsonian Office of Anthropology,
Bureau of American Ethnology Collection*

Three Taos men on horseback—an indication of the Plains Indian influence on Taos. By Vernon Bailey, 1904.

*Courtesy of the Smithsonian Office of Anthropology,
Bureau of American Ethnology Collection*

Men from Pueblo of Santa Clara, New Mexico. Left to right: Cajete, Doloreo, Guadalupe (seated), Bonifacio, Governor Diego Narango (seated), Geronimo, former Governor Jose Jesus Narango (seated), Casimiro. Possibly photographed by F. A. Rinehart at the Omaha Expedition, 1898.

U. S. Signal Corps Photograph, The National Archives

Two Cheyenne girls, 1876. Girl at right is granddaughter of William Bent.

The Suppression of the Comanchero Cattle Trade, 1867-1872

and twenty-seventh, he unknowingly passed within a few miles of Quitaque and barely missed Mackenzie's returning expedition, which was then in the vicinity of Silverton.[76] After resurveying the region around Clarendon, Gregg on August 30 began the journey home on a "well-defined wagon road leading northwest." Without any major incidents, he arrived at Fort Bascom on September 14, having made the first thorough exploration of the Red River from its sources to the foot of the Caprock. Significantly, he reported that there were no indications that the trail he had followed had been used by the cattle traders during the preceding two years. Prior to that time, he concluded, a very large trade had annually passed over it.[77]

In many respects, 1872 marked the climax of the struggle against the *Comancheros*. Hittson's raid had undoubtedly made the New Mexican ranchers hesitant about buying stolen cattle, and both Mackenzie and Granger had made threatening moves against the suppliers of the traders. Since these groups were less willing to take chances than were the daredevil *Comancheros*, much less pressure was required to persuade them to abandon the business. In addition, the pioneer marches of Mackenzie and Gregg had revealed the location of the trading grounds, portending similar scouts in subsequent years. Although some traders would doggedly range the plains until the last of the Indians had been subdued, most realized that the time had come to find other occupations, such as herding sheep on the new grazing grounds being wrested from their Indian allies or serving as guides and scouts for the increasing numbers of troops moving onto the plains. Even José Tafoya, onetime prince of the *Comancheros*, allegedly entered the service of Mackenzie and, according to the folklore of the range, was instrumental in the final defeat of his Indian trading partners.

The year closed much as it had begun—with the Kwahadi Comanches making another attempt to maintain their ties with New Mexico. Cohepa, one of their leading chiefs, sent word to

[76] Wallace, *op. cit.*, 73.
[77] Gregg, "Report of a Scout to Quitta Que," *loc. cit.*

Colonel Granger that his people and some Kiowa groups would come in and remain at peace if they could have a reservation on the Canadian or Pecos rivers. Although Granger recommended that the Indians, if they "are acting in good faith as we have every reason to believe," should be granted a reservation in New Mexico,[78] the Indian Department took no action, even as it had done nothing to implement the earlier recommendations of Superintendents Collins, Steck, and Norton. The Washington officials were determined to place the Kwahadis on the reservation in Oklahoma; within a few years they would have enough troops to accomplish the task.

[78] Granger to Pope, November 8, 1872, Dist. of N. Mex., LS, Vol. 46, 31, Army Commands, RG 98, NA.

10
The End of a Long Road

AT THE BEGINNING OF 1873, a major change had taken place in the *Comanchero* commerce. The relentless military harassment during the preceding two years had crippled the once-great cattle trade so severely that traders returned only with a few horses, buffalo robes, and barely enough cattle to suggest the halcyon days of the past. Nevertheless, venturesome New Mexicans would continue to go forth to barter as long as an Indian roamed the plains or possessed trade items valuable enough to make the long trek to the Indian Territory reservations worth while.

Aware that warm weather might see a renewal of trading activities, Colonel Gregg, once again in command of the District of New Mexico, sent Captain S. B. M. Young with two companies of the Eighth Cavalry to reoccupy Fort Bascom in May, 1873. Young stationed one company at the fort to protect the ranchers in the area and dispatched the other to patrol the road linking Bascom with old Fort Sumner. His efforts were futile, however, for the *Comancheros*, always alert to exploit weaknesses in the picket lines, immediately shifted their trade routes to the region north of the Canadian. By July, according to rumors circulating in Las Vegas, they had driven five hundred head of stolen cattle across the Canadian in the vicinity of Fort Union.

Emboldened by these successes, other traders rushed to the plains. So confident had they become that one, Juan Pieda, even challenged "all the troops in the country" to catch him.[1] Although Captain Young pleaded for reinforcements in order to extend his patrol lines, General Pope, to whom the request was

---

[1] Young to Gregg, July 17, 1873, N/233, Dept. of the Missouri, LR, Army Commands, RG 98, NA.

forwarded, replied illogically that "two companies are deemed sufficient . . . if properly rotated."

In early July, a party of traders, returning with a few head of horses and cattle, insolently passed within sight of Fort Bascom itself and easily eluded a pursuit by eleven troopers.[2] A few weeks later, however, one Juan Lucero, on his way in from the plains with thirteen ponies, was apprehended near the mouth of Utah Creek. The suspected *Comanchero* was detained with his animals at Fort Bascom, but he immediately appealed to New Mexico Supreme Court Justice J. G. Palen. Palen issued a writ of habeas corpus ordering Lucero's delivery to the San Miguel authorities. They quickly released him on bail.[3] Judge Palen then issued another writ commanding the return of Lucero's horses, but Young refused to comply, stating that as a commissioned officer acting in obedience to military instructions, he was not amenable to the laws of New Mexico.[4] Although his superiors commended him on his stand, they decided there was not enough evidence to convict Lucero and therefore ordered the restoration of his animals.

The lackadaisical attitude of Captain Young's superiors toward the *Comancheros* ended abruptly in late August when Lieutenant Colonel J. B. Brooks, commander at Camp Supply, Indian Territory, complained vociferously to General Pope that New Mexican traders were introducing large quantities of whisky to the Cheyennes in the Antelope Hills region and implied that the troops in New Mexico were doing little to stop them. Questioned about the matter by Pope, Colonel Gregg hotly declared that Captain Young was doing everything feasible with the small force at his disposal. He then pointedly observed that Fort Bascom was at least five times as far from the Antelope Hills as was Camp Supply and asked why Brooks could not apprehend the traders. It would be much easier, he maintained, to guard the immediate approaches to the Indian camps than to prevent the traders, who

[2] Rogers to Young, July 15, 1873, enclosed with *ibid.*
[3] Young to Palen, August 14, 1873, enclosed with Young to Gregg, August 14, 1873, N/269, Dept. of the Missouri, LR, Army Commands, RG 98, NA.
[4] Young to Palen, August 20, 1873, copy enclosed with Young to Gregg, August 20, 1873, Y/20, Dist. of N. Mex., LR, Army Commands, RG 98, NA.

The End of a Long Road

were "the boldest and most unscrupulous portion of this frontier population" and had "all the inhabitants of the country in full sympathy with them," from going to the plains.[5]

Nevertheless, Gregg ordered Captain Young to reconnoiter the entire length of the eastern frontier, from Las Portales in the south to the Santa Fe Trail on the north.[6] With fifty men and rations for twenty-six days, Young left Fort Bascom on August 28 and marched southwestward to Las Cañaditas, a favorite *Comanchero* watering spot northeast of Fort Sumner. From there he turned southeast and reversed Mackenzie's trail of the previous year past Tule Lake and Las Portales all the way to Blanco Canyon, where he arrived on September 8. Discovering the tracks of wagons and cattle leading north, he followed them across the Red River to the Washita. There, on September 16, he overtook his quarry, a company of fifty Texan surveyors selecting lands for a grant to the Houston and Great Northern Railroad. W. S. Mabry, leader of the surveyors, noted in his diary that the troops "had followed our trail from Canyon Blanco, thinking we were Mexicans out trading guns and ammunition to the Indians for horses and cattle."[7]

Young then led his command to Camp Supply to replenish his rations and give the troops a rest before beginning the homeward journey. He returned by following Wolf and Palo Duro creeks, tributaries of the North Canadian, across the eastern half of the Texas Panhandle and then striking across the plains to reach the South Canadian near Adobe Walls. From there he retraced Kit Carson's trail of 1864 to Fort Bascom. Finding that it had already been abandoned for the winter, he marched on to Fort Union, where he arrived on October 24.

In fifty-eight days, he had marched more than a thousand miles without finding a single *Comanchero*.[8] Young concluded from his

[5] Gregg to Pope, August 29, 1873, Dist. of New Mex., LS, Vol. 46, 268, Army Commands, RG 98, NA.
[6] Lt. J. P. Willard to Young, August 21, 1873, *ibid.*, p. 260.
[7] W. S. Mabry, "Early West Texas and Panhandle Surveys," *Panhandle-Plains Historical Review*, II (1929), 35.
[8] Young to Willard, November 1, 1873, Y/27, Dist. of N. Mex., LR, Army Commands, RG 98, NA.

reconnaissance that "not one dollar's worth" of contraband goods had passed between old Forts Bascom and Sumner during the year but that north of the Canadian, considerable trading had apparently been carried on "without fear of hindrance."[9]

More ominously, Young discovered that the entire upper part of the Texas Panhandle was "full of buffalo parties," killing the animals for their hides.[10] He pointedly warned that an Indian outbreak would occur unless these illicit activities were curtailed. Although no notice was given to his prediction, it was only too true.

The following summer, the southern Plains Indians, irritated by the failure of the government to fulfill its annuity promises, goaded by New Mexican traders who plied them with whisky, and inflamed by the exhortations of a mystical young medicine man named Ishatai, took to the warpath. On June 27, some 260 Kiowas, Comanches, and Cheyennes struck a supply camp for the buffalo hunters at Adobe Walls. The raiders were repulsed by the 28 occupants of the post, but the former were soon joined by hundreds of their fellow tribesmen, who poured off the reservations to ravage the frontier along a 600-mile arc from the Arkansas to the Pecos. The isolated ranchers in eastern New Mexico, never before faced with a determined onslaught from the plains, were particularly hard hit. Before the forays let up in late July, scores of settlers had been killed in the Cimarron Valley and 9 at Fort Bascom. Even John Chisum, headquartered far down on the Pecos, had 300 horses stolen.[11]

In response to the raids, the cattlemen on the upper Pecos and Canadian met in Santa Fe on July 26 to petition Colonel Gregg for protection.[12] Their plea was unnecessary, however, because the authorities were already moving rapidly to end the Indian menace for all time. On July 19, Secretary of War W. W. Belknap issued orders authorizing the troops to follow the hostiles onto the reservations in order to punish them. With the Quaker Peace Policy thus discarded, Lieutenant Colonel John W. David-

[9] *Ibid.*
[10] *Ibid.*
[11] *Daily New Mexican*, July 23, 1874, August 3, 1874.
[12] *Ibid.*, July 27, 1874.

The End of a Long Road

son, commander at Fort Sill, ordered all Indians to register at their agencies by August 3. Those who did not would be considered hostile and punished. Five separate columns, operating out of bases in Texas, New Mexico, Kansas, and the Indian Territory, then converged on the headstreams of the Red River, the favorite haunts of the holdouts. The troops completely outmarched, outfought, and demoralized the erstwhile masters of the plains and forced band after band to surrender dejectedly at their agencies.

Few *Comancheros* were detected during the campaigns, for those who unwittingly ventured into the maelstrom hastily retreated to New Mexico. On August 28, 1874, Major William B. Price with four companies of the Eighth Cavalry left Fort Bascom and followed the Fort Smith road toward the Antelope Hills. Discovering "the fresh trail of Mexican Comanche traders" about 150 miles below the fort, Price traced it for 8 miles before it merged with an Indian trail and veered away in a southeasterly direction. Although the three former *Comancheros* serving Price as guides assured him that by following the trail he could strike a large Indian village on the headwaters of the Red River, he adhered to his orders and continued toward the Antelope Hills.[13] He found no further signs of *Comancheros*.

Colonel Mackenzie, operating out of Fort Concho, also utilized New Mexican guides, one of whom allegedly was José Tafoya.[14] According to one of the favorite stories of the plains, Mackenzie encountered Tafoya venturing over the prairie "in pursuit of trade," questioned him about the location of the Indians, and (when the *Comanchero* refused to talk) "propped up the tongue of a wagon and hanged Tafoya to the end." The terrified trader then supposedly led Mackenzie and his command to the Comanche village in Palo Duro Canyon.[15] In reality, however, a half-

[13] Price to the Asst. Adj. Gen., Dept of the Missouri, September 23, 1874, in Joe F. Taylor (comp.), "The Indian Campaign on the Staked Plains, 1874-1875," *Panhandle-Plains Historical Review*, XXXIV (1961), 47.
[14] In 1893, Tafoya stated that he had served as a guide for Mackenzie. Deposition of José Tafoya, June 26, 1893, Indian Depredation Case No. 9133, Records of the U.S. Court of Claims, RG 123, NA.
[15] Haley, "Comanchero Trade," *loc. cit.*, 175. Nothing in contemporary records

blood New Mexican scout named Johnson located the camp and set the stage for the most decisive victory of the campaign. In a dawn attack on September 28, Mackenzie's force routed the Indians and captured 1,424 of their best horses, killing more than 1,000 of them to ensure that they would never again be used for hunting or fighting.[16]

After a four-day rest, Mackenzie resumed his search for the Indian escapees. Circling the head of Palo Duro Canyon, he encountered, on the upper part of Mulberry Creek, fifteen *ciboleros*, three of whom he allowed to join his command as guides. The following day, October 8, he captured five *Comancheros* who had carried a load of supplies to the hostiles. After breaking up their wagon for firewood and slaughtering their oxen to feed his troops, Mackenzie placed the unlucky New Mexicans under arrest.[17] Although he scouted the Staked Plains and the brakes beneath their eastern escarpment until Christmas, no more traders were apprehended.

The army campaign was as effective as it was brutal. By June of 1875, the last of the Indians to surrender, the proud Kwahadis, had joined their chastened brothers on the reservations. With the spirit of the Indians broken, thousands of their best horses confiscated, and many of their leaders imprisoned in distant Florida, the basis on which the *Comanchero* trade had been built was demolished.

For the *ciboleros*, too, the sudden ascendancy of the Anglos was disastrous. Those who continued to make trips to the plains

---

corroborates this story. A possible basis for it was related by Henry Strong, who also served as a scout on the expedition. Mackenzie captured four New Mexicans who claimed to be buffalo hunters, held them for two days, and released them. After they had been turned loose, Strong tried to force one to talk by suspending him from a rope over the edge of a precipice. The New Mexican, however, was so obstinate that Strong "gave it up as a bad job." In the course of fifty years, the story of this near-lynching and the well-known name of Tafoya could have become fused together in the folklore of the plains. Strong, *op. cit.*, 63.

[16] Mackenzie, "Itinerary of the March of the 1st Southern Column," September 29–November 8, 1874, File 4262, Dept. of Texas, 1874, Army Commands, RG 98, NA.

[17] Wallace, *op. cit.*, 151.

The End of a Long Road

encountered a situation far different from that which had greeted their forerunners. Rather than hunting in a majestic solitude that liberated them for a few days from their usual drudgery, they now had to compete with Anglo hunters. The clashing styles of hunting employed by the two races led inevitably to conflict. The *cibolero* still mounted his favorite horse and made his kill while riding full speed, an arm's length from death and surrounded by a hundred fear-crazed beasts. The American, on the other hand, killed by stealth. Once he got a "stand" on a herd, he systematically and monotonously decimated its ranks while the dim-witted survivors continued to graze uneasily amidst the carnage. Where the *cibolero* dashed, no Anglo could obtain a stand; where the Anglos waited, no *cibolero* dared venture.

Few of the clashes which occurred between the two peoples have been recorded, but those which have illustrate the sad plight of the New Mexicans. W. S. Glenn, an unusually articulate Anglo hunter, recalled that an American had tediously worked his way to a crest overlooking a small valley in which a herd of buffalo awaited execution when a group of New Mexicans, lances high, dashed from the opposite ridge toward the herd and stampeded it. Enraged at being deprived of his kill, the American in short order shot the horses of four of the *ciboleros*. The chastened Mexicans, their chances for a successful hunt destroyed, withdrew.[18] A similar incident involved an Anglo hunter named George Causey. When a band of *ciboleros* ruined his stand, Causey first killed several of their horses and then condescendingly offered to allow them to skin the animals he killed in return for the meat.[19] Painfully aware of the hungry *niños* awaiting their return, the hapless lancers accepted the offer.

The New Mexican hunters were never secure from Anglo aggressions. In 1877, twenty-seven Texans who had followed the trail of some stolen horses into Blanco Canyon encountered a band of *ciboleros* who possessed thirty horses, *one* of which was

[18] Rex W. Strickland (ed.), "Recollections," *loc. cit.*, 37.
[19] Frank Collinson, "George Causey, Buffalo Hunter and Cowman," MS, Panhandle-Plains Historical Museum Library, Canyon, Texas, 1937.

recognized by the Texans. Although the New Mexicans stated that they had recently received this animal in trade and offered to return it, the Texans took *all* their horses at gun point and divided them among themselves, "believing that they were stolen property." After thus despoiling their victims, the Texans turned them loose with the warning that if they were ever "caught down there again they would be killed."[20]

In spite of such humiliations, the *ciboleros* doggedly contested for the last remnants of the herds. The tradition of the last Taos buffalo hunt, occurring in 1884, was recorded by Blanche Grant:

> Right after the San Gerónimo fiesta . . . forty or fifty left for the east. . . . Guns for the most part had displaced the bows and arrows but there were still some who trusted more to a good bow than any white man's shooting stick . . . They found the buffalo . . . grazing peacefully among the cattle. Fifty-four were soon killed and the meat jerked. . . . A grand powwow, described as "mostly noise," was held at the pueblo. The buffalo hunt was over—over forever.[21]

Memories of the hunts lingered on, however. A privileged visitor in a Taos apartment many years later was proudly shown a seven-foot lance suspended on a wall. This spear, the host related, "was used by my grandfather in hunting the buffalo. He was good at it. . . . Many Indians used to join in the hunt. Taos always had buffalo meat for the fiestas and holidays."[22]

Other remembrances were highly acrimonious. One aged *cibolero* reflected: "Had not the *Americanos* come in with their guns, we might still be enjoying the sport, but it did not take them long with their rifles to clear the Llano of buffaloes."[23]

For the *Comancheros*, the last years of their operations on the plains were even more hectic. Texans who were content with depriving the buffalo hunters of their horses were likely to kill the Indian traders. In August, 1874, the *Daily New Mexican*

[20] "Notes of a Conversation with P. W. Reynolds," MS, Rister Papers, Southwest Collection, Texas Technological College, Lubbock.
[21] Blanch C. Grant, *The Taos Indians*, 84.
[22] Fernando Solaz, "The Ageless Village," *New Mexico Magazine*, XXVII (March, 1942), 37.
[23] Cabeza de Baca, *op. cit.*, 42.

The End of a Long Road

reported in cryptic fashion that seven *Comancheros* returning from the Indian country with a "large drove of horses bartered from the Indians" had been waylaid by a party of Texans who professed to recognize some of their animals. Six of the traders were killed outright; the seventh, grievously wounded, succeeded in reaching home but, according to the news account, "it is not supposed he will recover."[24]

In an incident even more vaguely reported, about thirty Anglo buffalo hunters, in hot pursuit of a band of Indian thieves in the late 1870s, encountered twelve *Comancheros* on the Pease River and, presuming that they were in league with the Indians, "killed the *Comancheros* to a man."[25]

Although the elaborate patrols along the eastern border of New Mexico were discontinued after the close of the Red River War, the military occasionally apprehended *Comancheros*. In August, 1875, a scout under Lieutenant Theodore Baldwin found nine armed New Mexicans leading a string of pack mules across the central Panhandle. Baldwin "took them" back to Camp Supply on the supposition that they had been trading with the Indians, but they would tell nothing and were eventually released.[26]

The greatest threat to the *Comanchero* trade, however, was the destruction of the buffalo. With the end of the cattle trade, the New Mexicans were limited to bartering for buffalo robes, and these were fast becoming unobtainable. The decline in value of the robes sold by the Comanches and Kiowas to their official traders between 1876 and 1879 graphically illustrates the progressive annihilation of the southern buffalo herd: in 1876, $70,400; in 1877, $64,500; in 1878, $26,375; and in 1879, only $5,068.[27] The number traded to the *Comancheros* possibly declined at an even greater rate.

[24] *Daily New Mexican*, August 13, 1874.
[25] John McCarty, *Maverick Town*, 15.
[26] L. F. Sheffy (ed.), "Letters and Reminiscences of Gen. Theodore L. Baldwin," *Panhandle-Plains Historical Review*, XI (1938), 11.
[27] "Report of P. H. Hunt, August 30, 1879," in *Annual Report of the Commissioner of Indian Affairs*, 1879, 171.

The last full-scale buffalo hunt by the Comanches, in January, 1879, was a tragic failure. A large band of tribesmen, driven by habit and hunger, secured permission from their agent to hunt. For the first time, however, the plains failed them. According to their agent, they found almost no buffalo on the frigid prairies, and soon they were

> in a suffering condition. When I learned of this, I sent out . . . the interpreter, with some supplies for their relief, and with instructions to bring them in as soon as it was possible for them to move. The ground being covered with snow, so that their ponies, already poor, could not graze, some time elapsed before they reached the agency.[28]

To compound the Indians' humiliation, a company of the Texas Frontier Battalion under the command of Captain George W. Arrington shot one, scalped him, and possibly would have massacred the others had it not been for the timely appearance of a detachment of Negro cavalry.[29]

Nevertheless, the Pueblos were most reluctant to give up the ancient commerce and for some time made trading trips to the reservations in Oklahoma. With the approach of the traditional trading season in September, 1880, the Santo Domingans and their kinsmen from Sandía and Santa Ana optimistically prepared for such an excursion. By chance, the youthful A. F. Bandelier, making his first anthropological tour of New Mexico, was invited to the organizational meeting. Asked to keep a record of those selected to go on the trip, Bandelier listed sixty-three names —forty-five from Santo Domingo, fourteen from Santa Ana, and four from Sandía. He termed the meeting "one of the most interesting" he ever saw,[30] but his description, unfortunately, was quite vague. After watching the traders depart on what seemed to be the apex of high adventure, Bandelier wrote to a friend: "How I should like to have gone along on the trip, but the journey alone, both ways, will take two months."[31]

[28] *Ibid.*, 170.
[29] *Ibid.*; G. W. Arrington to J. B. Jones, January 20, 1879, Day and Winfrey, *op. cit.*, IV, 409-10.
[30] Bandelier, "Journal of 1880," entry of September 26.
[31] George P. Hammond and Edgar F. Good (eds.), *A Scientist on the Trail*, 33.

The End of a Long Road

The expedition was anything but a success. The Pueblos were received hospitably by the Comanches and Kiowas, but they were dismayed to find that their hosts lacked buffalo robes or other desirable trade goods. Seemingly realizing that this was the end of an era, the Pueblos leisurely visited in camp after camp before making the last long trek homeward.[32] The buffalo were dead, the Pueblos and Comanches were separated by a quarter of a continent, and the Anglos reigned supreme over the plains.

IT IS QUITE EVIDENT that the Plains Indians and the New Mexicans made a deep and lasting impact on each other. Since the two regions where they resided constituted a natural economic unit, it was inevitable that trade would develop between them. So important was this commerce before the arrival of the Spaniards that Pecos, easternmost of the pueblos, became the largest and strongest settlement in New Mexico. Following the Spanish occupation under Don Juan de Oñate in 1598, New Mexico's relations with the Plains Indians—despite the disturbing effects of slave raids—were remarkably tranquil for a full century because of the close commercial ties. Indeed, in the case of the Cuartelejo, Jicarilla, and Faraon Apaches, contact with the pueblos and Spaniards led Plains Indians to adopt, to an astonishing degree, the more advanced culture. They not only began to engage in farming under Pueblo tutelage, but they also began to build pueblo-like dwellings and to manufacture pottery. By the end of the seventeenth century, moreover, some of them were also expressing a rudimentary interest in the New Mexicans' religion.

The Comanches' adaptation to the horse and their rapid conquest of the southern plains inaugurated a new era in the history of New Mexican–Plains Indian relations. But even though the Comanches had the power to devastate New Mexico, their desire for trade goods kept them peaceful until French and Taovaya traders began to supply their trade needs. When the Comanches, under the leadership of Cuerno Verde, resorted to all-out war in the 1770s, the collapse of the province was averted only by the

[32] Mooney, "Calendar History," *loc. cit.*, 347.

A History of New Mexican–Plains Indian Relations

timely arrival of a military and diplomatic genius named Don Juan de Anza, who succeeded in slaying Cuerno Verde. In a conference with Ecueracapa, an Indian statesman of the first rank who had become the most significant figure among the Comanches, Anza negotiated a never-to-be-broken peace treaty in 1786, a pivotal event in the histories of both New Mexico and the Comanches. Without it, New Mexico, if its earlier devastation and the later agony of Chihuahua and Durango mean anything, could not have endured; with it, the New Mexicans enjoyed unprecedented prosperity until 1820. For their part, the Comanches obtained an abundant source of supplies for their wars with Texas and Old Mexico.

For a time, it also seemed likely that the Comanches' way of life would be modified considerably by their close contacts with the New Mexicans. Near the end of the eighteenth century, their chiefs were being confirmed by the New Mexico governors, some of their children were being educated at Santa Fe, and one of their leaders had even expressed an interest in building a pueblo for his people. In addition, significant numbers of Comanches were apparently settling permanently in the frontier villages of New Mexico. All of these promising developments came to naught, however, and the Comanches adopted few of the cultural ways of the New Mexicans. With their acquisition of larger and larger herds of horses and their perfection of hunting and raiding techniques, they were no longer attracted by the sedentary life of the Spaniards and Pueblos.

Despite this disappointment, the ties already established continued to flourish, largely because of the steady procession of New Mexican *Comancheros* going to the plains to trade. After 1846, this constant bartering led to the spontaneous formation of an informal alliance between the two peoples against the Anglo intruders who had occupied the Southwest. Although attempts by the Americans to break up the *Comanchero* commerce were begun soon after the occupation and were continued persistently during the following three decades, they were greatly hampered by the unceasing co-operation of the New Mexicans and the

Indians. In late 1864, for example, a *Comanchero* warning of an impending attack helped the Kiowas and Comanches to force the noted Kit Carson to retreat from the Battle of Adobe Walls. In addition to this, the traders were so adroit at evading the patrols of the military that their illicit trade actually hit its peak during the late 1860s. They purchased thousands of head of cattle from the Comanches and thereby inspired them to take a heavy toll upon the advancing American frontiersmen. By the mid-1870s, however, irresistible military force had converted their Indian associates into miserable, reservation-confined paupers. With this development, the books were closed forever upon both the *Comanchero* trade and the strangest alliance of southwestern annals.

THE YEARS OF CLOSE CONTACT with the Plains Indians produced a significant modification in the culture of the New Mexicans. Wesley Hurt, a young anthropologist who made a detailed study of the isolated village of Manzano in the 1930s, found that the inhabitants had not only borrowed material items, such as bows, arrows, lances, moccasins, and buckskin clothing, from the Indians, but that they had also adopted some of their ceremonies, such as the scalp dance. Timio Luna, an old farmer, recalled the return from the plains of a party of hunters with "the scalps of many Indians" tied to their saddles. That night, the scalps, lofted atop a long pole, were jubilantly paraded through the town, and afterward a scalp dance was held to celebrate the victory.[33]

The Pueblos were probably affected more profoundly by the Plains Indians than were the Spanish-Americans. In 1846, Lieutenant W. H. Emory, while visiting Santo Domingo, was greeted with a dazzling Pueblo display of horsemanship that could scarcely have been surpassed by the Comanches themselves:

> When within a few miles of the town we saw a cloud of dust rapidly advancing, and soon the air was rent with a terrible yell. . . . The first object that caught my eye through the column of dust was a fierce pair of buffalo horns, overlapped with long shaggy hair. As they approached, the sturdy form of a naked Indian revealed itself

[33] Wesley Hurt, "Indian Influence," *loc. cit.*, 246-47.

beneath the horns, with shield and lance, dashing at full speed, on a white horse, which, like his own body, was painted all the colors of the rainbow; and then, one by one, his followers came on, painted to the eyes, their own heads and their horses covered with ... horns, skulls, tails, feathers, and claws.[34]

After allowing their horses to rest, the Santo Domingans put on a brisk mock battle for their visitors: "The opposite files met ... and kept up a running fight, with muskets, lances, and bows and arrows. Sometimes a fellow would stoop almost to the earth to shoot under his horse's belly, at full speed, or to shield himself from an impending blow." These traits had obviously been learned from the Plains Indians.

Pueblo dances likewise reveal Plains Indian characteristics. The buffalo dance at many of the pueblos was quite similar to that of either the Comanches or the Kiowas, and the war dance was styled simply the "Comanche dance."[35] At San Ildefonso in 1921, an Anglo observed an age-old Comanche dance which re-enacted, by means of "chanting, movements, and pantomime," a mythical victory over the denizens of the plains. The first act concerned the news of the approach of the Comanches and the invocation of the "Sky-Father's" aid; the second, the preparations of the Pueblo warriors for battle and their departure; the third, the return of the victors, the mockery of the prisoners, and the thanksgiving to the Sky-Father.[36]

Of all the pueblos, Taos had the closest ties with the Plains Indians. There is even a puzzling linguistic similarity between Tanoan and Kiowan that defies explanation. Anthropologist John P. Harrington first studied and described this phenomenon, and Alice Marriott noted that "some Kiowas recognize a resemblance between their language and that of Taos."[37]

[34] Ross Calvin (ed.), *Lieutenant Emory Reports*, 64.
[35] Charles H. Lange, "A Reappraisal of Evidence of Plains Influences among the Rio Grande Pueblos," *Southwestern Journal of Anthropology*, IX (Summer, 1953), 220.
[36] "Comanche Dance at San Ildefonso, January 23, 1921," *El Palacio*, X (February, 1921), 6.
[37] Marriott, *op. cit.*, viii.

The End of a Long Road

In another area, the noted anthropologist Alfred M. Kroeber found that Taos, in "material culture and dress," was "half Plains."[38] Typical of the pervasive influence was its music. "Plains music is as common as any other there," observed Helen Roberts, the foremost authority on Amerindian music, and during the "famous song contests of moonlit summer nights . . . quantities of beautiful songs of typical Plains character are heard."[39] Taos continued to be influenced by the Comanches and Kiowas after the close of the frontier, contracting from them early in the twentieth century the Peyote Cult.[40]

The influence left by the long years of intimate relations with the Plains Indians was nowhere more conspicuous than in New Mexican folk drama. In many isolated villages, even the traditional Nativity play revolved (and conceivably still does) around a Comanche abduction of the Christ Child and ended with the Comanche chief recognizing the sovereignty of his Divine Hostage and offering Him blankets, bows, and arrows. The action of the play was advanced entirely by "sinuous" dancing to chants which, according to folklorist A. L. Campa, were "simply Comanche songs learned directly from the members of this tribe and handed down by oral tradition."[41] A typical stanza (translated by Campa) goes:

> At the stroke of twelve this evening
> We have come to look for Him
> We the Comanche Indians
> Have come here to dance for Him.[42]

A more famous folk drama recounted in epic form a victory over the mighty Comanche chief Cuerno Verde, whom the New Mexicans, as if somehow in awe of the sheer ferocity of his blood-

---

[38] Lange, "Reappraisal of Evidence," loc. cit., 221.
[39] Helen H. Roberts, "Musical Areas in Aboriginal North America," Yale University Publications in Anthropology, No. 12 (1936), 110–11.
[40] Weston LeBarre, "The Peyote Cult," Yale University Publications in Anthropology, No. 19, (1938), 40–41.
[41] Campa, "Los Comanches," loc. cit., 13.
[42] Ibid., 14.

thirsty forays, had enshrined as a character of Arthurian proportions:

> I am that mighty captain
> At whose name men shake with fear
> I am the brave, the bold, the terrible,
> This horn which you can see
> Green and golden, see it glisten
> All its fame it takes from me.[43]

In staging the epic, Taos Indians (riding bareback) and scions of pioneer Spanish families re-enacted the roles of Comanches and New Mexicans so vigorously that Professor Campa contended their performance was seldom equaled in "realism, color, and thrills anywhere in the world." After the orations and counter-orations had been exchanged in the open-air arena, the two sides clashed in a mock battle. Campa described, in almost blow-by-blow fashion, one of the last performances near Taos in the early 1930s:

> The battle is enacted with all the realism of a primitive encounter. Indians ride sideways letting arrows fly over the backs of their ponies. Many a rider is thrown as the horses become unmanageable in the constant discharge of firearms . . . . The battle begins to subside. The Indian ranks are thinning down with the effectiveness of the Spanish charge, and ponies head for the hills nearby at a full gallop. Except for those who remain behind lying in the dust, the Comanches beat a hasty retreat and disappear. Riderless mounts run in all directions, frightened by the uproar, and the Spanish army proceeds to gather the stock as the battle ends.[44]

Attesting to the popularity of the drama, Aurelio M. Espinosa, writing in 1907, stated that "up to some twenty years ago," it was performed in many parts of New Mexico at important feast days. So dear was it to the people, he reported, that "very few New Mexicans over fifty years of age are not able to recite large por-

---

[43] Gilberto Espinosa (trans.), "Los Comanches," *New Mexico Quarterly*, VII (May, 1931), 137.
[44] Campa, "Los Comanches," *loc. cit.*, 19-22.

tions of 'Los Comanches' from memory."[45] To have permeated so completely both New Mexican religious and heroic folk drama, the extent of the Comanche impact must have had few parallels in the history of America.

Thus a strong cultural affinity of the New Mexicans and the Plains Indians must be added to the economic importance of the trade between them, their maintenance of peace, and the desperate but futile alliance against the Anglo conquerors in order to judge fully the significance of the New Mexican–Plains Indian relationship. In view of this, it is little wonder that mention of the Comanches, which in Texas evokes visions of barbarous outrages, in New Mexico brings back only nostalgic memories.

[45] Aurelio Espinosa, "Los Comanches," *loc. cit.*, 19.

Bibliography

PRIMARY SOURCES

Unpublished Materials

"Abstract of Title to the Antonio Ortiz Grant Situated in San Miguel County, New Mexico." Typescript copy in Coronado Library, University of New Mexico, Albuquerque.

Amangual, Francisco. "Diary of the Incidents and Operations Which Took Place in the Expedition Made From the Province of Texas to the Province of New Mexico [1808]." Typescript translation by J. Villasana Haggard. Bexar Archives, University of Texas, Austin.

Archivo General de la Nación, Provincias Internas, Vol. CII. Photostatic copy in Coronado Library, University of New Mexico, Albuquerque.

Archivo Nacional de la Nación, Historia, Vol. XLIII. Typescript copy in Coronado Library, University of New Mexico, Albuquerque.

Bandelier, Adolph F. "Journal for 1880." New Mexico Historical Museum Library, Santa Fe.

Bent, Charles. Papers. Benjamin Read Collection, New Mexico Historical Museum Library, Santa Fe.

Brown, Lorin W. (ed.). "Manuel Maes." MS CL-1057, New Mexico Historical Museum Library, Santa Fe, 1937.

Collinson, Frank. "George Causey, Buffalo Hunter and Cowman." Panhandle-Plains Historical Museum Library, Canyon, Texas, 1937.

——. "The Old Mexican Buffalo Hunters." Panhandle-Plains Historical Museum Library, Canyon, Texas, 1936.

Court Docket for San Miguel County, 1871–1876. Special Collections Division, University of New Mexico Library, Albuquerque.

East, James. "Recollections." Panhandle-Plains Historical Museum Library, Canyon, Texas, 1926.

Folmer, Henri. "French Expansion Towards New Mexico in the Eigh-

Bibliography

teenth Century." Unpublished M.A. Thesis, University of Denver, 1939.

Montoya, Samuel. "A Buffalo Hunt." New Mexico Historical Museum Library, Santa Fe, 1935.

New Mexico Archives, 1787–1841. Photostatic copies in Coronado Library, University of New Mexico, Albuquerque.

Rister, Carl Coke. Papers. Southwest Collection, Texas Technological College, Lubbock.

Romero, Vicente. Typescript copy of an interview with L. B. Brown, April 6, 1937. New Mexico Historical Museum Library, Santa Fe.

Steck, Michael. Papers. Nine file boxes in Special Collections Division, University of New Mexico Library, Albuquerque.

United States Court of Claims. Indian Depredation Case Records. Record Group 123, National Archives, Washington.

United States Department of Justice. Records of the Attorney General's Office, 1865–1871. Record Group 60, National Archives, Washington.

———. Chronological Files, 1865–1873. Record Group 60, National Archives, Washington.

United States Department of State. Territorial Papers, New Mexico, 1850–1873. Record Group 59, National Archives, Washington.

United States Department of War. Records of the Adjutant General's Office, 1865–1875. Record Group 94, National Archives, Washington.

———. United States Army Commands, 1851–1875. Record Group 98, National Archives, Washington.

 Department of the Missouri, 1865–1875. Letters Received and Letters Sent.

 Department of New Mexico, 1849–1866. Letters Received and Letters Sent.

 Department of Texas, 1866–1874. Letters Received and Letters Sent.

 District of New Mexico, 1866–1874. Letters Received and Letters Sent.

United States Office of Indian Affairs. Field Office Papers of the New Mexico Superintendency, 1851–1875. Record Group 75, National Archives, Washington.

———. Letters Received from the Kiowa Agency, 1854–1875. Record Group 75, National Archives, Washington.

——. Letters Received from the New Mexico Superintendency, 1851–1875. Record Group 75, National Archives, Washington.

——. Letters Sent, 1851–1875. Record Group 75, National Archives, Washington.

Walker, Clarabel (ed.). "Selected Spanish Archives Translations." Coronado Library, University of New Mexico, Albuquerque.

Wallace, Ernest. "The Habitat and Range of the Kiowa, Comanche and Apache Indians Before 1867." Unpublished MS report for the United States Department of Justice in the possession of Ernest Wallace, Lubbock, Texas, 1959.

Published Documents

Abert, Lt. J. J. "Report on the Upper Arkansas and the Country of the Comanche Indians," 29 Cong., 1 Sess., *Senate Executive Document No. 438*. Washington, Government Printing Office, 1846.

Abert, Lt. J. W. "Report of Lt. J. W. Abert of His Examination of New Mexico," 30 Cong., 1 Sess., *House Executive Document No. 41*. Washington, Government Printing Office, 1848.

Beale, Lt. J. H. "Report on Construction of a Wagon Road," 36 Cong., 1 Sess., *House Executive Document No. 42*. Washington, Government Printing Office, 1859.

Carter, Clarence E. (ed.). *The Arkansas Territory*. Vol. XIX in *The Territorial Papers of the United States*. Washington, Government Printing Office, 1954.

——. *The Territory of Louisiana-Missouri, 1803–1806*. Vol. XIII in *The Territorial Papers of the United States*. Washington, Government Printing Office, 1948.

——. *The Territory of Louisiana-Missouri, 1806–1814*. Vol. XIV in *The Territorial Papers of the United States*. Washington, Government Printing Office, 1948.

Day, James M., and Dorman Winfrey (eds.). *Texas Indian Papers, 1825–1916*, Vol. IV. 4 vols. Austin, Texas State Library, 1959–1961.

Emory, William H. "Report on the United States and Mexican Boundary Survey," 34 Cong., 1 Sess., *House Executive Document No. 135*. Washington, Government Printing Office, 1855.

Gordon, Clarence. "Report on Cattle, Sheep, and Swine," *Tenth Census of the United States, 1880*, Vol. III. 22 vols. Washington, Government Printing Office, 1883–86.

Bibliography

Harrington, John P. "The Ethnogeography of the Tewa Indians," *Twenty-Ninth Annual Report of the Bureau of American Ethnology*. Washington, Government Printing Office, 1883.

Marcy, Captain Randolph B. "Report," 31 Cong., 1 Sess., *House Executive Document No. 45*. Washington, Government Printing Office, 1850.

———. "Report," 31 Cong., 1 Sess., *Senate Executive Document No. 64*. Washington, Government Printing Office, 1850.

Mooney, James. "Calendar History of the Kiowa Indians," *Seventeenth Annual Report of the Bureau of American Ethnology*. Washington, Government Printing Office, 1898.

Simpson, Lt. J. H. "Report on the Route from Fort Smith to Santa Fe," 31 Cong., 1 Sess., *Senate Executive Document No. 12*. Washington, Government Printing Office, 1850.

United States Commissioner of Indian Affairs:

Annual Report for 1857. Washington, Government Printing Office, 1857.

Annual Report for 1858. Washington, Government Printing Office, 1858.

Annual Report for 1864. Washington, Government Printing Office, 1864.

Annual Report for 1866. Washington, Government Printing Office, 1866.

Annual Report for 1867. Washington, Government Printing Office, 1867.

Annual Report for 1869. Washington, Government Printing Office, 1869.

Annual Report for 1870. Washington, Government Printing Office, 1870.

Annual Report for 1871. Washington, Government Printing Office, 1871.

Annual Report for 1879. Washington, Government Printing Office, 1879.

United States Congress. "Condition of the Indian Tribes," 39 Cong., 2 Sess., *Senate Report No. 156*. Washington, Government Printing Office, 1867.

———. *Congressional Record*. 49 Cong., 1 Sess., Vol. XVII.

———. "The Pastoral Lands of America," 43 Cong., 2 Sess., *House Executive Document No. 13.* Washington, Government Printing Office, 1875.

United States Secretary of the Interior. "Annual Report for 1859," 36 Cong., 1 Sess., *Senate Executive Document No. 2.* Washington, Government Printing Office, 1860.

———. *Explorations and Surveys for a Railroad Route from the Mississippi River to the Pacific Ocean,* Vol. III. 12 vols. Washington, Government Printing Office, 1855–60.

———. "Private Land Claims in New Mexico," 36 Cong., 2 Sess., *House Executive Document No. 28.* Washington, Government Printing Office, 1861.

———. "Texas Border Troubles," 45 Cong., 2 Sess., *House Miscellaneous Document No. 64.* Washington, Government Printing Office, 1878.

United States Secretary of War:

"Annual Report for 1844," 28 Cong., 2 Sess., *Senate Executive Document No. 2.* Washington, Government Printing Office, 1844.

"Annual Report for 1855," 34 Cong., 1 Sess., *Senate Executive Document No. 2.* Washington, Government Printing Office, 1856.

"Annual Report for 1858," 35 Cong., 2 Sess., *Senate Executive Document No. 1.* Washington, Government Printing Office, 1859.

"Annual Report for 1860," 36 Cong., 2 Sess., *Senate Executive Document No. 1.* Washington, Government Printing Office, 1861.

"Annual Report for 1872," 42 Cong., 3 Sess., *House Executive Document No. 1.* Washington, Government Printing Office, 1872.

War of the Rebellion, Official Records, Series 1, Vols. IX, XV, XXXIV, XLI, XLVIII. 130 Vols. Washington, Government Printing Office, 1881–98.

Wislizenus, Frederick A. "Memoir of a Tour of Northern Mexico," 30 Cong., 1 Sess., *Senate Miscellaneous Document No. 26.* Washington, Government Printing Office, 1846.

Newspapers

The Colorado Chieftain (Pueblo), 1873.
Daily New Mexican (Santa Fe), 1868–75.
The Daily Statesman (Austin), 1873.
Dallas Herald, 1865–70.
The New Mexico Union (Santa Fe), 1872.

The Republican Review (Albuquerque), 1869–70.
Rio Abajo Weekly Press (Albuquerque), 1863–65.
The Rocky Mountain News (Denver), 1871–73.
San Antonio Express, 1865–71.
Santa Fe Weekly Gazette, 1860–67.
Santa Fe Weekly Post, 1870–72.
Weekly New Mexican (Santa Fe), 1865–74.

Books

Abel, Annie Heloise (ed.). *The Official Correspondence of James S. Calhoun While Indian Agent at Santa Fe and Superintendent of Indian Affairs in New Mexico*. Washington, Government Printing Office, 1915.

Barker, Anselm H. *Diary of 1858 from Plattsmouth, Nebraska Territory, to Cherry Creek Diggings, the Present Site of Denver, Colorado*. Ed. by Nollie Mumey. Denver, Golden Bell Press, 1959.

Battey, Thomas C. *The Life and Adventures of a Quaker Among the Indians*. Boston, Lee and Shepard, 1875.

Bieber, Ralph P. (ed.). *Southern Trails to California in 1849*. Vol. V in Ralph P. Bieber (ed.), *Southwest Historical Series*. 12 vols. Glendale, Calif., Arthur H. Clark Co., 1931–42.

Bolton, Herbert Eugene (trans. and ed.). *Spanish Explorations in the Southwest, 1542–1706*. New York, Charles Scribner's Sons, 1916.

Calvin, Ross (ed.). *Lieutenant Emory Reports: A Reprint of Lieutenant W. H. Emory's Notes of a Military Reconnoissance*. Albuquerque, University of New Mexico Press, 1951.

Carroll, H. Bailey, and J. Villasana Haggard (transs. and eds.). *Three New Mexican Chronicles: The Exposición of Don Pedro Bautista Pino, 1812; the Ojeada of Lic. Antonio Barreiro, 1832; and Don Agustín de Escuredo, 1849*. Albuquerque, The Quivira Society, 1942.

Coues, Elliott (ed.). *The Expeditions of Zebulon Montgomery Pike*, Vol. II. 3 vols. New York, Francis P. Harper, 1895.

——. *The Journal of Jacob Fowler*. New York, Francis P. Harper, 1898.

Domínguez, Fray Francisco Atanasio. *The Missions of New Mexico, 1776*. Ed. and trans. by Eleanor B. Adams and Fray Angelico Chavez. Albuquerque, University of New Mexico Press, 1956.

Farnham, Thomas. *Travels in the Great Western Prairies, the Anahuac and Rocky Mountains, and in the Oregon Territory*. Vols. XXVIII and XXIX in Reuben Gold Thwaites (ed.), *Early West-*

ern Travels, 1784–1846. 32 vols. Cleveland, Arthur H. Clark Co., 1904–1907.
Field, Matt. *Prairie and Mountain Sketches.* Ed. by Kate L. Gregg and John F. McDermott. Norman, University of Oklahoma Press, 1957.
Forrestal, Peter P., C.S.C. (trans. and ed.). *Benavides' Memorial of 1630.* Washington, Academy of American Franciscan History, 1954.
Frémont, John C. *Narrative of the Exploring Expedition to the Rocky Mountains in the Year 1842 and to Oregon and North California in the Years 1843–1844.* New York, D. Appleton & Co., 1846.
Gálvez, Bernardo de. *Instructions for Governing the Interior Provinces of New Spain, 1786.* Ed. and trans. by Donald E. Worcester. Berkeley, The Quivira Society, 1951.
Garrard, Lewis. *Wah-To-Yah and the Taos Trail.* Vol. IX in Ralph P. Bieber (ed.). *Southwest Historical Series.* 12 vols. Glendale, Calif., Arthur H. Clark Co., 1931–42.
Gregg, Josiah. *Commerce of the Prairies.* Ed. by Max Moorhead. Norman, University of Oklahoma Press, 1954.
Gregg, Kate L. (ed.). *The Road to Santa Fe: The Journal and Diaries of George Champlin Sibley and Others Pertaining to the Surveying and Marking of a Road from the Missouri Frontier to the Settlements of New Mexico, 1825–1827.* Albuquerque, University of New Mexico Press, 1952.
Hackett, Charles W. (trans. and ed.). *Historical Documents Relating to New Mexico, Nueva Vizcaya and Approaches Thereto, to 1773,* Vol. III. Collected by Adolph F. Bandelier. 3 vols. Washington, Carnegie Institution, 1923–37.
———. *Pichardo's Treatise on the Limits of Louisiana and Texas,* Vols. II, III. 4 vols. Austin, University of Texas Press, 1934–46.
———. *Revolt of the Pueblo Indians of New Mexico and Otermín's Attempted Reconquest, 1680–1682.* 2 vols. Albuquerque, University of New Mexico Press, 1942.
Hafen, LeRoy R., and Ann W. Hafen (eds.). *Relations with the Indians of the Plains, 1857–1861.* Vol. IX in *The Far West and the Rockies Historical Series.* 15 vols. Glendale, Calif., Arthur H. Clark Co., 1955–61.
———. *Rufus Sage: His Letters and Papers, 1836–1847, With an Annotated Reprint of His "Scenes in the Rocky Mountains and in Oregon, California, New Mexico, Texas, and the Grand Prairies."*

Bibliography

Vols. V and VI in *The Far West and the Rockies Historical Series*. 15 vols. Glendale, Calif., Arthur H. Clark Co., 1955-61.

Hammond, George P. (ed.). *Campaigns in the West, 1856-1861: The Journal and Letters of Colonel John Van Deusen Dubois*. Tucson, Arizona Pioneers Historical Society, 1949.

——, and Edgar F. Good (eds.). *A Scientist on the Trail: Travel Letters of A. F. Bandelier, 1880-1881*. Berkeley, The Quivira Society, 1949.

Hammond, George P., and Agapito Rey (transs. and eds.). *Don Juan de Oñate, Colonizer of New Mexico, 1596-1628*. 2 vols. Albuquerque, University of New Mexico Press, 1942.

——. *Expedition into New Mexico Made by Antonio de Espejo, 1582-1583*. Los Angeles, The Quivira Society, 1929.

——. *The Gallegos Relation of the Rodríguez Expedition to New Mexico*. Santa Fe, The Rydal Press, 1927.

——. *Narratives of the Coronado Expedition, 1540-1542*. Albuquerque, University of New Mexico Press, 1940.

Hodge, Frederick Webb, George P. Hammond, and Agapito Rey (transs. and eds.). *Fray Alonso de Benavides' Revised Memorial of 1634*. Albuquerque, University of New Mexico Press, 1956.

Hulbert, Archer Butler (ed.). *Southwest on the Turquoise Trail: The First Diaries on the Road to Santa Fe*. Denver, Denver Public Library, 1933.

Hunter, J. Marvin (ed.). *The Boy Captives: Clinton L. and Jeff D. Smith*. Bandera, Tex., The Frontier Times, 1927.

James, Edwin. *James' Account of S. H. Long's Expedition, 1819-1820*. Vols. XIV-XVII in Reuben Gold Thwaites (ed.), *Early Western Travels, 1784-1846*. 32 vols. Cleveland, Arthur H. Clark Co., 1904-1907.

James, Thomas. *Three Years Among the Indians and Mexicans*. Ed. by Milo Milton Quaife. Chicago, R. R. Donnelley and Sons, 1953.

Jones, Jonathan H. *A Condensed History of the Apache and Comanche Indians Prepared from the General Conversations of Herman Lehmann, Willie Lehmann, Mrs. Mina Keyser, Mrs. A. J. Buchmeyer and Others*. San Antonio, Johnson Brothers, 1899.

Kendall, George Wilkins. *Narrative of the Texan Santa Fe Expedition*. Chicago, The Lakeside Press, 1929.

Kinnaird, Lawrence (trans. and ed.). *The Frontiers of New Spain:*

Nicolás de Lafora's Description, 1766–1768. Berkeley, The Quivira Society, 1958.

Lee, Nelson. *Three Years Among the Comanches.* Albany, N. Y., B. Taylor, 1859.

McCoy, Joseph G. *Historic Sketches of the Cattle Trade of the West and Southwest.* Vol. VIII in Ralph Bieber (ed.), *Southwest Historical Series.* 12 vols. Glendale, Calif., Arthur H. Clark Co., 1931–42.

Marcy, Randolph B. *Thirty Years of Army Life on the Border.* Philadelphia, J. B. Lippincott Co., 1963.

Margry, Pierre (ed.). *Découvertes et Éstadlissements des Francais dans l'Quest et dans le Sud de l'Amerique Septentrionale,* Vol. VI. 6 vols. Paris, Maisonneuve, 1879–88.

Maury, Dabney H. *Recollections of a Virginian in the Mexican, Indian, and Civil Wars.* New York, Charles Scribner's Sons, 1894.

Mumey, Nollie (ed.). *March of the First Dragoons to the Rocky Mountains in 1835: The Diaries and Maps of Lemuel Ford.* Denver, Eames Brothers Press, 1957.

Nasatir, A. P. (ed.). *Before Lewis and Clark: Documents Illustrating the History of Missouri, 1785–1804.* 2 vols. St. Louis, Historical Foundation, 1952.

Otero, Miguel. *My Life on the Frontier, 1864–1882.* New York, Press of the Pioneers, 1935.

Parker, W. B. *Notes Taken During the Expedition Commanded by Capt. R. B. Marcy, U.S.A., Through Unexplored Texas in the Summer and Fall of 1854.* Philadelphia, Hayes & Zell, 1856.

Pattie, James Ohio. *The Personal Narrative of James O. Pattie of Kentucky.* Vol. XVIII in Reuben Gold Thwaites (ed.), *Early Western Travels, 1784–1846.* 32 vols. Cleveland, Arthur H. Clark Co., 1904–1907.

Russell, Mrs. Hal (ed.). *Land of Enchantment: Memoirs of Marian Russell Along the Santa Fe Trail.* Evanston, Ill., The Branding Iron Press, 1954.

Strong, Henry W. *My Frontier Days and Indian Fights on the Plains of Texas.* Waco, Tex., n.p., 1926.

Sunder, John E. (ed.). *Matt Field on the Santa Fe Trail.* Norman, University of Oklahoma Press, 1960.

Thomas, Alfred Barnaby (trans. and ed.). *After Coronado: Spanish Exploration Northeast of New Mexico, 1696–1727.* Norman, University of Oklahoma Press, 1935.

Bibliography

———. *Forgotten Frontiers: A Study of the Spanish Indian Policy of Don Juan Bautista de Anza, 1777–1787.* Norman, University of Oklahoma Press, 1932.

———. *The Plains Indians and New Mexico, 1751–1778.* Albuquerque, University of New Mexico Press, 1940.

———. *Teodoro de Croix and the Northern Frontier of New Spain, 1776–1783.* Norman, University of Oklahoma Press, 1941.

Articles

Abel, Annie Heloise (ed.). "Indian Affairs in New Mexico Under the Administration of William Carr Lane; From the Journal of John Ward," *New Mexico Historical Review*, XVI (April, 1941), 206–32.

———. "The Journal of John Greiner," *Old Santa Fe*, III (July, 1913), 189–242.

Adams, Eleanor B. (trans. and ed.). "Bishop Tamaron's Visitation of New Mexico, 1760," *New Mexico Historical Review*, XXVIII (July, 1953), 192–221.

"Bishop Crespo to the Viceroy, September 25, 1730," *New Mexico Historical Review*. XXVIII (July, 1953), 222–33.

Bloom, Lansing (ed.). "Bourke on the Southwest," *New Mexico Historical Review*, XI (July, 1936), 217–82.

———. "From Lewisburg to California in 1849: Notes from the Diary of William H. Chamberlain," *New Mexico Historical Review*, XX (January, 1945), 14–58.

Bolton, Herbert Eugene (ed.). "New Light on Manuel Lisa and the Spanish Fur Trade," *Southwestern Historical Quarterly*, XVII (July, 1913), 61–66.

Concha, Don Fernando de la. "Advice on Governing New Mexico, 1794" (trans. by Donald E. Worcester), *New Mexico Historical Review*, XXIV (July, 1949), 236–54.

———. "Diary, 1788" (trans. by Adlai Feather), *New Mexico Historical Review*, XXXIV (October, 1959), 286–89.

"Extracts from the Diary of Major Sibley," *Chronicles of Oklahoma*, V (June, 1927), 196–218.

Greiner, John. "Private Letters of a Government Official in the Southwest" (ed. by Tod Galloway), *Journal of American History*, III (July, 1909), 546–56.

Lewis, Anna (trans.). "LeHarpe's First Expedition in Oklahoma," *Chronicles of Oklahoma*, II (December, 1924), 331–49.

Mabry, W. S. "Early West Texas and Panhandle Surveys," *Panhandle-Plains Historical Review*, II (1929), 33–48.

Martin, Mabelle E. (ed.). "From Texas to California in 1849: Diary of C. C. Cox," *Southwestern Historical Quarterly*, XXIX (July, 1925), 36–51.

Pike, Albert. "Narrative of a Journey on the Prairie," *Arkansas Historical Association Publications*, VI (1906), 38–130.

Rister, Carl Coke (ed.). "Evans' Christmas Day Indian Fight," *Chronicles of Oklahoma*, XVI (September, 1938), 275–301.

Sheffy, L. F. (ed.). "Letters and Reminiscences of Gen. Theodore L. Baldwin: Scouting After Indians on the Plains of West Texas," *Panhandle-Plains Historical Review*, XI (1938), 6–19.

Strickland, Rex. W. (ed.). "The Recollections of W. S. Glenn, Buffalo Hunter," *Panhandle-Plains Historical Review*, XXII (1949), 28–49.

Taylor, Joe F. (comp.). "The Indian Campaign on the Staked Plains, 1874–1875: Military Correspondence from the War Department, Adjutant General's Office, File 2815–1874," *Panhandle-Plains Historical Review*, XXXIV (1961), 1–156.

Thomas, Alfred Barnaby (trans. and ed.). "Anonymous Description of New Mexico, 1818," *Southwestern Historical Quarterly*, XXXIII (July, 1929), 50–75.

———. "Documents Bearing upon the Northern Frontier of New Mexico, 1818–1819," *New Mexico Historical Review*, IV (April, 1929), 146–77.

———. "San Carlos on the Arkansas River, 1787," *Colorado Magazine*, VI (May, 1929), 79–92.

Tyler, S. Lyman, and H. Daniel Taylor (transs.). "The Report of Fray Alonso de Posada in Relation to Quivira and Teguayo," *New Mexico Historical Review*, XXXIII (October, 1958), 285–314.

Utley, Robert M. (ed.). "Captain John Pope's Plan of 1853 for the Frontier Defense of New Mexico," *Arizona and the West*, V (Summer, 1963), 149–64.

SECONDARY SOURCES

Books

Bailey, Jessie Bromilow. *Diego de Vargas and the Reconquest of New Mexico*. Albuquerque, University of New Mexico Press, 1940.

Bibliography

Bancroft, Hubert Howe. *The History of Arizona and New Mexico.* Vol. XVII in *The Works of Hubert Howe Bancroft.* 39 vols. San Francisco. A. L. Bancroft and Co., 1882–1890.

Bandelier, Adolph F., and Edgar L. Hewett. *Indians of the Rio Grande Valley.* Albuquerque, The University of New Mexico Press, 1937.

Beck, Warren A. *New Mexico: A History of Four Centuries.* Norman, University of Oklahoma Press, 1962.

Benedict, Ruth. "Tales of the Cochití Indians," Bureau of American Ethnology *Bulletin 98.* Washington, Government Printing Office, 1931.

Bolton, Herbert Eugene. *Athanase de Mézières and the Louisiana-Texas Frontier, 1768–1780.* 2 vols. Cleveland, Arthur H. Clark Co., 1914.

———. *Coronado on the Turquoise Trail: Knight of Pueblos and Plains.* Albuquerque, University of New Mexico Press, 1949.

Cabeza de Baca, Fabiola. *We Fed Them Cactus.* Albuquerque, University of New Mexico Press, 1954.

Carroll, H. Bailey. *The Texan Santa Fe Trail.* Canyon, Tex., Panhandle-Plains Historical Society, 1949.

Carter, Robert G. *On the Border with Mackenzie; or, Winning West Texas from the Comanches.* New York, Antiquarian Press, 1961.

Castañeda, Carlos E. *Our Catholic Heritage in Texas, 1519–1936,* Vol. V. 7 vols. Austin, Van Boeckmann-Jones Co., 1942–57.

Chavez, Fray Angelico. *Archives of the Archdiocese of Santa Fe, 1678–1900.* Washington, D.C., Academy of American Franciscan History, 1957.

Cook, John. *The Border and the Buffalo.* Chicago, The Lakeside Press, 1938.

Davis, W. W. H. *El Gringo; or, New Mexico and Her People.* New York, Harper and Brothers, 1857.

Emmett, Chris. *Fort Union and the Winning of the Southwest.* Norman, University of Oklahoma Press, 1965.

Espinosa, J. Manuel. *Crusaders of the Rio Grande: The Story of Don Diego de Vargas and the Reconquest and Refounding of New Mexico.* Chicago, Institute of Jesuit History, 1942.

Forbes, Jack D. *Apache, Navaho, and Spaniard.* Norman, University of Oklahoma Press, 1960.

Foreman, Grant. *Advancing the Frontier, 1830–1860.* Norman, University of Oklahoma Press, 1933.

Grant, Blanche C. *The Taos Indians*. Taos, N.M., n.p., 1925.
Grinnell, George Bird. *The Cheyenne Indians: Their History and Ways of Life*. 2 vols. New Haven, Yale University Press, 1924.
Hackett, Charles W., George P. Hammond, and J. Lloyd Mecham (eds.). *New Spain and the Anglo-American West*. 2 vols. Lancaster, Pa., n.p., 1932.
Hafen, LeRoy R. *The Overland Mail, 1849–1869*. Cleveland, Arthur H. Clark Co., 1926.
———. *Ruxton of the Rockies*. Norman, University of Oklahoma Press, 1950.
Haley, J. Evetts. *Charles Goodnight, Cowman & Plainsman*. Norman, University of Oklahoma Press, 1949.
Hallenbeck, Cleve. *Land of the Conquistadores*. Caldwell, Idaho, The Caxton Printers, 1950.
Hewett, Edgar L., and Bertha P. Dutton (eds.). *The Pueblo Indian World*. Albuquerque, University of New Mexico Press, 1916.
Hollon, W. Eugene. *The Lost Pathfinder: Zebulon Montgomery Pike*. Norman, University of Oklahoma Press, 1949.
Hyde, George E. *Indians of the High Plains*. Norman, University of Oklahoma Press, 1961.
———. *The Pawnee Indians*. Denver, University of Denver Press, 1951.
Inman, Henry. *The Old Santa Fe Trail*. New York, The Macmillan Co., 1897.
Keleher, William. *Turmoil in New Mexico*. Santa Fe, The Rydal Press, 1952.
Kidder, Alfred V. *The Artifacts of Pecos*. New Haven, Yale University Press, 1932.
———. *Pecos, New Mexico: Archaeological Notes*. Vol. V in *Papers of the Robert S. Peabody Foundation for Archaeology*. Andover, Mass., Phillips Academy, 1958.
———. *The Pottery of Pecos*. 2 vols. New Haven, Yale University Press, 1931.
Kirkpatrick, John Erwin. *Timothy Flint: Pioneer, Missionary, Author, Editor, 1780–1840*. Cleveland, Arthur H. Clark Co., 1911.
LeFarge, Oliver. *Santa Fe: The Autobiography of a Western Town*. Norman, University of Oklahoma Press, 1959.
McCarty, John. *Maverick Town: The Story of Old Tascosa*. Norman, University of Oklahoma Press, 1946.

McConnell, Joseph C. *The West Texas Frontier*. 2 vols. Palo Pinto, Tex., n.p., 1935–39.
Marriott, Alice. *The Ten Grandmothers*. Norman, University of Oklahoma Press, 1945.
Nye, Wilbur S. *Bad Medicine and Good: Tales of the Kiowas*. Norman, University of Oklahoma Press, 1959.
Oglesby, Richard Edward. *Manuel Lisa and the Opening of the Missouri Fur Trade*. Norman, University of Oklahoma Press, 1963.
Richardson, Rupert Norval. *The Comanche Barrier to South Plains Settlement*. Glendale, Calif., Arthur H. Clark Co., 1933.
Rister, Carl Coke. *Border Captives: The Traffic in Prisoners by Southern Plains Indians, 1835–1875*. Norman, University of Oklahoma Press, 1940.
———. *Comanche Bondage*. Glendale, Calif., Arthur H. Clark Co., 1955.
———. *The Southwestern Frontier, 1865–1881*. Cleveland, Arthur H. Clark Co., 1928.
Robbins, Wilfred W., John P. Harrington, and Barbara Freire-Marreco. "Ethnobotany of the Tewa Indians," Bureau of American Ethnology *Bulletin 55*. Washington, Government Printing Office, 1916.
Stanley, F. *Fort Bascom, New Mexico: Kiowa-Comanche Barrier*. Pampa, Tex., Pampa Print Shop, 1961.
Towne, Charles W., and Edward H. Wentworth. *Shepherd's Empire*. Norman, University of Oklahoma Press, 1945.
Twitchell, Ralph Emerson. *The Spanish Archives of New Mexico*. 2 vols. Cedar Rapids, Iowa. The Torch Press, 1914.
Wallace, Ernest. *Ranald S. Mackenzie on the Texas Frontier*. Lubbock, West Texas Museum Association, 1964.
———, and E. Adamson Hoebel. *The Comanches: Lords of the South Plains*. Norman, University of Oklahoma Press, 1952.
Wedel, Waldo R. *An Introduction to Kansas Archeology*. Bureau of American Ethnology *Bulletin 174*. Washington, Government Printing Office, 1959.
———. *Prehistoric Man on the Great Plains*. Norman, University of Oklahoma Press, 1962.

Articles

Boyd, E. "Troubles at Ojo Caliente, a Frontier Post," *El Palacio*, LXIX (November, 1957), 353–58.

Campa, Arthur L. "Los Comanches: A New Mexican Folk Drama," *University of New Mexico Bulletin*, Language Series, No. 7 (1932).

Chávez, Amado. "The Defeat of the Comanches in 1717," Historical Society of New Mexico *Publication No. 8* (1906).

Chavez, Fray Angelico. "Early Settlements in the Mora Valley," *El Palacio*, LXII (November, 1955), 318-23.

"Comanche Dance at San Ildefonso, January 23, 1821," *El Palacio*, X (February, 1921), 10-21.

Dunn, William E. "Apache Relations in Texas, 1718-1750," *Texas State Historical Association Quarterly*, XII (January, 1911), 198-275.

Espinosa, Aurelio. "Los Comanches," *University of New Mexico Bulletin*, Language Series, No. 1 (1907).

Espinosa, Gilberto (trans.). "Los Comanches," *New Mexico Quarterly*, VII (May, 1931), 128-50.

Foreman, Grant. "Antoine Leroux, New Mexican Guide," *New Mexico Historical Review*, XVI (October, 1941), 367-78.

Gunnerson, Dolores. "The Southern Athabascans: Their Arrival in the Southwest," *El Palacio*, LXIII (November, 1956), 346-65.

Haley, J. Evetts. "The Comanchero Trade," *Southwestern Historical Quarterly*, XXXVIII (January, 1935), 157-77.

Holden, William Curry. "Excavation of Saddle-Back Ruin," *Texas Archaeological and Paleontological Society Bulletin*, V (1933), 39-52.

Hurt, Wesley. "Buffalo Hunters," *New Mexico Magazine*, XIX (November, 1941), 9-36.

———. "Indian Influence at Manzano," *El Palacio*, XLVI (November, 1939), 245-54.

Kelley, J. Charles. "Factors Involved in the Abandonment of Certain Peripheral Southwestern Settlements," *American Anthropologist*, New Series, LIV (July, 1952), 352-87.

Kenner, Charles Leroy. "The Great New Mexico Cattle Raid, 1872," *New Mexico Historical Review*, XXXVII (October, 1962), 243-59.

Krieger, Alex D. "The Eastward Extension of Puebloan Datings Towards the Cultures of the Mississippi Valley," *American Antiquity*, XII (September, 1947), 141-48.

Lange, Charles H. "A Reappraisal of Evidences of Plains Influences Among the Rio Grande Pueblos," *Southwestern Journal of Anthropology*, IX (Summer, 1953), 212-30.

LeBarre, Weston. "The Peyote Cult," *Yale University Publications in Anthropology*, No. 19 (1938).
Pettis, Captain George H. "Kit Carson's Fight with the Comanche and Kiowa Indians," Historical Society of New Mexico, *Personal Narratives of the Battles of the Rebellion* (1908), 7-35.
Reeve, Frank D. "Navaho-Spanish Diplomacy, 1770-1790," *New Mexico Historical Review*, XXXV (July, 1960), 200-36.
Rister, Carl Coke. "Harmful Practices of the Indian Traders of the Southwest," *New Mexico Historical Review*, VI (July, 1931), 228-45.
Roberts, Helen H. "Musical Areas in Aboriginal North America," *Yale University Publications in Anthropology*, No. 12 (1936).
Scholes, France V. "Troublous Times In New Mexico, 1659-1670," *New Mexico Historical Review*, XII (July, 1937), 380-433.
Secoy, Frank E. "Changing Military Patterns on the Great Plains," *Monographs of the American Ethnological Society*, No. 21 (1953).
———. "The Identity of the 'Paduca': An Ethnohistorical Analysis," *American Anthropologist*, New Series, LII (January, 1951), 525-47.
Shaeffer, James B. "The Alibates Flint Quarry, Texas," *American Antiquity*, XXIV (October, 1958), 188-91.
Smith, Ralph A. "The Scalp Hunter in the Borderlands, 1835-1850," *Arizona and the West*, VI (Spring, 1964), 5-23.
Solaz, Fernando. "The Ageless Village," *New Mexico Magazine*, XXVII (March, 1942), 18, 37-38.
Walker, Lennie Merle. "Picturesque New Mexico Revealed in Novel as Early as 1826," *New Mexico Historical Review*, XIII (October, 1938), 325-28.
Wallace, Ernest. "Colonel Ranald S. Mackenzie's Expedition of 1872 Across the South Plains," *West Texas Historical Association Year Book*, XXXVIII (October, 1962), 4-22.
Wendorf, Fred. "The Archaeology of Northeastern New Mexico," *El Palacio*, LXVII (April, 1960), 55-65.

Index

Abert, Lieutenant John W.: 80, 82f., 86, 97, 116, 155
Ácoma Pueblo: rebels against Spanish rule, 12
Adams, Andrew M.: 171 n.; loses cattle herds, 167–68
Adobe Walls (on the Canadian River): 150, 151, 153, 203; description of, 132n.
Adobe Walls, Battle of: in 1864, 148–49, 149n., 213; in 1874, 204
Agriculture: by Plains Indians, 21 n., 24, 26, 30
Agua Azul Creek (Texas): 112
Akerman, Anthony G. (Attorney General): 190
Alamo Gordo Creek (New Mexico): 191, 192; peace conference at, 136
Albuquerque: 34, 138
Alexander, Major A. J.: complains of *Comancheros*, 176
Alexico, José (*cibolero*): 103f.
Alibates flint: 4, 10
Alvarado, Hernando de: 8
Alvarez, Manuel: 76
Amalla, Jesus (*Comanchero*): 149
Amangual, Don Francisco: 107; describes Comanche attire, 57
Amarillo: 163n.
Anadarko Indians: 153n.
Anglo-Americans: 23, 79, 87f., 96, 101, 153; fear of New Mexicans, 119n.; attempt to dominate *Comanchero* trade, 161; killed by Navahos, 183; *see also* buffalo hunters, Anglo; ranchers, Anglo; and Texans
Anglo traders: 53, 54; bad influence on Plains Indians, 68; hostile to *Comancheros*, 90–91; sell whisky to Indians, 97, 171 n.

Antelope Creek people: 98; trade with New Mexico, 5; vanish after 1450, 6
Antelope Hills: 128, 202, 205
Antón Chico (New Mexico): 29, 63, 65, 115, 120, 122
Anza, Don Juan Bautista de: 29n., 38, 45, 50, 53, 56f., 67, 78, 100, 212; regulates trade fairs, 40; campaign against Comanches, 50–51; negotiates peace treaty, 52; constructs pueblo for Comanches, 58–59
Apache Indians: 19f., 38, 44, 52, 55, 60f., 63, 94, 107, 118, 120, 150; arrival in Southwest, 9n.; enslaved by Spaniards, 15; used as spies, 42; attacked by Comanches, 59f.; raid New Mexico, 76; *see also* Plains Apaches and specific Apache bands
Apaches *del Acho*: 19; join in Pueblo revolt, 20
Arapaho Indians: 74, 87f., 90, 97, 153n.; attack New Mexico, 75–76
Archeleta, Juan de: 15
Arkansas River: 25, 30f., 34, 67, 75, 88, 91f., 92, 102, 108, 109, 110n., 204
Armijo, Manuel: mishandles Indian affairs, 75
Arny, W. F. M. (Pueblo agent): 189; charges illegal seizure of trade goods, 161
Arrington, Captain George W.: 210
Arrocha, Don Juan José: negotiates with Comanches, 71–72
Ashenfelter, S. M. (district attorney): fails to convict *Comancheros*, 189
Augur, Major General C. C.: 192; commends Mackenzie, 193

Baca, Celco (cattle thief): 197

235

Baca, Julian (*Comanchero*): testimony, 172
Baca, Matias (trader): 89
Backus, Captain William H.: 140 f.
Baja Sol (Comanche chief): 119 & n.
Baldwin, Lieutenant Theodore: captures *Comancheros*, 209
Ballinger, Texas: 99, 169
Bandelier, Adolph A.: 89f.; records names of traders, 210
Barreiro, Antonio: 107; describes buffalo hunting, 101
Battey, Thomas C.: on Indian trading, 171 n.
Beale, Lieutenant J. H.: describes Hatch's Ranch, 123
Bears, F. M. (Comanche chief): 146
Beck, Preston (rancher): 120; ranch, 121
Belknap, William W.: 204
Benavides, Fray Alonso de: 19; describes Indian trade, 14
Bent, Charles: 76, 119; tries to prevent Arapaho attack on New Mexico, 75-76; death of, 119n.
Bent, William: 132; supports Cheyennes against *ciboleros*, 109
Bent's Fort, Colorado: 75f., 91, 109,
Bergmann, Captain E. H.: 140, 144, 150, 167, 176; gives presents to Comanches, 142; supplies *Comancheros*, 156; involved in *Comanchero* trade, 157
Blanco Canyon, Texas: 192, 203, 207
Blunt, General James G.: 147
Bolton, Herbert Eugene: 8
Bonaparte, Joseph: 79
Bonneville, Colonel B. L. E.: seeks conference with Comanches, 127-28
Bosque Redondo, New Mexico: 60, 80n., 120, 130, 187; location of, 71; reservation at, 162
Bourgmond, Étienne Veniard de: visits Padouca Indians, 35
Bourke, Lieutenant John: 87
Brazos River, Texas: 192
Bread, New Mexican: as a trade item, 84-85
Brooks, Lieutenant Colonel John B.: complains of *Comancheros*, 202
Brooks, Major J. H.: 122

Brown, Aaron (Postmaster General): 127
Bucareli, Viceroy Antonio María de: 47f., 50
Buffalo Eaters: *see* Kotsoteka Comanches
Buffalo hunters, Anglo: 114; invade Panhandle, 204; clash with *ciboleros*, 207-208; kill *Comancheros*, 209
Buffalo hunters, New Mexico: 52, 80, 98f.; accompanied by interpreters, 56; *see also ciboleros*
Buffalo hunting, New Mexican: growth of, 101; techniques, 103; preserving meat, 104; uses for buffalo, 104-105; dangers of, 105-107
Bunsham (employee of Samuel Watrous): killed by Comanches, 124-25
Bustamante, Governor Juan Domingo de: 100; describes Jicarilla Apaches, 32
Butterfield Trail: 142

Cabello, Governor Domingo: 34
Caddo Indians: 153n.; enslaved by Apaches, 17
Calhoun, Governor James S.: 81, 96, 117f.; seeks to rescue captives, 94; council with Comanches, 118; death, 119; threatened, 119n.
Caliente Valley, New Mexico: 46
Camp Easton, New Mexico: 141, 142, 185
Camp Jackson, New Mexico: 130, 131
Camp Napoleon, Indian Territory: conference, 153n., 154
Camp Supply, Indian Territory: 202, 209
Campa, Arthur L.: 215; translates "Los Comanches," 29n.; describes performance of "Los Comanches," 216
Canadian, Texas: 182
Canadian River: 21, 24, 60, 65, 67, 80, 107f., 118, 124, 128, 130, 132n., 139, 141 & n., 143n., 157, 182, 197, 200, 201, 203
Canadian valley: 4, 69, 98, 102, 116, 120, 132, 159; site of farming by Plains Indians, 5; attempt to survey, 126; fertility of, 140 n.; description, 143

Index

Canagiap (Comanche chief): confirmed by Spaniards, 56
Canby, Colonel E. R. S.: 138
Cañon del Infierno, New Mexico: 90
Cañon del Rescate, Texas: 80n., 163n., 191
Cañon de Quele, New Mexico: 128
Canyon, Texas: 198
Caprock: 198
Captives: 81; sale of Comanche, 33; Apache, 61; trade in Mexican, 93-94; ransom of Anglo, 94-96; Mexican, 111; aid Comanches, 124
Caraher, Lieutenant Andrew: 188 & n.; captures Pueblo traders, 186
Carlana Apaches: 24; attacked by Comanches, 30
Carleton, Brigadier General James H.: 139, 140, 145, 148f., 154, 158f., 176; describes *cibolero* hunts, 113; seeks Comanche friendship, 141; supplies Comanches, 142-43; quarrels with Indian Department, 144; organizes Adobe Walls campaign, 147-48; bans *Comanchero* trade, 150; seeks peace conference, 152; replaced, 178
Carretas: 98, 104, 108, 112, 185; description of, 86-87
Carson, Colonel Christopher (Kit): 111, 132n., 153, 203, 213; in Adobe Walls campaign, 147-48; blames *Comancheros* for defeat, 149
Castañeda, Pedro de: 7, 8
Castillo, José (*Comanchero*): 149
Cather, Willa: 74
Catholic medals: used by Indians, 14
Caudle, Malinda: captured by Comanches, 170
Causey, George (buffalo hunter): kills *ciboleros'* horses, 207
Cazadores (buffalo lancers): 102; skill, 103-104
Chacón, Governor Fernando: 56; settles Indians on Pecos, 64
Chamuscado, Fray Francisco Sánchez: 10
Chaparito, New Mexico: 133, 136, 139, 182; establishment, 123
Chapius, Jean (French trader): 42
Cháves, Amado: describes Comanche campaign in 1717, 29; sources of article, 29n.; on Comanche peace, 74

Chavet, Jean (interpreter): 67f.
Chavez, Fray Angelico: 64
Chavéz, Don Féliz (rancher): 128
Chavéz, J. Francisco (Congressman): 66; elected to Congress, 151 n.
Chavéz, Manuel (*Comanchero*): 161
Cherokee Indians: 153n.
Cheyenne Indians: 74, 76, 85f., 88, 90 f., 91 n., 97, 144, 153n., 162, 204; war with *ciboleros*, 108-12; attack New Mexican frontier, 110 & n.; make peace with Taos, 111
Chickasaw Indians: 96, 153n.
Chihuahua: 42n., 50, 53, 66f., 73, 77, 93, 97, 101, 212; New Mexican efforts to protect, 71; treaty with Comanches, 119n.
Childress, H. M. (rancher): description, 195n.
Chisum, John (rancher): 204; herd of cattle stolen, 168
Choctaw Indians: 153n.
Cibola Creek: *see* Mulberry Creek
Ciboleros: 80, 98ff., 116, 182, 206; origins, 98-101; description, 101-102; efforts to restrict, 101, 113-14; reputation, 105; dangers, 105-107; threatened by Indians, 106-108; war with Cheyennes, 108-112; complaints against, 112; massacred by Indians, 112-13; trouble with Anglo hunters, 207-208; last hunt at Taos, 208; *see also cazadores*, buffalo hunters, buffalo hunting, and New Mexicans
Cimarron River: 108, 130, 204
Cincinnati, Ohio: 71
Claramonte, Father (Franciscan friar): 38
Clarendon, Texas: 198
Clements, R. E. (surveyor): captured by Comanches, 126
Clendenin, Major D. R.: 186; reports on *Comancheros*, 185; scout to Portales Spring, 187
Coahuila: 77
Cochiti Pueblo: early trade with Plains Indians, 11
Cohepa (Kwahadi chief): 199
Collins, J. L.: 124, 134, 140, 144, 150, 200; seeks conference with Comanches, 127-28; reports on Alamo

237

Gordo Creek conference, 136 & n.; blames *Comancheros* for Indian trouble, 137; proposes Comanche agency in New Mexico, 141 & n.
Collinson, Frank: 102
Colyer, Vincent: 183
Comanche Indians: 22f., 35n., 40f., 50, 53, 60, 63f., 68, 74n., 76, 78f., 85f., 88f., 93f., 100, 107, 111, 115, 117f., 121f., 124, 129, 135n., 139, 144, 147, 150, 154n., 157, 163, 165n., 178, 180, 191, 211, 213f., 217; origins of, 28; drive Apaches from plains, 30–34; at Taos trade fairs, 37; steal livestock, 40; attack Taos valley, 43; defeated by Portillo, 44; attack Ojo Caliente, 46; defeated by Fernandez, 47; ravage New Mexico, 47–48; defeated by Anza, 51; Gálvez's policy towards, 54f.; gifts to, 54–55; confirmation of chiefs, 56–57; attire, 57; pueblo for on Arkansas, 58–59; aid New Mexico against Apaches, 59f.; make peace with Kiowas, 62; settle at San Juan, 64; strategic importance of, 66–67; raid Chihuahua, 71; reasons for peace with New Mexico, 73–74; trade goods, 94n.; threaten *ciboleros*, 108; visit New Mexican settlements, 115; paid to kill Apaches, 119n.; rumored alliance with Mexico, 119–20; move closer to New Mexico, 120–21; destroy Anglo ranch, 124–25; favoritism to New Mexicans, 125, 145; oppose expansion of Anglo settlement, 126; burn mail wagon, 127; avoid Collins and Phelps, 128; raid frontier, 128–29; escape Major Ruff, 131; steal cattle, 133; at Alamo Gordo conference, 136; proposed agency for, 141 & n.; visit Fort Bascom, 142–43; massacre teamsters, 145; seek Confederate alliance, 152; resume friendship with New Mexico, 154; trade with, 166f.; escort *Comancheros*, 166; as cattle thieves, 167–69; atrocities of, 169–71; seek reservation in New Mexico, 182; attack Adobe Walls, 204; last hunt of, 210; relations with New Mexico, summary, 211–13; New Mexican effect upon, 212

Comancheros: 78ff., 89f., 97, 101, 112, 115f., 123, 134, 145, 150, 152, 157ff., 177, 179, 184ff., 190, 192, 194, 197, 209, 212; beginnings of, 78–79; origin of term, 78n.; reputation, 78, 155, 172; licensing of, 79, 81–82, 150, 177; trails, 80, 86; description of, 82–83; trade goods, 84–85, 92, 96–97; social relations with Indians, 85–86, 164; range of, 87–88; as guides, 88–89, 131–32, 205; danger from Indians, 89–90; supply Anglo trading posts, 91–92; ransom Anglo captives, 93–96; give false information to military, 130–32; as messengers to Comanches, 134–35; as scouts, 139–40; restrictions against, 140; incite Comanches, 144, 175; oppose Adobe Walls campaign, 146–47; warn Comanches and Kiowas, 148–49; encourage Indians to raid Texas, 163; attacked by Texans, 166, 208–209; steal cattle, 166–67; financed by merchants, 173; denounced by press, 170–71; attitude towards profession, 171–72; released by judicial authorities, 177, 180, 189; change occupation, 199; shift trade routes, 201; captured by Mackenzie, 206; *see also* Comanchero trade, Pueblo traders, and trade goods

Comanchero trade: 81, 184; changing character of, 97, 155; cattle trade, 155–61, 173–75; bartering techniques, 164–66; flourishes after Civil War, 176; decline of, in 1867, 180–82; attacked by press, 185; hurt by Hittson's raid, 197; change in, after 1872, 201; basis of, demolished, 206; effect of buffalo destruction upon, 209–210

Concha, Governor Fernando de la: 58; use of interpreters, 55–56; aids Comanches against Pawnees, 61–62; allows traders to go to plains, 78

Confirmation of Indian chiefs: 56–57

Connelly, Governor Henry: refuses to call out New Mexico militia, 148

Cooke, Colonel Philip St. George: suspicious of *Comancheros*, 95; jus-

Index

tifies Cheyenne raid on New Mexico, 110
Cooley, D. N.: 159
Cordero (Comanche chief): 61, 71; attire, 57
Cordova, New Mexico: 140
Cordova, José María (Taos war chief): 111
Coronado, Francisco de: 7
Cortéz, Don José (Spanish engineer): 60; on Comanches, 58
Creek Indians: 128, 153n.
Crespo, Bishop Benito: 35
Crittenden, Lieutenant Colonel George B.: 135; defeats Comanches, 133-34
Croix, Teodoro de: 34, 51; conference at Chihuahua, 50
Crosbyton, Texas: 192
Crow Indians: 88
Cuartelejo Apache Indians: 24ff., 60, 211; ask for Spanish aid, 25, 31; release Picurís captives, 25-26; search for Comanches, 30; defeated by Comanches, 33-34
Cuerno Verde: 29 & n., 67, 211-12; description, 45; leads massive raids on New Mexico, 49; death, 51; as folk drama hero, 215-26
Cuervo, Governor Francisco de: sends expedition to El Cuartelejo, 24
Cumanches *Orientales* (eastern Comanches): raid Mexico, 69
Cumanches *Occidentales* (western Comanches): remain at peace, 69

Daily New Mexican (Santa Fe): 164, 166, 172, 183, 185, 208; denounces *Comancheros*, 170; on size of cattle trade, 174
Davidson, Lieutenant Colonel John W.: 205
Davis, Judge W. W. H.: 87, 95, 107, 112; describes *ciboleros*, 102
Deaf Smith County, Texas: 198
Delgado, Felipe: 149, 158, 176
Department of the Missouri: 189
Department of New Mexico: 120, 134, 138
Department of Texas: 192
Deus, Captain Charles: 146
Diplomacy: Spanish-Comanche, 28; Vélez and Comanches, 44; Minand Comanches, 46; Anza-Ecueracapa conference, 1786, 52; New Mexican-Comanche in 1820's, 71-72; Alamo Gordo conference, 136; Camp Napoleon conference, 153; Little Arkansas treaty, 154
Dismal River Complex: Pueblo influence upon, 26
District of New Mexico: 176, 192, 201
Division of the Missouri: 176
Dogs: as pack animals, 7, 11, 14, 16
Dohasen (Kiowa chief): 115
Dole, William (Commissioner of Indian Affairs): 141; refuses to supply Comanches, 144
Domínguez, Fray Francisco Atanasio: 39, 48f.
Donley County, Texas: 198
Double Mountain Fork of the Brazos River: 192
Dubois, Lieutenant John V.: castigates New Mexicans, 131
Duck Creek, Texas: 163
Duncan, Jim (trooper): 161, 195
Duncan, Captain Thomas: attacks Comanches, 136
Durango Province, Mexico: 64, 69, 71, 73, 77, 93, 119n., 212
Du Tisne, Claude: 34

Ecueracapa (Comanche chief): 53f., 56f., 78, 100, 116, 212; description, 51; confers with Anza, 52; expedition against Apaches, 59-60
Eighth Cavalry: 201
El Cuartelejo, Pueblo of: 25, 31, 99; built by runaway Pueblos, 15; as proposed site of presidio, 31
Elkins, Stephen B.: 177; appeals decision, 180
Elliott, Captain W. L.: establishes military post at Hatch's Ranch, 122-23
El Manco (buffalo hunter): 106
El Parral, mines of: 18
El Paso, Texas: 34
Embudo, New Mexico: 65
Emory, Lieutenant William H.: on treaty between Chihuahua and the Comanches, 119n.; visit to Santo Domingo, 213-14

239

Esaquipa (Comanche chief): 122, 144; negotiates with Anglos, 136; attacked at Chaparito, 136; visits Fort Bascom, 142
Española, New Mexico: 40
Espejo, Antonio de: leads expedition to New Mexico, 10–11
Espinosa, Aurelio M.: 216; edits "Los Comanches," 29n.
Evans, Major A. W.: expedition down Canadian, 182

Fairs, trade: in 1694, 20; at Taos, 36–40, 44, 46, 85; economic importance of, 40; at Pecos, 40, 52, 62–63
Falconer, Thomas: 88
Faraon Apache Indians: 19f., 27f., 32, 211; meet with Vargas, 20–21; raid New Mexico, 23; defeated by Comanches, 30–31
Farnham, Thomas Jefferson: describes Fort El Pueblo, 92
Fauntleroy, Colonel T. T.: 134, 135
Fernandez, Don Carlos: 29n.; defeats Comanches, 29, 47
Field, Matt: describes Fort El Pueblo, 92–93; describes *cibolero* hunt, 103–104
First New Mexico Volunteers: at Adobe Walls, 148
Fish, Hamilton: 194
Fitzpatrick, Thomas: 109
Five Civilized Tribes: 154
Flechas de Palo Apaches: 24
Flint, Timothy: rewrites Pattie's account, 71; edits *Personal Narrative*, 73n.
Florida: Indians imprisoned in, 206
Folmer, Henry: on Padouca Indians, 25n.
Folsom men: 4
Forbes, Jack D.: 8
Ford, Captain Lemuel: describes *Comancheros*, 83
Fort Arbuckle, Indian Territory: 129
Fort Atkinson, Kansas: 108
Fort Bascom, New Mexico: 65, 112, 143n., 144f., 148, 150, 152, 156f., 162, 167, 173, 176, 178, 182f., 186, 188, 190, 193, 197, 199, 201; proposed agency at, 141; establishment, 143; garrison intimidated, 177; formal abandonment of, 185
Fort Biddle, New Mexico: proposed name for Hatch's Ranch, 123
Fort Butler, New Mexico: proposed replacement for Fort Union, 140n.
Fort Cobb, Indian Territory: 182
Fort Concho, Texas: 167, 168, 191
Fort Craig, New Mexico: 124n., 138
Fort *El Pueblo* (New Mexican settlement in Colorado): description, 92f.
Fort Griffin, Texas: 167
Fort Laramie, Wyoming: 92
Fort Larned, Kansas: 147
Fort Lupton, Colorado: 92
Fort Riley, Kansas: 129
Fort Sill, Indian Territory: 197, 205
Fort Smith, Arkansas: 69, 141
Fort Smith Road: 128, 156, 178, 179, 184, 197, 205
Fort Stanton, New Mexico: 134, 139, 187
Fort Stockton, Texas: 167
Fort Sumner, New Mexico: 71, 139, 167, 178, 184, 193, 201, 203, 204
Fort Union, New Mexico: 95, 124, 130, 133f., 136, 138f., 154, 182, 185, 188, 195, 201, 203; proposed replacement of, 140n.
Fowler, Jacob: on Comanche–New Mexican relations, 73; describes *Comancheros*, 83
Fowler, John (Indian agent): 69
Francis Berniam: novel by Timothy Flint, 72n.
Franciscans: 12, 63
Fredericksburg, Texas: 169
Frémont, Captain John Charles: 92
French traders: 22, 36, 211; aid Pawnees, 25, 30f.; aid Cuartelejo Apaches, 33
Freshwater Fork of the Brazos River: 192
Friend, John: seeks news of son, 170
Friend, Mrs. John: wounded by Comanches, 170
Friend, Lee Temple: captured, 170

Gail, Texas: 163
Galisteo Pueblo, New Mexico: 23, 47; attacked by Comanches, 41–42, 48–

Index

49; friendship with Apaches, 42; decline in population, 49
Gallegos, Colonel J. G.: 138
Gallinas River: 65, 71, 116, 122f., 179n.
Gálvez, Viceroy Bernardo de: Indian policy of, 53f.; significance of his instructions, 55n.
Garcia Lake, Texas: 198
Garland, Colonel John: 120, 122, 126; justifies Cheyenne attack on New Mexico, 110
Garrard, Lewis: 84, 91; anti-Mexican bias, 9n.
Garron, Vicente (Isleta chief): pleads for right to hunt buffalo, 113–14
Genizaros: definition, 63–64
Geranucano (Comanche chief): attacks Apaches, 60
Getty, Colonel George Washington: 179, 183, 184; establishes "picket posts," 178; arrests Comanche leaders, 182
Giddings, James M. (rancher): 120, 122; ranch raided, 121, 123
Giddings, Governor Marsh: 194, 196
Gifts, Indian: by Spaniards, 24, 53; amount, 55; shortage of in New Mexico, 68; by military at Fort Bascom, 142
Gila Apaches: campaign against, 60 n.
Glenn, W. S. (buffalo hunter): 207
Glorieta Pass, New Mexico (battle at): 138
Gomes, Diego (resident of Ojo Caliente): 46
Gonzales, Manuel (trader): purchases cattle, 173
Goodnight, Charles: 172; estimates size of *Comanchero* cattle trade, 174; seeks to recover cattle, 179 & n.
Granger, Colonel Gordon: 192, 199, 200; supports Hittson, 193; patrols New Mexico frontier, 197
Grant, Blanche: 208
Grant, Ulysses S.: 189
Greenhorn Mountain, Colorado: 51
Greenwood, A. B. (Commissioner of Indian Affairs): 127
Gregg, Colonel John Irwin: 185, 187, 188n., 199, 201 ff.; reinforces Fort Bascom, 186; expedition to Quitaque, 197–99

Gregg, Josiah: 64, 76, 84, 87f., 96, 103, 105, 107; on sheep industry, 66; on Comanche-New Mexican relations, 73; coins term *Comanchero*, 78n.; describes *ciboleros*, 101–102
Greiner, John: 82, 88f., 120; records trade licenses, 81–82; fears Comanche attack, 119–20; opinion of New Mexicans, 119n.
Grinnell, George Bird: 85
Guatamo (Arapaho chief): 111
Guerro, José Cristobal (*genizaro*): 64
Gunnerson, Dolores: 9n.
Guns, trade in: 85, 96f.; at Taos, 38; by Taovayas, 45; advocated by Gálvez, 54; by Osages, 97; by Anglos, 171
Guterous, Don Feliciano (rancher): attacked by Comanches, 128

Hall, Jacob: captured by Comanches, 127
Hammond, George P.: 8
Hancock, General Winfield Scott: 160
Harrington, John P.: 214
Harris, Mrs.: ransomed by *Comancheros*, 95
Harvey, Thomas H.: 97
Hatch, Alexander: 120; ranch raided by Indians, 122; supplies military, 123; negotiates with Comanches, 135–36
Hatch, Major John: 191; escorts cattle herds, 169
Hatch's Ranch, New Mexico (military post): 126, 128f., 132, 134, 136, 138f., 160; description and establishment, 122–23; proposed Comanche agency at, 141 n.
Healy, Lieutenant Patrick Henry: 158, 165n.; secures trade license, 159; sublets licenses to *Comancheros*, 161
Henderson, John D. (Indian agent): 176; issues trade permits, 160; forbidden to issue permits, 177
Hennissee, Lieutenant A. G.: loses cattle, 188
Hittson, Jesse: attacked by Comanches, 169
Hittson, John (rancher): 166, 173, 194n., 199; on origins of *Comanchero* cattle trade, 155n.; on cattle stealing, 169; on size of *Comanchero* cattle

241

trade, 174; cattle raid into New Mexico, 193–97; tactics, 194; trouble with courts, 196; reputation, 197n.
Hopi Indians: 11
Horn, Sarah Ann: ransomed by *Comancheros*, 94–95
Horses, trade in: 54; beginning of, 16; at Taos, 37
Horsehead Crossing (Pecos River): 139, 169
Houston and Great Northern Railroad: 203
Hubbell, Charles: alleged thief, 178n.
Hubbell's Ranch ("picket post"): 178 & n.; location, 178n.
Hughes and Church (merchants): 192
Hurt, Westly (anthropologist): 213
Hurtado, Juan Paez: expedition against Faraon Apaches, 27–28
Hyde, George E.: on Padouca Indians, 35n.

Independence Springs, Texas: 168
Indian Department: 143; refuses to locate Kwahadis in New Mexico, 200
Indian Policy, New Mexican: guidelines for, 53f.; threatened by United States, 66; in 1820's, 70–73
Indian Territory: 201, 205
Inman, Colonel Henry: 106
Interior Provinces, Commandancy-General of: created, 50
Interpreters, New Mexican: duties, 55–56; to Pawnees, 67–68
Ishatai (Comanche leader): 204
Isleta Pueblo, New Mexico: 49, 82, 90, 113
Isletans: captured with stolen cattle herd, 186; released, 188

James, Thomas (trader): 57, 61; almost killed by Comanches, 70
Jémez Pueblo, New Mexico: 75, 101
Jennings, Lieutenant Charles J.: 159, 177, 179; in *Comanchero* trade, 158f.; sublets trade license, 161–62
Jewett, Captain Horace: berates New Mexican merchants, 173; captures *Comancheros*, 184
Jicarilla Apache Indians: 24, 62, 110n., 147, 211; defeated by Comanches, 30, 32–33; scout for Spaniards, 42; aid Anza, 50; gifts to, 55; seize sheep, 117
Johnson (scout): guides Mackenzie to Comanche camp, 206
Jumanas Pueblo, New Mexico: rebels against Spaniards, 12; trade center for Vaquero Apaches, 14
Jumano Indians: 8, 14, 45, 99; *see also* Taovaya Indians
Jupe Comanches: 58

Kansas Indians: 67
Keithly, Levi (rancher): 129; blames military for Comanche hostility, 137
Kelley, J. Charles: 9
Kendall, George Wilkins: 88
Ketcham, H. T.: vaccinates Plains Indians, 156
Kickapoo Indians: 96, 97
Kidder, Alfred V.: 10
Kiowa Indians: 63, 71, 79, 88f., 111f., 122f., 129f., 139, 145, 147, 150, 155, 163, 168, 200, 209, 211, 213f.; peace with Comanches, 62; attack *Comancheros*, 89–90, 162; surprised by troops, 124n.; hostile to New Mexicans, 153; steal cattle, 156; stampede Gregg's cattle, 198; attack Adobe Walls, 204
Kiowa-Apache Indians: 80
Kiowan language: 214
Kotsoteka Comanche Indians: 56, 71; raid Maxwell's ranch, 121; seek New Mexican reservation, 182
Kroeber, Alfred M.: 215
Kwahadi Comanche Indians: 183, 200; incited by *Comancheros*, 175; seek New Mexican reservation, 182, 199–200; seek peace with New Mexico, 190; surrender of, 206

Labadi, Lorenzo (Indian agent): 156, 167, 190
Labadi (alleged cattle thief): 197
LaCuesta, New Mexico: 63, 191
LaFora, Don Nicolás: 44
LaHarpe, Bénard de: 32, 34, 35
Laitane Indians (Comanches): 36
La Jicarilla, valley of, New Mexico: 30, 31
Lane, Governor William Carr: 81

Index

Largo, Francisco (Comanche guide): 64
Las Cruces, New Mexico: 138
Las Lenguas Creek, Texas (Pease River): 163n.
Las Portales: 203
Las Tecovas: 163n.
Las Truchas: 191, 197
Las Vegas, New Mexico: 110, 122, 133, 151, 179n., 180, 194, 194n., 201; founding of, 75
Leavenworth, Jesse (Comanche agent): 159; complains of *ciboleros*, 112; treaty of the Little Arkansas, 154; condemns Comancheros, 158–59, 175
Lee, Nelson: saved by Comancheros, 96
Lehmann, Herman (white captive): 164, 165, 167
Leroux, Antoine (guide): 132 & n.
Letterman, Captain George F.: 180; inventories trade goods, 162, 178; impounds cattle, 179
Lewis, Meriwether: 67
Lipan Apaches: 8, 60, 153n.
Lipiyane Apaches: 60
Lisa, Manuel: 87, 107
Little Arkansas, Treaty of: 154
Little Buffalo (Comanche chief): aids Union troops, 142
Little Hawk (Cheyenne warrior): 86
Llanero Apaches: 60
Llano County, Texas: 170
Llano Estacado: 155, 174, 177, 191, 192, 198; *see also* Staked Plains
Loma Parda, New Mexico: 196; gunfight at, 195
Long, Lieutenant Stephen: 80
López, Anirecha (buffalo hunter): 112
Loring, Colonel W. W.: 135, 136; seeks to protect Texas from Comanches, 135n.
Los Cibolos, plains of: 33
"Los Comanches" (folk drama): 216–17
Louisiana: 66, 67
Loving, Oliver (cattleman): 156
Lower Cimarron Springs, massacre at: 145–46
Lubbock, Texas: 80n.

Lucero, Juan (interpreter): warns Comanches against Anglos, 69
Lucero, Juan (*Comanchero*): captured, 202
Luna, Timio: 213

Mabry, W. S. (surveyor): 203
McClellan Creek, Texas: 163n.
McCoy, Joseph C.: 195n.
McCusker, Philip (interpreter): states *Comanchero* trade ended, 180
Mackenzie, Colonel Ranald Slidell: 169, 197, 199, 203, 206n.; discovers trading stations, 163; pursues Comancheros across Llano, 192–93; campaign in 1874, 205–206
McLaughlin, Captain N. B.: expedition to Mucha Que, 192
Madrid, Spain: 49
Mallet brothers (French traders): visit Santa Fe, 36
Manrique, Governor Joseph: 71
Manuel el Comanche (guide): 64–65
Manzano, New Mexico: effect of Plains Indians upon, 213
Manzano Mountains (New Mexico): 10, 14, 90
Marcy, Captain Randolph B.: 65, 80, 116
Mares, José: 59
Marín del Valle, Governor Francisco Antonio: pursues Comanches, 43
Marriott, Alice: 214
Martínez, Father Antonio José: on Comanche peace, 74
Maxwell, Lieutenant J. E.: investigates Indian raid, 108
Maxwell, Lucien (rancher): 120, 121, 130
Mead, J. R. (interpreter): 175
Medicine Lodge Conference: 146n.
Medina, José (*Comanchero*): 166
Melgares, Governor Facundo: 56, 63, 69; expedition to plains, 67
Mendinueta, Governor Pedro Fermín de: 44, 46f., 50, 66; garrisons Ojo Caliente, 46
Mendizábal, Governor Bernardo López de: 17f.
Mendoza, Captain Juan Domínguiz de: hunts buffalo, 99
Merino, Don Manuel: 60

243

Meriwether, Governor David R.: 95f., 109f., 120, 121; supports *ciboleros* against Cheyennes, 109-10
Mesa Verde: 4
Mescalero Apaches: 34, 60, 119n., 120, 134, 141, 144
Mestes, Manuel (interpreter): 71
Mexico: 87, 119n.; deterioration of Indian affairs under, 70f.
Mexico City, Mexico: 78
Mézieres, Athanase de: 56n.
Miera map (1780): 46
"Milk Fort": see Fort El Pueblo
Miller, Robert (Indian agent): 124
Missions, Spanish: on the Río Trampas, 33
Missouri: 97, 127f., 147
Montoya, Pablo: land grant, 65-66
Monument Creek, Texas: 182
Moore, William B. (contractor): 135
Mora, New Mexico: 94
Mora County, New Mexico: 151, 196
Mora Valley, New Mexico: 140; first settlement in, 65
Morris, Captain Louis: 182n.
Morrison, Arthur: reports Comanche hostility, 152-53
Mountain Men: 84
Mow-way (Comanche chief): aids Union troops, 142; seeks peace in New Mexico, 182
Mucha Que Valley, Texas: 163, 191, 192
Mulberry Creek, Texas: 198, 206
Muleshoe, Texas: 6
Munroe, Colonel John: 115

Natchitoches, Louisiana: 56
"Nations of the North" (Indian tribe): 74n., 107; raid New Mexico, 74-75
Nava, Pedro de: 61
Navaho Indians: 33, 55, 63, 120, 122, 124n., 147; trouble with Comanches, 62; hostility of, 90; attack *Comancheros*, 162; kill New Mexicans, 183
Negro cavalry: rescue Comanches, 210
Neosho, Missouri: 127
New Mexicans: 23, 40f., 47, 54, 82, 91f., 104, 108, 138, 201, 208; as soldiers, 41; educate Comanche children, 57; join Comanches in wars, 60-61; promote peace among Indian tribes, 62; reject *genizaros*, 63; rivalry with Americans, 67f.; influence over Comanches, 70; explain the Comanche peace, 73-74; numbers of traders, 82; as workers for Anglos, 92; settle on Arkansas River, 92-93; disguised as Indians, 97; give false reports to military, 129; aid Comanches, 130-32; as Union soldiers, 153; attitude towards Texans, 171; effect of Plains Indians upon, 213-17; folk drama of, 215f.; feeling for Comanches, 217; *see also ciboleros, Comancheros, pastores,* and Spaniards
New Mexico: 15, 25f., 28f., 47f., 50f., 67, 82, 85, 92, 96f., 101, 107f., 113, 133f., 155, 161f.; relations with Plains Indians after 1700, 23f.; conditions after 1786, 53f.; Comanche settlers in, 64-65; expansion of frontier, 63-66, 116-17; conditions after Anglo conquest, 115f.
New Mexico Union (Santa Fe): condemns Hittson's raid, 195-96
New Orleans Picayune: 88
New Spain: 14, 53
New York Evening Post: 197n.
North, Robert (squawman): accuses *Comancheros* of inciting Plains Indians, 144
North Platte River: 91, 109
Norton, A. B. (Supt. of Indian Affairs): 158, 159, 161, 165, 176, 179, 182, 200; revokes trade permits, 159; on *Comanchero* trade, 165n.
Nueva Vizcaya: 15, 50

Ojo Caliente, New Mexico: attacked by Comanches, 45-46
Oldham County, Texas: 5
Olona, Manuel (*Comanchero*): attacked by Navahos, 162
Oñate, Don Juan de: 11f., 19, 98, 211
Ortega, Juan de: describes Indian trade, 11
Ortiz, Antonio: land grant, 65
Ortiz, Polonio (*Comanchero*): 167, 198; reveals operations of *Comancheros*, 191-92
Osage Indians: 67f., 85, 97, 120, 153n.

Index

Ossorio, Governor Philip de: enslaves Vaqueros, 14
Otermín, Governor Antonio de: 19
Otero, Don Manuel: protests against Texan atrocities, 194
Otero, Manuel Jr.: 194

Padilla, Don Juan de: alleged expedition against Comanches, 29 & n.
Pahanca (Comanche chief): 121
Palo Duro Canyon, Texas: 163; described by Col. J. I. Gregg, 198; battle of, 205
Palo Duro Creek, Texas: 198, 203
Paloma Apaches: attacked by Utes, 30
Paracasqua (Comanche chief): 136
Paranquita (Kotsoteka chief): 71
Parunarimuco (Comanche chief): requests pueblo on Arkansas, 58–59; deserts pueblo, 59
Parvaquivista (Comanche chief): 71–72
Parker, W. B.: 94n.
Pastores (New Mexican sheepherders): 116; description, 116–17
Patterson, James (rancher): 196
Pawnee Indians: 32, 61, 67f.; attack Cuartelejo Apaches, 25, 30; defeat Villasur, 31; attack *ciboleros*, 107
Pecos Cattle Trail: 167f.
Pecos Pueblo, New Mevico: 8, 9n., 15f., 24, 26f., 55f., 58, 79, 100, 129, 137, 211; eastern bastion of New Mexico, 5; as trade center, 9; influence on Faraon Apaches, 27; attacked by Comanches, 41–42, 48–49; friendly with Apaches, 42; decline in population, 49; site of peace conference, 52; relations with Comanches, 65n.; abandonment of, 75
Pecos River: 60, 64f., 69, 71, 75, 80n., 115, 123, 130, 162, 174, 187, 197, 200, 204, 209; boundary for Kiowas, 124n.
Pecos Valley: 4, 65, 117, 120; new settlements in, 63
Peñalosa, Governor Diego de: destroys El Cuartelejo pueblo, 15; bans Plains Indian trade at pueblos, 17
Penxaye Apaches: 28
Perea, Colonel Francisco: 151 f.; defeated in race for Congress, 151 n.
Pettis, Captain George H.: on Comanche peace, 74; on battle of Adobe Walls, 149n.
Peyote cult: 215
Phelps, Major J. S. (Congressman): 128; establishes mail route, 127
Picurís Pueblo, New Mexico: 11, 19f., 27, 65, 82, 99, 140; natives attempt to flee to plains, 19–22; refugees among Cuartelejos, 24–26
Pike, Albert: 65, 154; negotiates with Plains Indians, 154n.
Pike, Lieutenant Zebulon M.: expedition of, 67
Pile, Governor William: proclamation against *Comancheros*, 184–85
Pino, Don Pedro Bautista: 29n., 55, 57, 61, 101; alleged campaign against Comanches in 1717, 29
Plains Apaches: 16, 19, 23, 26f., 35n., 53; defeated by Comanches, 31–35, 60; aid New Mexicans, 42
Plains Indians: 23, 35, 64, 79, 86, 97, 128, 138, 144, 147, 161; move into Canadian valley, 5; described by Coronado, 7; beginning of trade with Pueblos, 12; trade with on plains, 16–17; opposed to *ciboleros*, 107–108; adopt New Mexican ways, 211; evaluation of relations with New Mexico, 211–13; effect on New Mexican culture, 213–17
Plaza Larga Creek (New Mexico): 116
Pluma de Aguilar (Comanche chief): visits Santa Fe, 118; negotiates with Anglos, 131
Plympton, Captain P. L.: complains of Comanches, 143
Pope, Major General John: 197, 201, 202; comments on Comanches, 117; proposes to try *Comancheros* in Texas, 189
Pope, Nathaniel (Supt. of Indian Affairs): releases Isletans, 188
Portales Springs, New Mexico: 187, 191
Porter, Lieutenant Colonel A. L.: searches for *Comancheros*, 132
Portillo y Urrisola, Governor Manuel del: defeats Comanches, 43–44
Posada, Fray Alonso de: describes Indian trade, 16
Presidio, Texas: 119n.
Price, General Sterling: 147

245

Price, Major William G.: 205
Probst and Kirchner (ranchers): regain cattle, 196
Pueblo, Colorado: 93
Pueblo Indians: 3, 32, 60, 101, 104, 119, 185; prehistoric contacts with Plains Indians, 3; expansion into Canadian valley, 4; fortify towns, 6; described by Oñate, 11; relations with Plains Indians, 12, 16; rebellions, 15–16, 19; used as auxiliary soldiers, 24, 31, 50; as guides, 25, 27; influence Plains Apaches, 26; cheat Comanches, 39; revolt of 1847, 91 n.; as hunters, 98; attacked by Kiowas, 113; effect of Plains Indians upon, 213–17; dances of, 214; *see also* Pueblo Traders
Pueblo Traders: 81–82, 83, 90, 176; as messengers to Plains Indians, 117–18, 120; captured by military, 134–35; trusted by Comanches, 165; slip by Fort Bascom, 184; last expedition of, 210–11; *see also Comancheros*
Puerto de Luna, New Mexico: 192, 193

Querecho Indians: 98; identity of, 7
Quitaque, Texas (trading site): 163, 193, 197; Gregg's mistaken location of, 198
Quitaque Creek, Texas: 88

Rabbit Ear Creek, New Mexico: 74
Rabbit Ear Mountain, New Mexico: 132
Ranchers, Anglo: provoke Indian problems in New Mexico, 120; request protection, 204
Randlett, Captain James F.: 186; captures *Comancheros*, 187; court-martialed for losing cattle, 188 & n.
Rath, Charles (trader): arms Kiowas, 171 n.
Raton Mountains: 4, 30, 111
Raton Pass: 24
Rayado Creek, New Mexico: 121
Red River: 32, 74n., 142, 198, 203, 205
Red River War, 1874–75: 175; causes, 204, 209
Reeve, Colonel J. V.: berates New Mexicans, 129

Republican Review (Albuquerque): condemns *Comancheros*, 171
Republican River, Nebraska: 130
Richardson, Rupert Norval: on Padouca Indians, 35n.
Río Conchas, New Mexico: 128
Río Grande: 3, 22, 26, 34, 40
Río Hondo, New Mexico: 130, 197
Río Trampas, New Mexico: 33
Rivera, Don Pedro de: describes Comanches, 32
Roberts, Helen: on Taos music, 215
Roswell, New Mexico: 130
Roxo, Josef Manuel (trader): 52
Rubí, Marqués de: 44, 50
Ruff, Major Charles F.: campaign against Comanches, 130–32; misled by *Comancheros*, 131; describes Adobe Walls, 132n.
Rodrígues, Fray Agustín: exploration of New Mexico, 10
Romero, Captain Diego de: visits camps of Plains Indians to trade, 17
Romero, Pabla (Taos chief): 120
Romero, Vicente (*Comanchero*): 166; meets Indians, 163; gambles and races horses with Indians, 164; return from trading trips, 172–73
Rosas, Governor Luís de: engages in slave trade, 15
Russell, Mrs. Marian: 157; memoirs, 158
Russell, Lieutenant Richard: trades for cattle, 158
Ruxton, George: 97

Saddle-Back excavation, Texas: 5
Sage, Rufus: 92f.
St. Louis, Missouri: 58, 61, 76, 111
St. Vrain's Fort, Colorado: 92
Salada (trading site): 191, 192
Salazar, Damasio: 108; asks compensation for death of son, 111
Salazar (son of Damasio): attacks Cheyennes, 108
Sanaco (Comanche chief): 121
San Angelo, Texas: 14
San Antonio, Texas: 57, 59
San Antonio Express: 168, 170
Sandía Mountains: 23
Sandía Pueblo, New Mexico: 210; attacked by Comanches, 48

Index

San Felipe Pueblo, New Mexico: 16
Sangre de Cristo Mountains: 4, 21, 64, 65, 76, 107
San Ildefonso Pueblo, New Mexico: Comanche dance at, 214
San José del Vado, New Mexico: 63, 64, 112
San Juan Pueblo, New Mexico: 64, 88, 89, 166
San Luis Valley, Colorado: 50
San Miguel del Vado, New Mexico: 64, 75, 94, 108; settlement, 63
Santa Ana Pueblo, New Mexico: 88, 101, 210
Santa Clara Pueblo, New Mexico: 134; repulses Comanche attack, 47
Santa Fe, New Mexico: 14, 18, 20, 24f., 28f., 55, 57, 59, 62, 68f., 72f., 72n., 75f., 80f., 88, 93f., 96, 107, 118, 119n., 127, 138, 150, 159, 165, 184, 194n., 196, 204, 212
Santa Fe Trail: 64, 94, 136, 140, 203
Santa Fe Weekly Gazette: 90, 133, 136n.; supports Carleton, 150
Santa Fe Weekly Post: condemns Comancheros, 171
Santo Domingans: 42, 108; last trading trip, 210–11; horsemanship of, 213–14
Santo Domingo Pueblo, New Mexico: 82f., 89, 211, 213f.
Scott County, Kansas: site of El Cuartelejo pueblo, 26
Seaman, Edward (police chief): killed by Texans, 195
Secoy, Frank E.: on Padouca Indians, 35n.
Sedgwick, Major John: expedition against Comanches, 129
Seminole Indians: 153n.
Senecal, Mr. (resident of San Miguel): 108
Serna, Captain Cristóbal de la: 28
Serrano, Fray (Franciscan friar): on excesses of trade fairs, 37
Sheep: 17; prosperity of sheep industry in early nineteenth century, 66; stolen by Apaches, 76
Sheer-kee-na-kwaugh (Comanche chief): 151, 152; visits Fort Bascom, 150

Sheridan, General Phillip: winter campaign of 1868, 182; orders confiscation of *Comancheros*' stock, 183
Sherman, General William Tecumseh: 189; complains of Anglo traders, 171 n.; proposes to search traders, 176
Shoshone Indians: 88
Sibley, Major George C.: 64
Sibley, General H. H.: invades New Mexico, 138
Sibley, Major John: 68
Sierra Blanca Mountains: 18, 60
Sierra Jumano Mountains: *see* Wichita Mountains
Siete Rios Apaches: attack Tompiro towns, 18
Silverton, Texas: 199
Simonson, Major John S.: on treachery of New Mexicans, 130
Simpson (rancher): killed by Texans, 195
Sioux Indians: 88
Slave raids: 14, 17–18
Slough, Judge J. P.: releases *Comancheros*, 180
Smith, Clinton (Indian captive): describes *Comanchero* trading, 164
Smith, Major General E. Kirby: 154n.
Smith, John (mountain man): 91 n.; harasses *Comancheros*, 90–91
Socorro, New Mexico: 76
Soguara (Comanche chief): 63
Sonora Province, Mexico: 42n., 50
South Plains: 3, 155
South Platte River: 87
Spaniards: 10, 15f., 19f., 25f., 35f., 49, 54f., 58f., 61, 67f., 74, 80, 87, 115; in lower Canadian valley, 69; *see also* New Mexicans, *Comancheros*, and *ciboleros*
Staked Plains: 162, 169, 193, *see also* Llano Estacado
Stapp, William B.: proposed as Comanche agent, 141
Steck, Dr. Michael (Supt. of Indian Affairs): 144, 149, 200; opposes Adobe Walls campaign, 146–47; issues illegal trade permits, 148–49; removed from office, 149
Stinnett, Texas: 132
Stockton, Thomas: 196

247

Strong, Henry (guide): tortures *cibolero*, 206n.
Sturgis, Captain S. D.: campaign against Comanches, 129
Suaso, Antonio José (Taos war chief): 111
Suazo, Santo (Tesuque Indian): 88
Summer Camp on the Canadian: 185
Sumner, Colonel E. V.: 119
Sutton's Fort (Texas Panhandle): 118

Tafoya, José (*Comanchero*): 206n.; supplied by Bergmann, 157; employed by Lt. Jennings, 160–61; ceases trading, 180; guide for Mackenzie, 199, 205
Tamaron, Bishop Pedro: 37, 42
Taos Indians: 111; flee to El Cuartelejo, 15; last hunt by, 208; act in folk drama, 216; see Taos Pueblo
Taos Pueblo: 4, 11 f., 19f., 27f., 33, 42f., 46, 49, 55, 63f., 72, 75, 82, 92, 101; trade fairs, 28f.; allow Spaniards to take refuge in pueblo, 46; raided by Comanches, 51; ties with Plains Indians, 214–15
Taovaya Indians: 32, 211; purchase Spanish captives, 45; Spanish interpreters among, 56n.
Tatum, Lawrie (Comanche agent): 163
Taylor, Nathaniel (Commissioner of Indian Affairs): 161; revokes trading licenses, 177
Tecolote, New Mexico: 110, 135, 158
Teja Indians: 8
Tejanos: hated by New Mexicans, 171; see also Texans
Ten Bears (Comanche chief): 146n.
Tesuque Pueblo, New Mexico: 88, 117, 134, 139
Texans: 153f., 169; invade New Mexico, 138f.; attack *Comancheros*, 166; fight Comanches, 168; attitude towards New Mexicans, 194; attack Loma Parda, 195; surveyors tracked by Young, 203; take *ciboleros'* horses, 207–208; kill *Comancheros*, 209; see also *Tejanos*
Texan–Santa Fe Expedition: 88, 108
Texas: 34, 53, 57, 68, 120, 135, 135n., 141, 154, 155, 163, 179, 189, 205, 212, 217; attacked by Comanches,

51; Indian raids upon, 167–71; see also Texans
Texas Panhandle: 21, 23, 116, 148
Texas Rangers: 166n.
Teya Indians: 9n., 98; identity of, 8
Thomas, Alfred Barnaby: on Padouca Indians, 35n.
Thomas & Slater: cattle stolen, 168
Throckmorton, Brigadier General James W.: at Camp Napoleon Conference, 153–54; negotiates with Comanches, 154n.
Tierra Blanca Creek (head of Red River): 193, 198
Tierra Blanca Lake (Texas Panhandle): 191
Tompiro Pueblos, New Mexico: 10, 14; devastated by Apaches, 18
Toroblanco (Comanche chief): murdered, 51
Towne, Charles W.: 116
Trade, Indian: Pueblo–Plains Indian, 10; jeopardized by Spanish occupation of New Mexico, 12; in early eighteenth century, 34ff.; at Taos, 47f.; licensing of, 148, 151; see also *Comancheros*, *Comanchero* trade, New Mexicans, and trade goods
Trade goods: shortage of, 68; prices, 70–71; confiscation of, 162; inventory of, 178–79; destruction of, 187
Trampas, New Mexico: 65
Tres Ritos Canyon, New Mexico: 65
Tucumcari, New Mexico: 116
Tucumcari Mountain, New Mexico: 59, 145
Tule Canyon, Texas: 193
Tule Lake, New Mexico: 191, 203
Tupatu, Don Lorenzo (Picurís leader): flees with Apaches, 20
Tupatu, Luis (Picurís chief): 20

Ugarte y Loyola, Don Jacobo: 59
Ulibarrí, Don Feliz (resident of Chaparito): 133
Ulibarrí, José (*Comanchero*): 154
Ulibarrí, Sergeant Juan de: 28, 99; expedition to El Cuartelejo, 24–26
United States of America: 119n.; rivalry with Spain over Plains Indians, 66ff.

Index

Utah Creek (tributary of Canadian): 128, 141, 143
Ute Indians: 28, 30, 40, 44, 55, 63, 75, 79, 88, 93, 110n., 120, 147; aid Anza, 50; trouble with Comanches, 62

Valencia County, New Mexico: 49, 162
Valverde, Governor Antonio de: 31; campaign against Comanches, 30; hunts buffalo, 99–100
Valverde, Battle of: 138
Van Buren, Arkansas: 65, 80
Vaquero Apaches: 12; trade with Pueblos, 14
Vargas, Governor Diego de: 21; reconquers New Mexico, 19–20; recaptures Picurís natives, 21–22; death of, 23
Valdéz, Lorenzo (*Comanchero*): reports Comanche hostility, 152
Vélez Cachupín, Governor Tómas: 42, 100; regulates trade at Taos, 37, 39; defends Pecos and Galisteo, 41–42; replaces Portillo, 44
Vetancourt, Fray Agustín: describes Indian trade, 16
Vial, Pedro: expeditions across plains, 57–58; threats against, 58; as an interpreter, 67f.
Vigil, Don Carlos (Governor of Tesuque Pueblo): 119 & n., 134, 139; visits Governor Calhoun, 117; attends Comanche council, 118
Vigil, Juan (Tesuque leader): captured by troops, 134
Villasur, Don Pedro de: defeated by Pawnees, 31
Vose, Lieutenant R. C.: 159, 161; in *Comanchero* trade, 158

Wainwright, Captain R. A.: at Alamo Gordo Creek Conference, 136
Wagon Mound, New Mexico: 140
Wallace, Ernest: on Padouca Indians, 35n.
Wallen, Major H. D.: praises Canadian valley, 143
Ward, John: 82, 88f.; records trade licenses, 81–82
Warfare: Plains Indian–Pueblo, 8–9; interpueblo, 10 n.; Apaches destroy Tompiro towns, 18; Pueblo revolt and Vargas' reconquest, 19–20; alleged campaign against Comanches in 1717, 28–29; Valverde campaign in 1719, 30; Villasur expedition, 31; Comanche-Apache, 32–36; Comanche–New Mexican, 40–51; New Mexican and Comanche campaigns against Apaches, 60ff.; in the 1830's, 74–76; *cibolero*-Cheyenne war of 1853, 108–12; Comanche campaign of 1860, 129–32; Adobe Walls campaign of 1864, 145–49; Sheridan's 1869 campaign, 182; Red River War, 204–205
Washington, D.C.: 127, 159
Washita River: 154, 203
Waters, Justice B. J.: complains of inept district attorney, 189
Watrous, Samuel (Anglo rancher): 120, 126; ranch destroyed by Comanches, 124–25
Watts, John S.: receives trade license
Weapons: of Plains Indians, 32; of New Mexicans, 41; Spanish shortage of in 1770's, 47–48; trade policy concerning, 54; given to Comanches by Spaniards, 59; trade in by *Comancheros*, 85; *see also* guns, trade in
Wedel, Waldo R.: 26f.
Weekly New Mexican (Santa Fe): attacks Carleton's Comanche policy, 150–52
Wentworth, Edward H.: on expansion of sheep industry, 116
Whipple, Lieutenant A. W.: 82f., 89, 116, 155
Whisky: illicit trade in, 96f.; dangers of trading, 165–66; sold by Anglos, 171 n.; *see also Comancheros*
Whitfield, J. W.: ransoms New Mexican captives, 111
Wichita Indians: 34
Wichita Mountains, Oklahoma: 87, 163, 182
Wilkinson, General James: on Comanche importance to control of plains, 66–67
Wilson, Mrs. Jane: rescued by *Comancheros*, 95

249

Wilson, Sergeant William: captures Polonio Ortiz, 191
Wilson, William J. (rancher): on origin of *Comanchero* cattle trade, 155
Wizlezenus, Frederick: 102, 107
Wolf Creek, Texas Panhandle: 203
Wood, Captain E. W.: 159, 161; seeks to enter *Comanchero* trade, 158

Ye, Juan de (Pecos chief): 20 f.

Yellowhouse Canyon: *see Cañon del Rescate*
Young, Captain S. B. M.: 201, 204; expedition against *Comancheros*, 203–204; discovers intrusion into Panhandle of Anglo buffalo hunters, 204

Zaldívar, Vicente de: 11 f.; conducts buffalo hunt, 98–99
Zuñi Pueblo: 9

A History of New Mexican–Plains Indian Relations has been set on the Linotype in 11-point Electra, an original face designed by W. A. Dwiggins, eminent American artist and illustrator.

The paper on which the book is printed bears the watermark of the University of Oklahoma Press and is intended to have an effective life of at least three hundred years.

Bradford College Library
E78.N65 K33 BCHA
Kenner, Charles L./A history of New Mexi

3 6660 00012 5137

970.1 Kenner, C.L.
K   A History of New Mexican Plains Indian Relations

Date Due

DE 17 '70			
NO - 7			
AP 23 '73			
FEB 12 '92			
MR 12 '92			

DISCARDED